Problems in Modern
Mexican History

LATIN AMERICAN SILHOUETTES

Series Editors: William H. Beezley and Judith Ewell

Recent Titles in the Series

The Birth of Modern Mexico, 1780–1824
 Edited by Christon I. Archer
Recollections of Mexico: The Last Ten Months of Maximilian's Empire
 By Samuel M. Basch, Edited and Translated by Fred D. Ullman
Plutarco Elías Calles and the Mexican Revolution
 By Jürgen Buchenau
State Governors in the Mexican Revolution, 1910–1952: Portraits in Conflict, Courage, and Corruption
 Edited by Jürgen Buchenau and William H. Beezley
The U.S.-Mexican Border Today, Third Edition
 By Paul Ganster and David E. Lorey
The Third Century: U.S.–Latin American Relations since 1889, Second Edition
 By Mark Gilderhus, David C. LaFevor, and Michael J. LaRosa
Revolution in Mexico's Heartland: Politics, War, and State Building in Puebla, 1913–1920
 By David G. LaFrance
Simón Bolívar: Venezuelan Rebel, American Revolutionary
 By Lester D. Langley
Simón Bolívar: Essays on the Life and Legacy of the Liberator
 Edited by Lester D. Langley and David Bushnell
Addicted to Failure: U.S. Security Policy in Latin America and the Andean Region
 Edited by Brian Loveman
The Women's Revolution in Mexico, 1910–1953
 Edited by Stephanie E. Mitchell and Patience A. Schell
Gringolandia: Mexican Identity and Perceptions of the United States
 By Stephen D. Morris
Brazil in the Making: Facets of National Identity
 Edited by Carmen Nava and Ludwig Lauerhass, Jr.
Artifacts of Revolution: Architecture, Society, and Politics in Mexico City, 1920–1940
 By Patrice Elizabeth Olsen
The Divine Charter: Constitutionalism and Liberalism in Nineteenth-Century Mexico
 Edited by Jaime E. Rodríguez O.

Francisco Solano López and the Ruination of Paraguay: Honor and Egocentrism
    By James Schofield Saeger
Integral Outsiders: The American Colony in Mexico City, 1876–1911
    By William Schell Jr.
Hacienda and Market in Eighteenth-Century Mexico: The Rural Economy of the Guadalajara Region, 1675–1820, 25th Anniversary Edition
    By Eric Van Young
Vagrants and Citizens: Politics and the Masses in Mexico City from Colony to Republic
    By Richard A. Warren
Problems in Modern Latin American History: Sources and Interpretations, Fourth Edition
    Edited by James A. Wood
Latin America since Independence: Two Centuries of Continuity and Change
    By Thomas C. Wright
State Terrorism in Latin America: Chile, Argentina, and International Human Rights
    By Thomas C. Wright

For a complete listing of titles, visit https://rowman.com/Action/SERIES/_/LTA.

Problems in Modern Mexican History

Sources and Interpretations

Edited by William H. Beezley
and Monica A. Rankin

ROWMAN & LITTLEFIELD
Lanham • Boulder • New York • London

Published by Rowman & Littlefield
A wholly owned subsidiary of The Rowman & Littlefield Publishing Group, Inc.
4501 Forbes Boulevard, Suite 200, Lanham, Maryland 20706
www.rowman.com

Unit A, Whitacre Mews, 26-34 Stannary Street, London SE11 4AB, United Kingdom

Copyright © 2017 by Rowman & Littlefield

All rights reserved. No part of this book may be reproduced in any form or by any electronic or mechanical means, including information storage and retrieval systems, without written permission from the publisher, except by a reviewer who may quote passages in a review.

British Library Cataloguing in Publication Information Available

Library of Congress Cataloging-in-Publication Data

Names: Beezley, William H., editor. | Rankin, Monica A., 1972– editor.
Title: Problems in modern Mexican history : sources and interpretations / edited by William H. Beezley and Monica A. Rankin.
Description: Lanham, Maryland : Rowman & Littlefield, 2017. | Series: Latin American silhouettes | Includes bibliographical references and index. | Description based on print version record and CIP data provided by publisher; resource not viewed.
Identifiers: LCCN 2017004181 (print) | LCCN 2017011543 (ebook) | ISBN 9781442241237 (electronic) | ISBN 9781442241213 (cloth : alk. paper) | ISBN 9781442241220 (pbk. : alk. paper)
Subjects: LCSH: Mexico—History—Sources.
Classification: LCC F1226 (ebook) | LCC F1226 .P964 2017 (print) | DDC 972—dc23
LC record available at https://lccn.loc.gov/2017004181

∞™ The paper used in this publication meets the minimum requirements of American National Standard for Information Sciences—Permanence of Paper for Printed Library Materials, ANSI/NISO Z39.48-1992.

Printed in the United States of America

We dedicated this book to two teenagers
who met in the preschool at the University of Arizona:
Kyla Rankin and Virginia Beezley

and to

Kyla's sister Shiloe and Virginia's cousins Matt, Max, and Nick

Contents

ACKNOWLEDGMENTS	xv
INTRODUCTION	1
CHAPTER 1. INDEPENDENCE, 1810–1820	**5**
1.1. Politics: "Grito" for independence	5
1.2. Church: Edict (of excommunication) issued by the bishop elect of Michoacán, Manuel Abad y Queipo	7
1.3. Military, Militia, and Police: The viceroy offers reward for Hidalgo, Allende, and Aldama	11
1.4. Family: Luis de León, *The Perfect Wife*	12
1.5. Popular Groups: The Virgin of Guadalupe versus The Virgin of Remedios	19
Additional Reading	21
Leer en español	21
CHAPTER 2: THE EARLY REPUBLIC, 1820–1848	**23**
2.1. Politics: The Plan of Three Guarantees	23
2.2. Military: Christon Archer, "Independence and the Generation of Generals, 1810–1848"	26
2.3. Church, Politics, and Society: The Constitution of 1824	35
2.4. Family and Gender: Honor code as custom takes precedence over written laws	36

    2.5. Popular Groups: Puzzles, Santa Anna memory cards, and baseball   38

    Additional Reading   42

    Leer en español   42

CHAPTER 3. THE LIBERAL ERA, 1848–1862   43

    3.1. Politics: The Treaty of Guadalupe Hidalgo   43

    3.2. Popular Groups: Children's history book   60

    3.3. Church: Pope Pius IX rejects the Constitution of 1857   64

    3.4. Military and Police: Benito Juárez orders the arrest of a priest who refused last rites to a dead mayor   65

    3.5. Family: Epistle of Melchor Ocampo—the civil marriage vows   66

    Additional Reading   67

    Leer en español   68

CHAPTER 4. THE FRENCH INTERVENTION, 1862–1876   69

    4.1. Military: The Battle of Puebla (Cinco de Mayo) (Choice of documents)   69

    4.2. Politics: Victor Hugo's 1867 letter to Benito Juárez concerning the execution of Maximilian   70

    4.3. Church: Mexican clerical and European secular reaction to Maximilian's execution   73

    4.4. Family: Maximilian did not die; John Lamperti, "Who Was Justo Armas?"   73

    4.5. Popular Groups: "Adiós, Mamá Carlota"   83

    Additional Reading   88

    Leer en español   88

CHAPTER 5. THE PORFIRIAN YEARS, 1876–1911   89

    5.1. Politics: Hat laws and pants laws   89

    5.2. Military and Militia: Stephen Neufeld, "The Sly Mockeries of Military Men: Corridos and Poetry as Critical Voice for the Porfirian Army"   91

    5.3. Church: The crowning of the Virgin   98

5.4 Family: Etiquette manuals   99
5.5 Popular Groups: Music and foreigners (Choice of documents)   105
Additional Reading   107
Leer en español   107

CHAPTER 6. THE REVOLUTION, 1910–1920   109

6.1. Military: Michael C. Meyer, "The Battle of Ciudad Juárez"   109
6.2. Politics: Javier Malpica, "La decena trágica"   111
6.3. Church: Religious provision and land provision of the Constitution of 1917   117
6.4. Family: American Grocery Company in 1912 set up a model electric kitchen   124
6.5. Popular Groups: National types reflected in "La Cucaracha" and in John Reed, "The Rise of Pancho Villa"   126
Additional Reading   133

CHAPTER 7. THE REVOLUTION AS LIVED EXPERIENCE, 1920–1936   135

7.1. Politics: *Mexicanerías—La construcción del México típico*   135
7.2. Church: Religion in everyday life   141
7.3. Military and Security: Mobile health brigades and the national campaign for vaccination   142
7.4. Family: Domestic radio programming and board game Lotería   146
7.5. Popular Groups: Cultural effervescence   147
Additional Reading   156
Leer en español   156

CHAPTER 8. THE APOGEE OF THE REVOLUTION, 1934–1940   159

8.1. Politics: Cárdenas expropriates the foreign oil industry   160
8.2. Family: The First Lady's memories of the oil expropriation   162
8.3. Military: Navy—the voyage of the *Durango*   163

8.4. Church: The president's commitment to the
secularization of society — 168

8.5 Popular Groups: A corrido and a ballet — 168

Additional Reading — 170

Leer en español — 171

CHAPTER 9. THE SECOND WORLD WAR, 1940–1945 — 173

9.1. Military: Mexican Public Television Channel 22, "Mexico in World War II. Aztec Eagles Squadron 201," *Memoria Viva* — 174

9.2. Politics: Internment of Japanese and Japanese-Mexicans — 182

9.3. The Military — 196

9.4. Church and Family: Francisco de Paula Entrala, *Bienaventuranzas*—the unofficial beatitudes of the family — 197

9.5. Popular Groups: *The Three Caballeros* and Los Panchos — 197

Additional Reading — 199

Leer en español — 199

CHAPTER 10. THE MIRACLE, 1945–1985 — 201

10.1. Introduction to the era through short story and film — 202

10.2. Politics: Two images — 225

10.3. Military and Police: Joe Richman and Anayansi Diaz-Cortes, "Mexico's 1968 Massacre: What Really Happened?" — 228

10.4. Family: Earthquake—film and corrido — 228

10.5. Popular Groups: Alonso Arreola, "10 Monsters of Pop Culture" — 228

Additional Reading — 232

Leer en español — 232

CHAPTER 11. THE LOST DECADES, 1982–2000 — 233

11.1. Politics: The democratization of Mexico — 233

11.2. Security: "Mexico Police and Law Enforcement Organizations" — 234

Contents   xiii

    11.3. Constitution: Carlos Salinas, "Shell Distinguished Lecture Series—Mexico: The Policy and Politics of Modernization"   238

    11.4. Family: NAFTA: Its background, commissions, and myths   238

    11.5. Popular Groups: The Zapatista Army of National Liberation   244

    Additional Reading   249

    Leer en español   249

CHAPTER 12. CONTEMPORARY ISSUES, 2000–   251

    12.1. Politics: Mauricio Merino, "The Fight against Corruption"   251

    12.2. Military and Police: "Mexico's Drug Trafficking Organizations: Source and Scope of the Rising Violence"   265

    12.3. Family: Daniela Molina, "Mexicans: More Pounds and Less Happy"   266

    12.4. Church: "In Oaxaca, indigenous females have their first pregnancy starting at 11 years"   274

    12.5. Popular Groups: Humor—Robben, Piñatas, and Peñatas   274

    Additional Reading   278

    Leer en español   278

APPENDIX: READINGS FOR ARMCHAIR HISTORIANS   279

INDEX   281

ABOUT THE EDITORS   287

Acknowledgments

Susan McEachern, an outstanding and patient editor, inspired this project and helped refine it over dinner at several conferences. We have also been helped immensely by colleagues and students, especially our friends and collaborators at the Oaxaca Summer Institute, Bill French, Maria Múñoz, and Gabriela Soto Laveaga. The dozens of students in the Oaxaca program in recent years participated in insightful discussions about many of the themes covered in this book. Dorothy Sloan, of Dorothy Sloan-Rare Books Inc. in Houston, Texas, provided us with a pdf of the intriguing Santa Anna memory cards. Donald (Bud) Budrejko at the National Archives helped with the documents of Japanese-Mexican internment. John Charlot gave permission to use the children's history book in the Jean Charlot Collection at the University of Hawai'i. Several colleagues helped with securing documents, and we especially thank Rob Buffington, Víctor Macías-González, Diana Montaño, and Natasha Varner (and Servando Ortoll helped make sense of them). Others too numerous to mention have contributed either knowingly or unknowingly,

Graduate students have made direct contributions. At the University of Texas–Dallas, Toni Loftin helped with translations and with proofreading. Claire Perrott of the University of Arizona provided research assistance and helped locate and scan documents. Clea Conlin helped with some translation points and infographics; Juan Diego Marroquin, Tristan Curtis, Osciel Salazar, Cristina Chenal, and Cristina Urea Espinosa also provided assistance in various ways.

In the final stages of the publication process, we received critical help and support from Rebeccah Shumaker, the new assistant editor at Rowman & Littlefield.

The cover image and a couple of others come from the Champion Folk Art Collection, Tucson, Arizona, and Oak Island, North Carolina. Cheryle Champion took the photograph used on the cover.

Documents, whether in original Spanish or translated into English, can remain opaque without a sense of Mexican culture, folklore, music, history, and eccentricities. Carmen Nava loves Mexico, especially Mexico City, and has breathed its essence all her life. She shared her knowledge in ways too pervasive to enumerate, and she puffed air into this book.

Many of the original documents are in Spanish. Unless otherwise indicated, the translations were done by William H. Beezley. Several of the documents in this collection come from digital archives that scholars and students, if they have not yet seen them, should become familiar with. Of tremendous value and utility is "500 años de México en documentos" (http://www.biblioteca.tv/artman2/publish/index.shtml), with a helpful introduction by Kelley Marriam Castro. The Rice University Fondren Library houses another interesting collection in its Digital Scholarship Archive (e.g., https://scholarship.rice.edu/jsp/xml/1911/20697/3/aa00005tr.tei.html).

Introduction

Mexico, with its history of disjointed politics, disrupted economy, and unequal society, has developed since independence through five enduring networks: politics, the church, security (military and police), family, and popular groups. When considered in context, these systems have shaped the nation's historical experience and created a lasting culture with world recognition. Mexicans have managed to work out each of these dimensions as they framed needs, difficulties, and crises as problems, and devised solutions that have been imaginative, foolhardy, resiliently conservative, and remarkably optimistic. The magic of Mexico becomes recognizable as individuals within the government, the church, the military, the family, and popular groups have defined these problems as puzzles and worked out their solutions as dimensions of life for the nation.

Problems in Modern Mexican History offers a collection of documents that illustrate Mexican efforts at solutions to problems or puzzles experienced within the framework of the five networks outlined above. Organized chronologically, beginning in the era of the wars for independence, the chapters offer compelling sources that address each of the five themes. Historical documents illustrate both the defining of problems and the addressing of solutions. Readers are invited to consider the ideas presented in the documents and also to think of alternatives that Mexicans dismissed or ignored. While the problems were not always uniquely Mexican, interpretations of those issues and strategies to resolve them most often reflect a distinctly Mexican character. This collection of documents comes from a wide array of sources, including those that present traditional narratives from official archives and others from noninstitutional collections that represent more popular perspectives. The latter sources include, among others, images, menus, music, comics, literature, prayer cards, crossword puzzles, and other objects.

SUGGESTIONS FOR
INTERPRETING THE SOURCES IN THIS COLLECTION

For each of the historical eras there are, in most cases, five documents of various types that give expression to the networks of politics, the church, the military and police, the family, and popular (including ethnic) communities. In a few instances we provide one long document that reflects aspects that pertain to more than one of the five networks under study. Although these instances will be obvious, they are noted, and readers should read the entire document and then sort out the parts that apply to the five societal themes. In addition, sources in each chapter are followed by suggested readings that should help broaden interpretations. For each era, there is also a supplemental reading in Spanish (Leer en español) for those who read Spanish or want to give it a try. These selections provide examples of how Mexican scholars interpret some events, objects, and persons in their society.

Generally, in examining the documents, we can use the interpretive process, with a nod to the hope of historian Carl Becker, of each person becoming an "armchair historian." The appendix includes links to Becker's article, "Everyman His Own Historian," historian Carlo Ginzburg's "Morelli, Freud, and Sherlock Holmes: Clues and Scientific Method," anthropologist Clifford Geertz's "Thick Description: Toward an Interpretive Theory of Culture," and *New York Times* correspondent Sam Roberts's "Object Lessons in History." Together they offer imaginative suggestions and methodological procedures for ways to examine, analyze, and discuss the documents and readings that this work presents to illustrate Mexico's experience since its struggle for independence, commencing around 1800, to the mid-2010s.

Readers can choose to interpret the documents as clues to the problems of national formation, as dimensions of the nationalistic evolution, or as expressions of the nation's historical episodes. Within each context, there are at least three ways to consider the documents. First, each can be considered on its own. Readers might examine a document and consider its origin; then, based on their lived experience, current knowledge, and insights into human behavior, they might list four or five initial conclusions about it, consult the suggested materials for the source, then review and possibly revise their initial conclusions in light of new information and their rereading of the document. At that point, they will be able to discuss or write about the document with confidence. Second, readers can place each document within the context of the others for a particular section, thereby creating an analysis based on relationships among the selections that may be seen as the mosaic of experience of the community. Again, it is useful to start by making a list of points after the initial reading, then read additional recommended works, and then reconsider the documents and revise the list of points, to be able to discuss their historical connections. Third, readers can consider all documents in a section at one time. They might make a list of the salient points that the documents seem to reveal about an era and decide whether there is cohesion among the documents. After reading additional recommendations, they might reconsider whether the documents have described an era or if they must ask additional questions in an effort to redefine the period. Historians call this latter analysis *historiography*. Above all, readers should enjoy both reading and thinking about the dimensions contained within the documents.

The documents often contain surprising or murky references. We have provided some help with the most obscure, with comments or synonyms or bracketed information, but for the most part we have left it to the readers to track down and understand the references. After all, the documents represent puzzles for which there may be multiple solutions. We have, in most cases, included complete documents, even though some are quite long at times. By editing them, we would be imposing our interpretation on them, and we want readers to form their own evaluations. Read the entire document, and then reread the portions that are relevant or significant to you. The documents are at times images or sounds, and at times the visuals are more than one frame. Some video and sound documents have direct links in the electronic version of the book. For the print version, we provide information on how to access them. Finally, we envision these documents as an interactive collection, and we welcome messages from readers, who can contact us through the publisher's website with questions, comments, and theories.

CHAPTER 1

Independence, 1810–1820

The struggle for independence, from 1810 to 1820, brought a fragmented ending to the colony of New Spain. The breaking of political ties with Spain ended many institutions of government, but some economic, social, and religious organizations and practices, including the military and marriage, did not change much. Independence had different meanings for different societal networks and in different aspects of national, community, domestic, and everyday life. The struggle began when Padre Miguel Hidalgo gave his shout for independence (1.1). The response to the insurgency included church officials using the power of excommunication (1.2) and colonial civic authorities issuing "wanted posters" for the rebel leaders (1.3). Ten years of incessant warfare to achieve independence did not change the institution of marriage, nor alter expectations for the role of the wife (1.4). Among popular groups, conflicting views on independence and the possibility of a new society were expressed through the symbols of the Virgin of Guadalupe and the Virgin of Remedios (1.5).

1.1. POLITICS: "GRITO" [OR CALL] FOR INDEPENDENCE

The fundamental document recognized as the beginning of the movement for independence was Father Miguel Hidalgo's Grito de Dolores *(Cry of Dolores), a call for independence made in the small town of Dolores (now called* Dolores Hidalgo*) in the early hours of September 16, 1810. Hidalgo's exact words were not recorded, but several reconstructions exist. Four examples are provided here.*

Text version 1.

"My children: a new dispensation comes to us today. Will you receive it? Will you free yourselves? Will you recover the lands stolen three hundred years ago from your forefathers by the hated Spaniards? We must act at once . . . Will you defend your religion and your rights as true patriots? Long live Our Lady of Guadalupe! Death to bad government! Death to the gachupines!"[1]

Text version 2.

[*Hidalgo*] declared that the time for action had now come. He asked, "Will you be slaves of Napoleon or will you as patriots defend your religion, your hearths and your rights?" and there was a unanimous cry, "We will defend to the utmost! Long live religion, long live our most holy mother of Guadalupe! Long live America! Death to bad government, and death to the Gachupines!"[2]

Text version 3.

>Mexicans!
>Long live the heroes that gave us the Fatherland!
>Long live Hidalgo!
>Long live Morelos!
>Long live Josefa Ortiz de Dominguez!
>Long live Allende!
>Long live Aldama and Matamoros!
>Long live National Independence!
>Long Live Mexico! Long Live Mexico! Long Live Mexico![3]

Text version 4.

Miguel Hidalgo's speech to the People of Dolores to begin the independence of Mexico.
Early morning of September 16, 1810.
My friends and compatriots:
Neither King nor [fair] taxes exist for us.
This shameful gabelle should be only for slaves; we weathered it three centuries ago as a sign of tyranny and servitude; a terrible stain that we know how to wash out through our efforts.
The moment of our emancipation has arrived; the hour of our liberty has sounded; and if you know its great value, help me defend it from the ambitious claw of tyrants.

In only a few hours thou can see me marching at the head of men who pride themselves on being free.

I invite thou to fulfill this duty. As fate would have it, we will always be a long way from happiness without homeland or liberty.

Thou already knows it has been indispensable to take the step, and it has been necessary to begin with something.

The cause is holy and God will protect it.

These events rush forward and I will not have the pleasure of talking longer with thou.

So long live the Virgin of Guadalupe!

Long live the America for which we are going to fight![4]

1.2. CHURCH: EDICT [OF EXCOMMUNICATION] ISSUED BY THE BISHOP ELECT OF MICHOACÁN, MANUEL ABAD Y QUEIPO (SEPTEMBER 24, 1810)

Independence leaders included Father Hidalgo and other parish priests, but the great majority of church leaders remained committed to the Spanish king and kingdom. The document provides one dimension of the struggle.

Every kingdom divided against itself will be brought to desolation [*in Latin*]. . . ." Every kingdom divided into factions will be destroyed and ruined," says Jesus Christ our Good [*Shepherd*], chap. XI of St. Luke, v. XVII.

Yes, my beloved faithful: the history of all centuries, of all peoples and nations, what has happened before our eyes in the French Revolution, what is currently happening in the Peninsula, in our beloved and unfortunate country, confirms the infallible truth of this divine oracle.

But the example most analogous to our situation, we have nearby in the French part of the island of Santo Domingo, whose landowners were the richest, most comfortable and happiest that were known on earth.

The population was composed almost like ours of French Europeans and French criollos [*French born in the Americas*], of Indians native to the country, of blacks and mulattos, and of castes [*individuals of mixed ethnicity*] resulting from the first classes.

Division and anarchy entered as the result of the aforementioned French Revolution and everything was absolutely ruined and destroyed. The anarchy in France caused the death of two million Frenchmen, that is, about two twentieths, the most select portion of both sexes that existed; it ruined its commerce and navy, and slowed its industry and agriculture.

But the anarchy in Santo Domingo slaughtered all the white French and criollos, without leaving a single one, and slaughtered four fifths of all the rest of the inhabitants, leaving only the fifth part of blacks and mulattos remaining in eternal hatred and deadly war who should be destroyed entirely.

It devastated the entire country, burning and destroying all the possessions, all the cities, towns, and settlements, in such a way that [what was the] best settled and cultivated in all the Americas is today a desert, a refuge for lions and tigers. Here is the grim, but true picture of the ravages of the anarchy in Santo Domingo.

New Spain, that Europe has admired for the most brilliant testimonies of loyalty and patriotism for the mother country, supporting and sustaining it with its treasures, with its opinions and writing, maintaining peace and concord in spite of the malicious acts and conspiracies of the rule of tyranny, is seen today threatened with the discord and anarchy and the misfortunes that follow that the previously mentioned island of Santo Domingo has suffered. A minister of the God of Peace, a priest of Jesus Christ, a shepherd of souls (I do not want to say this), the priest of Dolores don Miguel Hidalgo (who had merited until now my confidence and my friendship), associated with captains of the Queen's Regiment, D. Ignacio Allende, D. Juan de Aldama and D. José Mariano Abasolo, raised the banner of rebellion and lit the torch of discord and anarchy, leading astray a number of innocent tenants, he made them take up arms, and with them fell on the town of Dolores, the 16th of the current month at dawn, he surprised and arrested the European residents, sacked and robbed their belongings; later going at 7 at night to the town of San Miguel el Grande, he did the same thing, seizing both authority and government.

Friday the 21st, in the same way, he occupied Celaya, and, according to reports, it seems that he has already reached Salamanca and Irapuatro.

He has with him European prisoners, and among them, the sexton of Dolores, the priest of Chamacuero, and various Carmelite friars from Celaya, threatening that he will have to execute them if towns offer him any resistance.

And insulting religion and our sovereign Don Fernando VII, he painted on his flag the image of our august patron, Our Lady of Guadalupe, and he placed the following inscription: Long live Religion! Long live our Most Holy Mother of Guadalupe! Long live Fernando VII! Long live America! and Death to bad government!

As religion condemns rebellion, murder, the oppression of innocents, and the Mother of God cannot protect the crimes, it is evident that the priest of Dolores, painting on his flag of sedition the image of Our Lady, committed two most grave insults: to religion and Our Lady.

He insults equally our sovereign, belittling and attacking the government that represents him, oppressing innocent vassals, disturbing public order, and violating the oath of allegiance to the sovereign and the government, resulting equally in the perjury of the above mentioned captains.

Nevertheless, confusing religion with crime, and obedience with rebellion, he has successfully misled the innocence of the people and has given sufficient structure to the anarchy he wants to establish.

Evil will make rapid progress if the vigilance and energy of the government and the enlightened loyalty of the people do not stop them.

I, at thine request and without any cooperation on my part, am elevated to the high dignity of thine bishop, thine pastor and father, in defense of the flock that is confided in me, am going to meet this enemy, using reason and truth against the deception, and the terrible damnation of excommunication against the persistence and evil nature.

Yes, my dear and faithful beloved, I have undeniable rights to thine respect, to thine submission and obedience in the matter.

I am European by origin, but I am American by adoption through volition and residence of more than thirty years.

There is not a single one among thou that takes more interest in thine true happiness. Perhaps there is no other so painfully and deeply affected by thine misfortunes, because there is no other who has been so preoccupied and continues so preoccupied with them.

No one has worked as much as I in promoting the public good, in maintaining peace and concord among all the inhabitants of America and in preventing anarchy that I fear so much since my return from Europe. My character and my zeal are well known. Thus, you ought to believe me.

In these circumstances, and using the authority that I exercise as bishop elect and governor of this bishopric, I declare: that the abovementioned D. Miguel Hidalgo, priest of Dolores, and his henchmen the three said captains, are disturbers of the public order, seducers of the people, sacrilegious, perjurers, and that they have incurred the major excommunication of the Canon Siquis [sic] Suadente Diabolo, for having attacked the person and liberty of the sexton of Dolores, of the priest of Chamacuero, and of various friars of the monastery of Carmen in Celaya, taking them prisoner and keeping them under arrest.

I declare them despicable excommunicates and prohibiting, as I prohibit, that anyone give them relief, assistance, or favor under penalty of Major Excommunication *ipso facto insurrenda*, this edict serving as an admonition from now until I declare the offenders caught.

Also I exhort and require that the number of people seduced with the title of soldiers and comrades-in-arms that these people stop and return to their homes by the third day immediately following when they receive news of this edict, under the same penalty of major excommunication, from now until I declare them and all those who voluntarily enlisted under their banners or that in whatever manner gave them help and assistance subdued.

Item: I declare that the said priest Hidalgo and his henchmen are seducers of the people and slanderers of the Europeans. Yes, my faithful beloved, it is a well-known calumny.

The Europeans do not have nor can they have other interests than the same ones that thou the natives of the country have: namely, to help the mother country any way possible, defend these domains against any foreign invasion for the sovereign to whom we have sworn or any other of his dynasty, under the government that represents him, according to and in the form that is resolved by the nation represented in the parliament that, as is known, is meeting in Cadiz or the island of Leon, with substitute representatives for the Americas until the elected representatives arrive.

This is the aegis under which we must take refuge; this is the center of unity of all the inhabitants of this kingdom, placed in the hands of our worthy leader, His Excellency, the current Viceroy who, filled with military and political knowledge, energy and legitimacy, will make of our resources and will the most suitable use for the conservation of the peace, of public order, and for the exterior defense of the entire kingdom.

United all the classes of the state in good faith, in peace and harmony under a similar chief, are great resources of a nation like New Spain, and we can achieve anything.

But disunited, the restraints of the law broken, public order disrupted, and anarchy introduced as the priest of Dolores intended, would destroy this beautiful country.

Theft, looting, arson, murder, revenge torching the estates, the cities, towns and places, to destroy the inhabitants, and it will be a desert for the first invader who arrives on our shores.

Yes, my dear and faithful beloved, such are the inevitable and necessary effects of lawlessness. Detest it with all thine heart: arm thou with catholic faith against the diabolic seditions that trouble thou; fortify thine heart with the evangelical charity that bears everything and conquers all.

Our Lord Jesus Christ, who redeemed us with his blood, have mercy on us, and protect us in such tribulation, humble I beg you.

And so that the news comes to all and no one alleges ignorance, I have ordered this edict to be published in this Holy Church cathedral, and be fixed to its doors, according to practice, and that the same be executed in all the parishes of the episcopate, directing corresponding copies.

Given in Valladolid on the 24th day of the month of September of 1810.

Sealed with the seal of my [*coat of*] arms and endorsed by the undersigned Secretary.

Manuel Abad y Queipo, Obispo electo de Michoacán.

By order of His Illustrious Holiness, the Bishop, my liege Santiago Camina, secretary[5]

1.3. MILITARY, MILITIA, AND POLICE: THE VICEROY OFFERS REWARD FOR HIDALGO, ALLENDE, AND ALDAMA (SEPTEMBER 27, 1810)

The viceroy (the highest colonial official in New Spain) issued a call for the capture of the rebel leaders and offered a reward for them dead or live in order to restore personal and property security to New Spain.

The Royal Palace of Mexico, September 27, 1810
Secretariat of the City Council of Guanajuato
"Don Francisco Javier Venegas," Governor and Captain General of New Spain

The unprecedented and scandalous attacks that the priest of Dolores, Dr. D. Miguel Hidalgo, and the captains of the Queen's Regiment of the Provincial Dragoons, D. Ignacio Allende and D. Juan Aldama have committed and continue committing, that after having led astray unsuspecting residents of this town, have steered them into violence and into rebellion, first to the village of San Miguel el Grande and on to the village of Chamacuero, the city of Celaya and Salamanca Valley, making in all these places the most despicable display of their immorality and evil ways, stealing and plundering the houses of the most honorable inhabitants to quench their vile greed, and with impertinent insults desecrating religious cloisters and the holiest places: they have forced me to take prompt, effective and timely measures to restrain them and reprimand them and to send picked troops with commanders and officers known for military skill, valor, and patriotism who will know how to crush and destroy them with all of their supporters if they dare to hang on and do not now take the only recourse left to them to escape promptly from the terrible hand of the justice that will strike them with all severity and rigor of the law that corresponds to the enormity of their crimes, not only to impose on them the punishment that they deserve as troublemakers for disrupting the public tranquility, but also to vindicate the ever faithful Spanish Americans and natives of this happy kingdom, whose unsullied reputation, honor, and loyalty they have sought to tarnish by boldly trying to feign common cause against their European brothers, even reaching sacrilege to avail themselves of the sacred image of Our Lady of Guadalupe, patron and protector of this kingdom, to dazzle the gullible with this appearance of religion, which is nothing less than the most impudent hypocrisy.

And as it may happen that shrinking from their crimes and terrified by the news alone of the troops in pursuit of them, they may wander to other communities, similarly looting and attacking their own countrymen, as they did in the aforementioned village, inhumanely killing two Americans and mutilating another in San Miguel el Grande because faithful to their obligations they did not want to follow this evil faction; appropriately I have had this notice communicated to all cities, towns, peoples, missions, haciendas and ranches of this kingdom, so that no one will be surprised by this bandit mob and will be prepared to repel it with force seeking to arrest the bandits in any place where it can be achieved. With the view that those who will identify one of the three main leaders of the faction, or give them the death they so justly deserve for their horrific crimes, will be immediately rewarded with the sum of ten thousand pesos and will be recognized with other awards and distinctions due to those who restore the public calm, and with the knowledge that an equal award and compensation with pardon for his complicity will be given to anyone who has unfortunately followed them in this factional party, and laudably repentant surrenders them dead or alive.

And in order that this news reaches everyone, I order its publication by edict in this capital circulates promptly, and with the same ends, to the courts, magistrates, chiefs and the ministers who achieve its promulgation, intelligence and compliance.

Given in the Royal Palace of Mexico, September 27, 1810. Francisco Javier Venegas.[6]

1.4. FAMILY: LUIS DE LEÓN, *THE PERFECT WIFE* (1583)

Luis de León, perhaps Spain's greatest poet in his day and an Augustinian friar, published La perfecta casada (The Perfect Wife) *in 1583 in Spain. It had to be reprinted almost immediately and became the most important guide for young wives for the next several centuries. It soon appeared in Mexico and continued to be published there, with its most recent edition by the Porrúa publishing house issued in 1970. León directed the homily to Mary Varela (or Valera), whose identity remains unknown.*

II

The Heart of her husband doth safely trust in her, so that he should have no need of spoil.

After the Holy Spirit has brought forward the subject of His discourse, and, by praising it, has aroused in us an affection for it, He commences to specify its good points, and that of which it is composed, and what it is that constitutes its perfection. And to this end: that planting their feet in these very footprints, and following in these very steps, women may as wives become perfect. And because the perfection of man, in whatever may be his estate, consists, primarily, in well doing, therefore, the Holy Spirit does not deal here with the several aspects of this perfection of which He treats, but solely with those meritorious works, for the performance of which a wife, who aspires to goodness, is under obligation.

Of these, the first is that in the heart of her husband she should engender the utmost confidence, but it remains to be seen what this confidence is, and of what it is made up. Because, some will take for granted that a husband will require of his wife that she be honest. And although it is true that a woman must by her goodness win from her husband this golden opinion, yet, to my way of thinking, the Holy Spirit does not refer here to this matter, and the reasons for it are most just.

The first reason is that His intention, at this point, is to present to us a perfect wife, and fidelity in a wife does not count, nor should it count, among those qualities of which this perfection consists, rather is it like the foundation on which the entire superstructure is upbuilded. In a word, faithfulness is like the very marrow and innate being of a perfect wife. For if a wife is without honor, she is not a wife, but a treacherous harlot, the vilest mire, a reeking refuse-heap, and of all beings the most despicable. And as in a man, to be endowed with intelligence and power of reasoning, does not confer credit upon him, because to possess these is of the essence of his being (although were these wanting, he would be greatly lacking): so a wife is not so praiseworthy for being faithful, as she is abominable and perverted if she is not. Wherefore, God the Holy Ghost does not enjoin a wife to be honest, but takes for granted that she is, and to a faithful wife he points out what she still lacks and what she is to add in order to be complete and perfect.

Now as we have said before, all this which is here related is like making a portrait or a picture, and the artist does not make the panel, but on the panel presented and set before him he puts in the outlines, and introduces the colors and causing the highlights to stand out in their appropriate places and lowering the shadows where necessary, brings his figure to its due perfection. So, likewise, upon the honor of a wife which serves as a canvas, and which He doubts not is unblemished, God sets down the richest colors of virtue, all such colors as are needful to complete so admirable a painting. And all this constitutes the first reason.

The second reason why God does not mention here what pertains to fidelity is because He wishes that this matter of honesty and purity women may have so ingrained in their hearts that they may not even dream that the opposite is possible. Of Solon, who gave the Athenians their laws, it is related when he attached to each transgression its penalties, he forebore to assign a punishment for one who murdered his father, nor did he make a memorandum of the crime, because, said he, it was not befitting that men should consider such iniquity as possible, or as ever likely to occur. In such fashion, therefore, God does not take up this matter of chastity and fidelity with her who is a perfect wife, because He wills not that possibility of offending should present itself, even remotely, to her imagination. Indeed, if the truth must be told, the thought that she can never be unfaithful is for a virtuous woman almost like a suggestion of infidelity, as it is also that by not being unchaste, she is doing something to merit gratitude.

Consider the birds, how it is their nature to fly; so married women must regard honor and goodness as their natural endowment, from which there must be not the least deviation. They must be convinced that the slightest lapse is an unfortunate and hateful occurrence, a most horrible deed. To put it more tellingly, no infringement must be considered possible, any more it is in the nature of fire to be chilly, or snow to be hot. Let a wife lay this well to heart: for a woman to break her plighted troth to her husband is for the stars to lose their splendor, and the skies to fall; for nature to overturn all its laws, and everything to return to primordial chaos.

And women are not to think either that because their husbands possess them, they may consider themselves free in regard to their conversation, postures, and small matters of behavior. No appearances may all be in her favor, but a woman is not truly good, unless she is good through and through. All that is remote from wrong-doing, must also be removed from very image or semblance of wrong, because as a Latin poet has well said, she alone is chaste on whom not even lying gossip dares to cast a slur. Certain it is that as one who sets out for the shrine of St. James is called by us a pilgrim, although he may not reach his journey's end, so, without shadow of doubt, has she made a beginning towards being a loose woman, who permits herself to discuss such matters, for these are the way. Were not all this true, what confidence is this of which God speaks at this point? In what is said immediately after, this is made clear, because he adds: *Her husband shall have no need of spoils.*

By spoils, the Holy Spirit means, as some understand it, what are called in Spanish, valuables and house furnishings, or, as I consider more certain, spoils are those earnings which come by way of salable goods or wares. For, be it noted, men build up an income and maintain themselves and live, either by the cultivation of the soil, or by barter, and business transactions with other man. The first mode of acquiring property is a harmless and a blessed one, because it is purely natural; and for this reason, that a man eats of the kindly fruit of his labors, hurting or injuring no one, and neither at the expense, nor to the loss, of anyone. And further, in like manner as it is natural to mothers to nourish with their own milk the children born to them, and natural to the children guided by instinct to feed at the breast, so are we inclined and disposed by nature to draw from the earth, our mother and universal parent, whatever is needful for our sustenance.

As to the other manner of earning and acquiring, which makes profit and enriches itself from other men's property, either with the consent of their owners, as do merchants, and the masters, and artificers of other crafts, who sell their wares, or by force and under compulsion, as happens in war, this manner is little in accord with nature. Here, for the most part, a certain degree of injustice and violence enter in, and those persons, at whose expense, profit is made, ordinarily hand over their possessions sullenly and disconsolately. For which reason, everything gained in this way, is spoken of by the Scriptures, and for a fitting reason, spoils. Clearly, by what goes to swell the merchant's estate, by so much is he who bargains with him left bereft and impoverished, and through not by war, yet by means of a sort of warfare, not always very just.

Therefore, the Holy Spirit states at this point that the first quality, and the primary work in which a married woman is to perfect herself is to inspire her husband with confidence and assurance: that having her to keep his house well-supplied and rich, he has no need to sail the seas, or go to war, or put his money out at usurious interest, and still less, to entangle himself in base and underhanded transactions. On the contrary, by tilling his fields, and gathering his harvests, and by having her to safeguard and use to advantage what has been harvested, he possesses riches in abundance. And that this guardianship, and this turning to good account pertain to the office of the wife, and form part of her perfection is not only the teaching of the Holy Spirit but is also demonstrated by common sense.

Certain it is that nature ordained the marriage of men and women not only to the end that lineage and name should be perpetuated in their children, but also that they themselves, and in their own persons should be preserved; an impossible thing to a man alone, or to the woman, with the man. Because, in order to live, it does not suffice that one should increase one's goods, unless what is gained is not dissipated; if what is acquired is wasted, it is as if it had never been acquired. Furthermore, man who possesses strength to upturn the soil, and to break land, to wander over the earth, and to transact business with men by bartering his commodities, cannot remain in his home as its guardian, nor is this according to his nature. Contrariwise, woman lacking physical strength, and limited in endurance, is inclined to quietude and frugality, and for the very reason that she lacks aptitude for the labor and sweat of amassing goods, is thereby fitted for economical management. Therefore, nature provident in all things, bound the one to the other, so that each, adding unto the other his resources, both together might live, since asunder, they were bound to perish. Out of dispositions so diverse, as is done in music upon different strings, nature called forth a precious and beautiful harmony: the husband busy in the fields, the wife busy at her home-making, and the latter holding and employing to good purpose, whatsoever the other might gather together. A poet has rightly said that the foundation-stones of a home are the woman and ox: the ox to plough, the woman to save.

It is woman's very nature which produces in her this aptitude for thrift, and induces in her this virtue as a part of her perfection: indeed, it is one of the most important and outstanding characteristics of her perfection. And this trait is recognized by the many and good effects which it brings about only one of which Solomon mentions here when he says that *the heart of her husband doth safely trust in her, so that he shall have no need of spoil.*

He shall have no need of spoil! Because possessing her, he is content with the heritage of his forbears, with the cultivation and harvest of his fields, neither running into debt, nor, much less, enmeshing himself in the perils and disappointments of other means of gain and trade, all of which, regarded from any viewpoint, is an unspeakable blessing. From the point of view of conscience alone, the husbandman living off his patrimony leads an innocent life, and one void of offence; whereas it is only a miracle that other means of livelihood are blameless or above suspicion. If it is a matter of restfulness, the farmer finds his rest at home, but the trader spends the major part of his life in hostelries, or on the road. The wealth of the one calls forth no criticism from anyone, of his own, that of the other is gossiped about, and abhorred. The one gets his livelihood from the soil, which never grows weary, never grumbles about yielding up its treasures; the other is defamed by the very ones who enrich him. And if we have in mind a spotless reputation, certain it is that there is nothing more base, more discreditable to a man than to deceive and to lie, and it is only by exception if any business transaction is free from fraud.

What shall I say now about the rearing of children, the harmony of the family, the wholesomeness of body and mind, save that they all follow the same order? Because it is inevitable, that he who absents himself from home should discover therein many an unpleasantness which arises, and grows, and gathers strength from the absence of the master. Also, it follows infallibly that he who tries to cheat should be cheated in turn, and that he who traffics and has dealing with people different in disposition and customs from his own, should contract many bad habits.

On the contrary, life in the country, and the cultivation of one's fields, make, as it were, a school of innocence and rectitude. One is bound to learn from those with whom one deals and converses. And as the earth in that which is entrusted to it is faithful, and in its steadfastness stable and dependable; openhanded in putting forth and bring to light its riches, and generous and well-supplied for all just dealing; so seemingly, it engenders and impresses in the hearts of those who till it a peculiar kindliness, a sort of unaffectedness of disposition; an intercourse sincere and loyal, full of honesty, and good and time-honored customs; such as are found with difficulty in those who follow another mode of life. But over and above all this, mother earth brings up her children to be sturdy and courageous, merry-hearted, and disposed for every sort of goodness. And the source of all these benefits, the root from which all spring, are the thrift and diligence of the wife, as we have already explained.

Let us now consider in what this thrift consists. It consists in two particulars: first, that a wife be not extravagant; and second, that she be not slothful. We shall take each of these in turn.

The perfect wife is not to be extravagant or wasteful, for, indeed, she has no reason to be so. All the expenses we run into are either to provide for our needs, or for our pleasures: either to remedy the natural necessities we were born with, of hunger or nakedness, or to gratify the individual fancies and tastes, which through our own weakness, we have created for ourselves. As to the former, nature itself imposed great limitations upon women; as regards the latter, nature obliged them to impose great limitations upon themselves. If the truth must be told, and if we consider solely what is their nature, the wants and necessities of women are much less than those of men. In the matter of food, a little will suffice them, since naturally they are less hot than men, wherefore it is very unbecoming to them to be greedy about dainties, or to be gluttonous. And it is the same, neither more nor less, in matters of dress. Nature made women, on the one hand, slow in movement so that they might be easy on their clothes; and, on the other hand, made them very trim so that whatever they put on, be it ever so simple, might become them well. Therefore, those who imagine that by dint of clothes and makeups they can make themselves good-looking labor under a great delusion: a woman who is beautiful remains a beauty however much awry her clothes may be; and she who is homely remains homely, and looks it too, and the more she overdresses, the more unattractive she is. All the more reason why the perfect wife of whom we are treating, be she homely or handsome, should be unwilling to appear other than she is, as will be explained presently.

To sum up the matter: as concerning their needs, nature has liberated women from a great deal of expense; in respect to their hobbies and pleasures, it holds them back by very strict obligations so that they may not run into extravagance. One of these obligations comes from woman's very nature: self-effacing, modest, temperate. So it follows that although unrestraint and prodigality, and to give loose rein to vain and unnecessary desires is blameworthy in all sorts of people, in women, born as they are for submission and humility, all this is much more vicious and reprehensible. Their condemnation being greater, I cannot understand how women, under obligation, therefore, to use more self-restraint, yet when they do break bounds, are more unbridled and go to greater lengths than men, and there is no measure and no end to their improvidence. This constitutes the second reason why women should be very self-controlled in gratifying their caprices: let them once begin to be immoderate, and there is an end to moderation. They are like a bottomless well, never full, no matter how much is poured into it; or like wood-borer perpetually boring; or like a hidden blaze which spreads silently throughout the house and property, until everything is in ashes.

Evidently, this is not a case of spending for to-day only, but of spending every day; not an expense which is undertaken once in a life-time, but one which goes on for life; not, as they say, a matter of many little things, but of many and very great ones.

If women are fond of good living, then their whole life turns on luncheon, and the afternoon refection, and the garden, with a companion gossip, and there goes a well-spent day! If clothes are their predilection, this business passes the bounds of passionate fondness, and ends in unbelievable folly and madness. Because, it is one frock to-day and another to-morrow, and every feast-day my lady must come out in something new; and what they make one day, they rip up the next, and everything their eyes light upon becomes a fad. Furthermore in their frenzy they go to even greater lengths, and become the self-constituted designers and inventors of new modes and costumes, even making it a matter of reputation to come out in what nobody ever saw before. Now while all masters like to have pupils who imitate them, these are so perverted that when they see others appearing in fashions they themselves have set, they loathe them, and cogitate, and lose sleep over inventing new ones. So the madness grows, and now they are no longer pleased with what is charming and beautiful, but only with what is expensive and showy. The material must come from the ends of the earth. Their brocades must be more heavily beaded and embroidered, three layers high; their gloves must be bathed in amber perfume, as also the leathern jacket, and even their slippers, which, in addition, must sparkle with gold, and the head-dress as well. The mantle, too, must be more lavishly garnished than the overskirt: everything has to be up-to-date and just out—made yesterday, to be worn to-day, and flung aside to-morrow.

Even as runaway horses, once they get the bit in their mouths, become more ungovernable the harder they run, and like the stone which, dropped from a height, gains in velocity the lower it falls, so the thirst of such women increases with drinking, and some great piece of folly or rashness which they commit marks the beginning of one even greater, and the more they spend, the more they revel in spending.

Now herein another great evil: whenever men turn out to be spendthrifts, in the majority of cases they spend, possibly not on necessary things, but on things which are at least lasting or estimable, or which to some degree are both useful and profitable. Such are those who to some degree, are both useful and profitable. Such are those who build sumptuously, or maintain a large family circle, or those who love to keep up enormous stables. But the expenditures of women are all a puff of wind: lavish spending, and for all their spending, nothing valuable or distinguished in return. Furbelows and gloves, scents and perfumes, jet ornaments, glass-ware imitation stuff, and other store rubbish which one cannot look at without loathing, or handle without a stench. Why, it frequently happens that a scholar does not spend as much on his books, as does a woman on blondining her hair. God deliver us from so great a misery!

But I must not lay all the blame on the wives, nor am I so unchristian as to do so. Well I know that much of this comes from the short patience of the husbands. At this point I should like to digress with my pen and say somewhat about husbands were I not deterred by the compassion I feel for them. Verily, husbands may be to blame, but they pay for their wrongdoing until seventy times seven.

Wherefore, let not the perfect wife be extravagant; let her not stake her reputation on spending more than her neighbor; but let her house be better supplied, and more perfectly kept up than her neighbor's. Let her by her deftness and neatness make an old frock look like new; and see to it that by its spotlessness, any dress she puts on may look well on her. The worn, commonplace dress, because of her carefulness, may come to look fresh and unusual. For it is contrary to the office of a wife to be thriftless; her needs do not demand this, and for the indulgence of her whims, extravagance is both vicious and wrong—a never-ending business which destroys the home, impoverishes the indwellers, enmeshes them in a hundred and one snares, and in untold ways beats them down and degrades them.[7]

1.5. POPULAR GROUPS: THE VIRGIN OF GUADALUPE VERSUS THE VIRGIN OF REMEDIOS

For many individuals the struggle for or against the Spaniards and for or against independence was played out through the images of the two most popular symbols of the Catholic culture in New Spain. The Virgins of Guadalupe and of Remedios collided in a monumental conflict. Their representations, through close exam-

Miguel Hidalgo's The Virgin of Guadalupe banner.
Wikimedia Commons, by Ludovicus Ferdinandus.

The Virgin of Remedios banner of those against independence.
Wikimedia Commons, photo by Fregenal01.

ination and by placing them in context, tell much about popular views and the Spanish Catholic culture. Because the account of the appearance of The Virgin of Guadalupe is contained in general histories of Mexico, it is not included here. The Virgin of Remedios is less known, so along with the visual, following is a documentary account of this Spanish Virgin.

The Virgin of Remedios

There are numerous shrines dedicated to the small image of Nuestra Señora de los Remedios said to have been carried by one of Cortés's men. The image itself is in Mexico City at the National Cathedral. According to the legend this wooden figure was taken, a few days before the disastrous Noche Triste retreat from Tenochtitlan and hidden near Naucalpam, beneath a giant maguey. Twenty years later it was found by an Indian noble who carried it to his home, and made an altar for it. During the night it vanished, and the next day the man found it again under the maguey. He took the figure home again, put it in a chest and slept on the lid. Next morning it was gone again, only to be found once more beneath the maguey. The events were reported to a priest who announced that a miracle had been performed.

A shrine was built on the hill where the figure was found, and the tiny wooden doll was dressed in satins and pearls. Her powers of warding off epidemics and droughts were so great a larger shrine was soon built. She was so revered she was solemnly received by viceroys and bishops, and lavish gifts were thrust upon her. At the time of the War of Independence the Spanish royalists made her their protectoress (in opposition to the dark Virgin of Guadalupe who led the Mexico troops to ultimate victory), and she was made a General in the Royal Army. According to tales, when the Virgen de los Remedios was captured during battle, she was stripped of her uniform by a Mexican general, and she was ordered deported from Mexico. She was allowed to remain only when it was promised she would stay out of politics.[8]

ADDITIONAL READING

Rodríguez de la O., Jaime. *Down from Colonialism: Mexico's Nineteenth Century Crisis.* Los Angeles: UCLA Chicano Studies Research Center, 1983.

Leer en español

Villoro, Luis. "La revolución de independencia." In *Historia general de México: Versión 2000*, by Ignacio Bernal, 489–524. Mexico City: El Colegio de México, 2000.

NOTES

1. Susan Deeds and Michael Meyer, *The Course of Mexican History* (New York: Oxford University Press, 2015), 276.
2. William F. Cloud, *Church and State or Mexican Politics from Cortez to Diaz* (Kansas City, MO: Peck & Clark, Printers, 1896), 186.
3. This is the version often proclaimed by the president of Mexico to initiate the celebration of Independence Day. The president gives the *grito* on the central balcony of the national executive office building or at Padre Hidalgo's church in Dolores Hidalgo. For each line beginning ¡*Viva(n)*! ("Long Live!") recited by the president, the crowd responds with ¡*Viva(n)*! ("May He/She[They] Long Live!"). Local leaders often adapt this for state or town celebrations.
4. "Discurso de Miguel Hidalgo al Pueblo de Dolores para dar inicio a la independencia de México," 500 años de México en documentos, http://www.biblioteca.tv/artman2/publish/1810_115/Discurso_de_Miguel_Hidalgo_al_Pueblo_de_Dolores_pa_604.shtml.
5. Gloria Villegas Moreno and Miguel Angel Porrúa Venero, eds., *Enciclopedia Parlamentaria de México, del Instituto de Investigaciones Legislativas de la Cámara de Diputados, LVI Legislatura*, Series III, Documents, Volume I: "Constitutive Laws and Documents of the Mexican Nation" (Mexico City: First Edition, 1997), 71. Online at http://www.biblioteca.tv/artman2/publish/1810_115/Edictos_del_obispo_electo_de_Michoac_n_125.shtml.
6. Ernesto de la Torre Villar, "La independencia," in *Historia documental de México*, ed. Miguel León Portilla (Mexico City: Universidad Nacional Autónoma de México, 2005), 1: 318–20. Online at http://www.biblioteca.tv/artman2/publish/1810_115/El_Virrey_Venegas_ofrece_10_mil_pesos_por_las_cabezas_de_Hidalgo_Allende_y_Aldama.shtml
7. Luis de Leon, *The Perfect Wife*, trans. Alice Philena Hubbard (1583; Denton: Texas State College for Women, 1943). Reprinted by permission of Texas Women's College, Denton, Texas.
8. James Norman, *Terry's Guide to Mexico* (Garden City, NY: Doubleday & Company, Inc., 1965), 210, n. 19.

CHAPTER 2

The Early Republic, 1820–1848

The insurgent army occupied Mexico City and proclaimed the colony's independence on September 27, 1821. Replacing the crown and colonial rulers became the first challenge for the leaders of the independence movement; they used as a guide the Plan of Three Guarantees (2.1). In the decades immediately following independence, when some of the main institutions of society competed to fill the power void created by the demise of Spanish colonial rule, military officers, based on their service in the independence struggles, attempted to dominate politics and society (2.2). Much of the instability and turmoil that plagued the new nation in the years from the 1820s through 1850 can be directly tied to bitter struggles among the church, the government, and the military. The struggle between the popular Holy Virgins as religious symbols took on new political forms and contributed to the first constitution (2.3). At the same time, individuals at the popular level strived to make sense of the new realities and as they did so, honor codes proved more important than legislated rules (2.4). Among the people, amusements included puzzles and games, at times with political overtones (2.5). The US-Mexican War, with its terrible effects, concluded the era.

2.1. POLITICS: THE PLAN OF THREE GUARANTEES

The need for some kind of system of government in the former colony was anticipated by the document of the independence army called the Plan of Three Guarantees. *These guarantees would continue to define major political issues until midcentury as Mexicans struggled with the issues of independence.*

Agustín de Iturbide, *Plan de Iguala* (February 24, 1821)

PLAN OF THE COLONEL D. AGUSTÍN ITURBIDE
Copy of the Supplement to Number 14 of the Abeja Poblana [*The Puebla Bee*]
COMMUNICATED ARTICLE
Plan or indications to the government that must be provisionally installed with the objective of ensuring our sacred religion and establishing the independence of the Mexican Empire: and it will have the title of the North American Government Junta, proposed by Colonel D.Don Agustín de Iturbide to his Excellency, the Viceroy of N.S., Count del Venadito.

1. The Religion of New Spain is and shall be Catholic, apostolic and Roman, without toleration of any other.
2. New Spain is independent of the old and of any other power, including those within our Continent.
3. Its Government shall be a Monarchy moderated by the Kingdom's particular and flexible Constitution.
4. Its Emperor will be D.Don Fernando VII, and if he does not personally present himself to take the oath in Mexico within the term prescribed by the Courts [i.e., Parliament], his Most Serene Highness, the Prince Carlos, D.Don Francisco de Paulo, Archduke Carlos, or another individual of the Royal Household that the Congress considers suitable will be called upon to take his place.
5. While the courts [i.e., Parliament] convenes, a Junta will meet to assure compliance with the plan in all extents.
6. Said Junta, which will be designated as Governing, must be composed of representatives, as dictated by his Excellency, the Viceroy's official letter.
7. While D.Don Fernando VII presents himself in Mexico to be sworn in, the Junta will govern in the name of His Majesty by virtue of its oath to remain loyal to the nation; however the orders that he may have imparted will be suspended during the time in which he is not sworn in.
8. If D.Don Fernando VII does not consider it worthwhile to come to Mexico, the Junta or the Regency shall rule in the name of the nation while the issue of the Emperor to be crowned is resolved.
9. This government shall be supported by the army of the three guaranties that will be discussed later.
10. The courts [i.e., Parliament] shall resolve the continuation of the Junta, or its substitution with a Regency if deemed necessary, while awaiting the person who should be crowned.

11. The courts [i.e., Parliament] shall immediately establish the Constitution of the Mexican Empire.
12. All the inhabitants of New Spain, without any distinction between Europeans, Africans, or Indians, are citizens of this Monarchy, and have access to all employment according to their merits and virtues.
13. Every citizen's person and his properties shall be respected and protected by the government.
14. The secular and regular cleric will be preserved in all its rights and pre-eminences.
15. The Junta shall assure that all the branches of the state remain without any alteration and that all the political, ecclesiastic, civil, and military personnel [remain] in the same state as they exist today. Only those that manifest dissent with the plan shall be removed, replaced by those more distinguished by virtue and merit.
16. A protective army will be formed that shall be called [the army] of the three guarantees, and it will take under its protection: first, the conservation of the Roman Catholic apostolic Religion, cooperating by all means that are within its reach so that there will be no mixing with any other sect and opportunely attacking the enemies that could damage it; second, the independence under the manifested system; third, the intimate union of Americans and Europeans, thereby guaranteeing the bases so fundamental to the happiness of New Spain, sacrificing their lives for all individuals, from the first to the last, before consenting to their infringement.
17. The troops of the army will strictly observe the ordinances to the letter, and the chiefs and officers will continue to operate under the same laws as they do today: that is, in their respective classes with access to open employment as well as any posts that will be vacated by those who do not wish to toe the line, or for any other cause, and with access for those that are considered of necessity or convenience.
18. The troops of said army shall be considered regular troops.
19. The same will take place with those that follow this plan. Those that do not differ, those of the system prior to the independence that join said army immediately, and the countrymen who intend to enlist, shall be considered national militia troops, and the courts [i.e., Parliament] shall dictate all forms for the kingdom's domestic and foreign security.
20. Employment will be granted according to the true merit by virtue of reports from the respective chiefs and provisionally in the name of the Nation.
21. While the Courts are being established, delinquencies will be processed in total agreement with the Spanish Constitution [of 1812].

22. Conspiring against independence shall result in imprisonment without progressing to any other action until the Courts [i.e., Parliament] decides the penalty for the gravest of the delinquencies after that of Divine Majesty.
23. Those who encourage disunion shall be watched and shall be considered conspirators against independence.
24. Since the Courts [i.e., Parliament] to be installed shall be constituent, it is necessary that the deputies receive sufficient powers to that effect; and furthermore as it is of great importance that the voters know that their representatives will be for the Mexican Congress, and not for Madrid, the Junta shall prescribe the just rules for the elections and shall indicate the time necessary for them and for the opening of Congress. Since the elections may not be verified in March, the terms will be stretched as long as possible.
Iguala, February 24, 1821—This is a copy—Iturbide.
Printed in Puebla and reprinted in Mexico in the office of D. J. M., Benavente and Associates. Year 1821[1]

2.2. MILITARY: CHRISTON ARCHER, "INDEPENDENCE AND THE GENERATION OF GENERALS, 1810–1848"

Military officers had special privileges called Fueros *recognized in both colonial and later Mexican law. The development of the military caste of officers and of the militia units is the subject of this essay. After independence these individuals attempted to protect and to expand their unique social standing. Moreover, because of their service in arms, they had popular recognition that several parlayed into political authority and made military coups d'état a regular feature of government during the first half century after independence. Christon Archer here provides an analysis of the first generation of generals.*

Until 1810, few Mexicans (or Novohispanos) could have imagined that following the attainment of national independence in 1821, the army of New Spain might produce anything like a generation of dominant generals capable of controlling national politics and retaining power for many years. Indeed, before 1810, the regular army consisted of four regular infantry regiments each with officers, NCOs, and theoretically with complements of 961 soldiers (the Infantry Regiments of the Crown, New Spain, Mexico and Puebla), an expanded infantry battalion of 881 soldiers permanently stationed at the strategic port of Veracruz, two dragoon regiments, two artillery companies stationed at the fortress of San Juan de Ulúa, and two light infantry Companies of Catalonia. In fact, these units often were notoriously under strength and the Infantry Regiments of Mexico and Puebla were sent to help defend Havana and [were] not returned for many years. In the northern Provincias Internas (Internal Provinces), there were small frontier companies to protect against attacks by so-called "barbarian Indians" that included the Comanche and Apache tribes. Many enlisted men in the regular regiments entered military service unwillingly after having been sentenced to duty for petty crimes, immorality, or wandering as homeless vagabonds. Disease, desertion, and chronic drunkenness were persistent problems.

At the strategic port of Veracruz situated in the tropical lowlands, *vómito negro* (yellow fever) decimated soldiers from the temperate interior highlands who lacked any resistance to mosquito-borne diseases. In 1800–1802, very bad years for yellow fever, the Infantry Regiments of the Crown and New Spain suffered 1,220 disease deaths and 1,558 desertions by terrified soldiers—many of whom having witnessed the horrible deaths of their comrades sold their own uniforms to raise money and deserted. At Veracruz from 1787 [to] 1804, the Hospital Militar de San Carlos reported the deaths of 4,681 soldier patients and the Poor Hospital of Montesclaros the deaths of 6,729 patients some of whom were soldiers, army muleteers, and sutlers (suppliers). To replace these heavy losses, army recruiters scoured the jails and the countryside for new blood—often accepting recruits who were in trouble with the law for petty delinquency or already had been sentenced to lengthy terms of forced labor as *presidarios*. Although in theory the regular army was to have had an active force of about 5,800 troops, in reality these units were seldom popular with potential recruits. . . .

As a direct response to the British conquest and temporary occupation of Havana in 1762 during the Seven Years' War (1756–1763), the Spanish moved to establish a provincial army in New Spain. However, even before the American Revolution broke out in 1775, some metropolitan Spanish observers opposed the dangerous idea of arming overseas provincials who might seek to sever their ties with the metropolis. Following the loss of Havana, there was no other alternative to establishing some form of regulated military system. In order to inculcate martial values among the Novohispanos, at first the imperial regime rotated main line peninsular infantry regiments for overseas duty in New Spain. However, the remnants of the Spanish Infantry Regiment of Zamora that returned to Europe in the late 1780s were the last of the metropolitan infantry regiments to serve in New Spain until the Spanish expeditionary regiments arrived to fight against the Mexican insurgents during the War of Independence (1810–1821).

Although the framework for the army of New Spain had been established and approved by the crown, some observers believed that arming and organizing a provincial army of Novohispanos inevitably would pave the way for a future rebellion that Spain might not be able to suppress. This was the view held by Viceroy Juan Vicente de Güemes, 2nd Conde de Revillagigedo (1789–1794 as viceroy) who feared the negative example and influence of the French Revolution. He doubted the loyalty of the Novohispano population—particularly that of the mixed race *castas* and the Indians. He disbanded the *pardo* and *Moreno* (mulatto and Black) militias and even more surprisingly decided to set aside Crespo's plan to raise a provincial army. Revillagigedo believed that this approach would grant the Novohispano *criollos* (whites) far too much power and influence. Confident of success, Revillagigedo moved without authorization from Madrid to disband the existing provincial militia units. In the meantime, however, the Captain General of Cuba warned the imperial government that revolutionary French forces threatened Cuba, Florida, and Spanish Louisiana. Based upon this information, in April, 1792, the Minister of War in Madrid authorized the Captain General of Cuba to requisition the Infantry Regiment of New Spain for duty in Cuba—leaving Mexico protected by little more than the Infantry Regiment of the Crown. From the perspective of the Spanish metropolitan military authorities, the precarious situation in Europe, the West Indies and the Gulf of Mexico required immediate attention while a major attack on New Spain seemed unlikely because France would not be able to mobilize a large overseas invasion force. With three of the four regular Novohispano infantry regiments on duty already in Cuba and Louisiana, Revillagigedo decided to disband the existing militia system of New Spain and he moved to create his own alternative. His objective was to raise regular army regiments that would have strong contingents of European Spanish officers and soldiers. In the military reorganization plan of February 1790 Revillagigedo described militias as absolutely useless, and without awaiting authorization from the crown commenced to disband existing units and to promote his concept for new regular army units that required contingents of soldiers and officers from the Spanish army. His military plan failed to receive any support in Madrid where European events closer to home, such as the impact of the French Revolution, were of far greater concern.

In 1794, France declared war on Spain and dispatched an invasion force through the Pyrenees to occupy the city of San Sebastián. In New Spain, Viceroy Revillagigedo completed his term on July 12 with the arrival in Mexico City of his successor Viceroy Miguel de la Grúa Talamanca, Marqués de Branciforte, a Sicilian by birth. On his trip inland from Veracruz to Mexico City, Branciforte expressed concern that in his opinion the defenses of New Spain were almost nonexistent. Moreover, fearing attacks by French forces, the Spanish commanders in Louisiana, Florida, Cuba and other Caribbean jurisdictions clamored for additional funds and troop reinforcements from New Spain. Branciforte recognized that a potentially disastrous defensive situation in New Spain resulted from Revillagigedo's rejection of Crespo's Plan Militar and his failure to obtain authorization from Madrid to implement a new and more costly defense program. Although recently arrived, Branciforte recognized that the key to developing an effective defense system in New Spain lay in establishing close relationships with wealthy creole miners, landowners, and merchants. He observed that the bureaucrats who controlled the urban *cabildos* (city and town councils) were anxious to gain additional social recognition and higher public offices. Before long, he concluded that a provincial militia system could be implemented paid for by private donations of aspirants for commissions. Those who aspired to attain militia commissions received invitations to offer voluntary donations to raise a militia company or squadron, a battalion, or in the cases of the extremely wealthy, to underwrite the entire costs of uniforms, arms, and horses for cavalry and dragoon regiments. In 1795, an infantryman cost forty pesos to uniform and equip and a dragoon up to seventy pesos.

In some jurisdictions, many individual donors contributed relatively small sums to rebuild militia battalions or regiments. Elsewhere fabulously wealthy mining and landholding [magnates]—such as Diego Rul, the conde de Casa Rul, whose wife was a daughter of the deceased Conde de Valenciana and who was the richest miner in the history of Guanajuato—financed the military units.

By the beginning of 1810, Viceroy Lizana exhibited signs of exhaustion and was unable to respond to the external or internal threats. In April, 1810, reports arrived of the fall of Málaga, the entry of the French army into Sevilla, and the siege of Cádiz. News of the French occupation of Andalusia and the collapse of the Junta Central depressed loyal Novohispanos and for some others opened the way to eccentric schemes and more dangerous projects. After the weak efforts of Garibay and Lizana that failed to restore stability to New Spain, the Council of the Regency interim regime at Cádiz appointed Francisco Javier de Venegas, the acclaimed hero of the Battle of Bailén, to become viceroy and captain general of New Spain. He arrived at Veracruz on August 25, 1810, inspected the army units in the cantonment of Jalapa, and assumed office in Mexico on September 14, only two days before the outbreak of the great insurgency led by Cura Miguel Hidalgo y Costilla.

Although the provincial army of New Spain was successful in putting down minor uprisings, the message of Cura Hidalgo mobilized an almost spontaneous reaction from large segments of the Indian, mestizo, mulatto and casta population. Although it is difficult even to estimate the numbers involved, the messages of Hidalgo and other insurgent leaders resonated among the rural and village populations and in some regions they responded to the call to arms. The insurgents were highly successful in spreading their message and in recruiting numerous supporters. On the royalist side, the regular and provincial militia regiments were at first incapable of immediate responses. For years, the major task of the military had been to anticipate how to response to a landing by a British or French expeditionary army. In September 1810, the troops assigned to the garrison of Veracruz and those serving at the cantonment of Jalapa were for a short time distant from the regions disrupted by the contagion. Nevertheless, the messages of Hidalgo and other insurgent leaders soon spread beyond their home provinces and tapped into old grievances and complaints concerning landholding, privileges, distribution of resources, and arbitrary governance by local officials.

Brigadier Félix Calleja, a former protégé of the Conde de Revillagigedo, now commander of the Tenth Militia Brigade based at San Luis Potosí, learned about the uprising on September 19 at 10:30 in the morning. At the moment, he possessed no mobilized military force that he could commit to fight a skirmish let alone a major battle. Shocked by the news, Calleja faced the task of disciplining an army of green militiamen with not one previously well-trained soldier. He assembled the commanders of his militia brigade, gathered the untrained vaqueros from the nearby haciendas, and ordered blacksmiths and carpenters to manufacture lances, machetes, and swords. The muskets available in his brigade were a very old and worn out assortment belonging to the Provincial Dragoon Regiments of San Luis and San Carlos. On September 23, Calleja received a dispatch from the Intendant of Guanajuato, Juan Antonio Riaño, who reported that he was in dire straits, surrounded by insurgent forces and cut off from provisions. Irapuato had fallen the day previously and he knew that the large urban population had begun to waver. Riaño wrote more and more desperate notes until September 28, when he sent one last message stating that he was about to be attacked and would resist as long as he could. Within hours, the insurgents had sacked the granary and killed the intendant and all of the European and creole defenders.

Viceroy Venegas commanded Calleja to mobilize his brigade and to march immediately to Querétaro where he was to join forces with other militia units from Puebla. Horrified by this order, since his dispersed militia forces were not immediately available, Calleja had to defer for weeks until he could mobilize artisans to construct lances for his dragoons and to recruit Indian bowmen. Lacking artillery, Calleja assembled a junta of blacksmiths and other artisans to see if they possessed sufficient skills needed to cast iron and bronze artillery pieces. They claimed that they were capable, but in the end managed to produce only one barrel suitable enough to be mounted on a carriage. The rest of their gun barrels were either too small to cause much damage or more often flawed during the casting process making them dangerous even to test fire. In the meantime, on October 9, 1810, the Marqués del Xaral Berrio, Commander of Calleja's advanced guard patrols, sighted an enormous insurgent force likely much overestimated at 40,000 to 50,000 men that appeared to be marching toward San Luis Potosí. He described them as moving by roads and through barrancas like a swarm of ants loaded down with booty from their robberies and determined to incite the country to rebellion.

In spite of the apparent strength of the insurgent forces, their major advantage was more an illusion than a reality. While effective in guerrilla fights, the poorly armed Indian and *casta* soldiers could not withstand the firepower of well organized and disciplined infantrymen trained to fire volleys from smoothbore muskets and backed by charges with fixed bayonets. As the Marqués de Xaral Berrio reported, the insurgents viewed the breakdown of law and order as an opportunity to pillage cities, towns, villages, and haciendas. Even if a few better trained officers and NCOs on the insurgent side attempted to implement military training and proper use of firearms, they needed time and training before they could convert rural *campesinos* into good soldiers. This became evident first in the conventional battlefield confrontations between the insurgents and royalist forces at Aculco, Guanajuato, and Puente de Calderón, in which massed musketry and better discipline among the moderately well-trained militiamen produced royalist victories. When the rebels altered their tactics to construct fortifications on mountain peaks, on islands in lakes such Mezcala in Laguna de Chapala, or in other isolated situations, they gained some success in the short term. Inevitably and often at high cost in resources and lives, the royalists besieged and attacked these positions or starved out the unfortunate defenders.

In June, 1811, Calleja issued a document titled the Reglamento Político Militar that formulated a significant but also a very controversial counterinsurgency program. He recognized that a general fragmented insurgency employing guerrilla warfare would inevitably exhaust the regular and militia units of the royalist army. His clever artifice was to declare a unilateral end to the insurgency. By degrading the insurgent opposition to that of common bandits, thieves, and delinquents, Calleja sought to gain a propaganda victory and equally to demonize the enemy. Backing his program, he introduced a tiered system of defense based upon royalist militias organized in the cities, towns, and rural districts. Some observers criticized Calleja, declaring that it was premature to suggest that the insurgency was at an end—and for making such wild claims that might even stimulate the insurgents to launch gratuitous attacks to prove their capabilities. Calleja responded to his critics by stating that the goal was simply to organize patriot militia companies composed of local men recruited from the cities, towns, and rural districts. The objectives were to isolate and to marginalize the rural-based insurgents, and to strengthen city and town defenses so that the lightly armed insurgents would not dare to attack without artillery. He explained to the district subdelegados that the army could not be present everywhere and that the people of the province must take up arms in their own defense. When this took place, the royalist army commanders would be able to unite some garrisons and to concentrate their forces against the major foci of insurgency. Critics of Calleja's plan complained bitterly about the high costs of funding and that in Veracruz province, for example, most of the arable land belonged to absentee landlords. Most of the landless peasants wanted their own plots of land—using guerrilla warfare as a means to secure their control and to support their contraband trade with the port city.

Beginning in 1816, many historians identify a slowdown in the intensity of the level of combat between the royalists and the insurgents. Lucas Alamán suggested that the royalist army backed by effective counterinsurgency repression had restored communications and allowed Viceroy Juan Ruiz de Apodaca to amnesty many former insurgents. Except for mopping up operations in mountainous regions of Veracruz, Jalisco, and Michoacán, Alamán declared the insurgency ended. After 1816, there were fewer large insurgent groups operating in the field. If the army could exert sufficient force, the rebels who had families to support accepted royal amnesties, joined the provincial militias, or simply returned to their previous endeavors. This had not been the situation in 1815 when for months the bands of Veracruz insurgents closed all communications between Jalapa and Veracruz. One convoy languished in Jalapa for over six months. The Consulado of Veracruz reported a "mortal paralysis" of internal and external trade, criticizing the army for its failures and repressive policies. Travelers and merchants paid insurgent taxes levied for permission to move, while the army offered an inefficient and ineffective program of escorted convoys. To show good faith, the imperial government ordered General Pablo Morillo to transfer 4,000 troops from his expeditionary army in Venezuela, which did not arrive. Instead, an expedition under Field Marshal Pascual de Liñán and Brigadier Fernando Miyares y Mancebo about to sail from Cádiz for Peru, received instructions from the minister of war to alter their destination to Veracruz. The ministry placed priority emphasis on maintaining open communications between Veracruz and Mexico City—and in garrisoning a defended "camino military" with sufficient troops to repel the insurgents. Even so, this pressure from the imperial army leadership produced only temporary deterrence. In 1818, the Veracruz insurgents that had been dispersed once again coalesced to apply their own system of special tolls. This time Viceroy Venadito (Apodaca) dispatched Field Marshall Liñán to assume the governorship of Veracruz Province with orders to establish fortified villages, amnesty rebels, and crush recalcitrant insurgent bands.

Brigadier Domingo Luaces, commander of the 2nd battalion of the Infantry Regiment of Zaragoza, stationed at Querétaro in 1818, reported that notwithstanding years of counterinsurgency bands of 200 to 300 insurgents attacked the rural haciendas of the province almost daily. Their pressure intimidated and exhausted the local militia companies. Luaces described a growing state of exhaustion within his own command caused by constant patrols and pursuits of insurgent bands. He complained that his infantrymen had been given too many and that he needed a dragoon regiment to deploy flying detachments that might be able to recover some of the more isolated haciendas from rebel control. Luaces reported that his overburdened soldiers expressed feelings of hopelessness and anger that made them listless, demoralized, and amenable to desertion. In August 1818, the royal treasury owed his regiment 14,000 pesos in back payments that had not been made available. In some cases, officers borrowed money themselves in order to assist their men with the purchase of daily provisions. Uniforms, shoes, and equipment had deteriorated to the point that some officers reported that their men were almost naked and embarrassed to appear in public. Similar conditions prevailed in many garrisons and offered arguments to accept the proposal of Agustín de Iturbide to end the war with the Plan de Iguala and the concepts of "Independence," "Religion," and "Union."

Many officers who served in the Mexican army on the insurgent side in the period after Independence up to the Mexican American War were veterans who began their military careers in the years between 1810 and 1821. Seven former insurgents—Guadalupe Victoria, Nicolás Bravo, Vicente Guerrero, José María Tornel y Mendivil, Manuel Rincón, Juan Álvarez, and Melchor Muzquiz—achieved the senior rank of division general, and four others became brigade generals. Many more Mexican generals of the post-Independence epoch were creoles, though some were *peninsulares* who had been transferred from Spain before 1810 or arrived with their expeditionary regiments between 1812 and 1817. Well after Mexican Independence, many royalists continued to think of the insurgents as potentially dangerous savages—of low class origins and given to vandalism, drunkenness, and cruelty. Few well off or wealthy Mexican creole families of royalist origins wanted their sons and daughters to have anything to do with such barbarous and uncivilized persons. Indeed, the families of the old royalists and the old insurgents inhabited quite different solitudes.

Although it is difficult to follow the lives of the European Spanish officers in New Spain, many of them maintained contact with each other, exchanged information, and until 1821 expressed keen interest in promotions within the metropolitan Spanish Army. In an era during which patronage relationships were all important there were many bitter rivalries and enmities among officers concerning advancement. Senior commanders looked after their favorite subordinates and developed circles of friendship and assistance. For example, the Captain General and Governor of Nueva Galicia José de la Cruz maintained close ties with his subordinates such as Pedro Celestino Negrete, a *peninsular*, and Luis Quintanar, a creole. Both Negrete and Quintanar became powerful counterinsurgency commanders and later played important roles in regional and district administration. After 1821, both officers achieved high rank and position in the Mexican army and were influential in political life.

As might be expected, after 1821 the *gachupín* officers who severed their relations with their mother country and interrupted their military careers almost immediately found themselves central figures in a campaign to expel them from Mexico. The basis for this effort reflected creole resentments and memories of the vengeful cruelties of the royalist counterinsurgency campaigns. For many Mexicans, Iturbide and other military figures represented brutal repression, the destruction of the economy, and irreparable damage to society. There was a movement to expel the *"capitulados"* (the Spanish soldiers who surrendered) and even to remove those *gachupines* who supported the Plan de Iguala. After a decade of suffering, many Mexicans wanted particularly to expel any *gachupín* who had played a role in the counterinsurgency programs. The assassination of Colonel Manuel de Concha, who was one of the most brutal and efficient royalist counterinsurgency commanders, convinced some of his former colleagues that they should abandon Mexico while they could. Concha had received many threats and was murdered in Jalapa on his way to Veracruz to board a ship for Spain. Agustín de Iturbide, who for a short time managed to become the first emperor of Mexico, died before a firing squad in 1824 at the village of Padilla near Veracruz. For a long while, Mexico's destructive War of Independence left the economy damaged and society disrupted. After 1821, the new nation needed time to rebuild and to restore itself. Instead, leaders such as Antonio López de Santa Anna, and other generals who had developed their careers as royalist counterinsurgency commanders and in some cases fought on the insurgent side, seized control of the nation. Preoccupied by internal divisions and incapable of defending themselves against a much more powerful northern neighbor, the generals were poor stewards of their nation and of its population. . . .

Senior Spanish Officers who abandoned Spain and the Spanish Army in 1821 to serve Mexico.
Domingo Estanislao Luaces, Coronel de Infantería de Zaragoza
Manuel Torres Valdivia, antiguo Comandante en San Luis Potosí
Brigadier Pedro Celestino Negrete
Melchor Álvarez, Coronel de la Infantería de la Reyna
Joaquín de Arredondo, Comandante General, Provincias Internas de Oriente
Rafael Bracho, Coronel de Infantería de Zamora
Manuel Obeso, Teniente Coronel de la Infantería de la Reyna
Gregorio Arana, Comandante de la Infantería de Mallorca

Froilán Bocinos, Teniente Coronel de la Infantería de Zaragoza
Pedro San Julián, Teniente Coronel de la Infantería de Zaragoza[2]

2.3. CHURCH, POLITICS, AND SOCIETY: THE CONSTITUTION OF 1824

In the first years of the Early Republic, the Virgin of Remedios remained a Spanish symbol, associated with the Scottish Rite Masons and the creation of Mexico City as the Federal District; she was opposed by the Virgin of Guadalupe, the favorite of the York Rite Masons, who wanted Mexico City to remain a part of the state of Mexico.[3] The masonic struggle with their different patrons finally created the Constitution of 1824 that included the following description of the nation and its religion.

THE FEDERAL CONSTITUTION OF THE UNITED MEXICAN STATES, SANCTIONED BY THE GENERAL CONSTITUENT CONGRESS ON THE 4TH OF OCTOBER, 1824.
CONSTITUTION OF THE UNITED MEXICAN STATES.

TITLE I.

ONLY SECTION [Italics in source.]
Of the Mexican Nation, its Territory and Religion. [Italics in source.]

ARTICLE 1. The Mexican nation is for ever free and independent of the Spanish government and of every other power.

Article 2. Its territory comprehends the former vice-royalty of New Spain, the captain-generalship of Yucatan, the former commandancies of the internal provinces of the East and West and Upper and Lower California with the lands annexed and the adjacent islands in both oceans. A constitutional law will be made for designating the boundaries of the Federation as soon as circumstances will permit.

Article 3. The religion of the Mexican nation shall perpetually remain the Roman Catholic and Apostolic. The nation protects it by wise and just laws and prohibits the exercise of any other.

TITLE II.

ONLY SECTION. [Italics in source.]
Of the form of Government of the Nation, in its integral parts, and of the division of the Supreme Power. [Italics in source.]

Article 4. The Mexican nation adopts for the form of its government a popular representative and federal republic.

Article 5. The constituent parts of the Federation are the following States and Territories, viz: the States of Chiapas, Chihuahua, Coahuila and Texas, Durango, Guanajuato, Mexico, Michoacan, Nuevo Leon, Oajaca, Pueblo de los Angeles, Queretaro, San Luis Potosi, Sonora and Sinaloa, Tabasco, Tamaulipas, Vera Cruz, Jalisco, Yucatan, and Zacatecas; the Territories of Upper California, Lower California, Colima, and Santa Fe de Nuevo Mexico. A constitutional law will fix the character of Tlascala.

Article 6. The Supreme power of the Federation as to its exercise, is divided into the legislative, executive and judicial powers.

Among the powers of the General Congress, the Constitution enumerated the following, in TITLE III, SECTION 5, Article 50:

12th. To give instructions for the forming of Concordates with the Holy See, to approve and ratify the same, and to regulate the exercise of patronage (patronato) in the whole Union.[4]

2.4. FAMILY AND GENDER: HONOR CODE AS CUSTOM TAKES PRECEDENCE OVER WRITTEN LAWS

Many indigenous and *mestizo* peasants from the area and surrounding highlands of the Sierra de Álica constituted the primary workforce. Even Manuel Lozada and his gang members, who had found sustenance by preying on growing streams of commerce, spent their early years working on the region's haciendas. So, more than a geographic crossroads, the large central swath of Jalisco's seventh canton [*Tepic*] constituted a point of congregation, interaction, and investment for a diverse cross-section of local society.

But just because foreign merchants, mestizos, and Indians intermingled regularly in and around Tepic, the seventh canton did not constitute a proverbial melting pot. [Ireneo] Paz's words [*in the novel* Manuel Lozada: El Tigre de Álica] make this clear. The unarmed representative of the Barrón y Forbes Company was "respectably dressed" and traveled on a bridled horse. In addition to such markers of class, civility, and urbanity, his manner of speech suggested that he had enjoyed a formal education. Even if the representative had been born locally, he was linked to a small but growing community of mostly European foreigners who entered the region after the fall of the Spanish monopoly to find their fortune. In contrast, Lozada, and his gang were largely illiterate, humbly dressed, traveled by foot, and had never ventured too far from home. Although Paz dismissively and incorrectly refers to Lozada as a "little Indian" of limited mental agility, his language reveals an air of perceived ethnic distinction that had long divided the European and mestizo lowlanders—with whom Paz clearly identified—from the mestizo and indigenous residents of the foothills and highlands. Even if three hundred years of racial mixing and nearly thirty years of independence had rendered useless most legal measures of difference, a mélange of cultural markers constituted an enduring vocabulary upon which one could call to discern oneself from an inferior "other."

These tensions rarely surfaced, however, and they certainly did not limit commercial interaction across class lines. In fact many residents of Tepic exuded optimism about the economic and social potential for the region so long as certain obstacles to trade could be overcome. According to Paz, the representative of the Barrón y Forbes Company quickly revealed to Lozada that the primary impetus for his visit was to persuade Lozada to put his muscle and local knowledge to work for the merchants. Specifically, he wanted Lozada's gang to facilitate the illicit exchange of goods, describing them as "cargos of merchandise that sometimes enter via permitted ports in agreement with port employees, and other times via any coastal point, which have to be defended from the port attendants or any public force that tries to capture them." Despite the public prominence of the Barrón y Forbes Company, they and other commercial entities like them would go to great lengths to protect themselves from the onerous tariffs assessed on the imported goods as well as the *alcabalas* (sales taxes) assessed on the overland transit of these goods. When port officials could not be paid to look the other way, the area under their watchful eyes could be circumvented. Such practices were part of doing business in the seventh canton of Jalisco and speak to local economic interests that spanned social categories to the degree that white elites and mestizo toughs found common cause. By manipulating or defying the tax collectors, merchants padded their profits and ensured their local economic dominance. For his part, Lozada entered into contact with the very revenue streams that later would underwrite his authority as an arbiter of local politics.

If a specific set of environmental factors and financial incentives brought a diverse array of actors together, an amorphous honor code cultivated a sense of trust among them. In Paz's imagination, after agreeing to the terms under which Lozada would provide protection for illicit trade, the Barrón y Forbes representative learned that Lozada's illiteracy prevented him from faithfully executing a written contract. Without hesitation, the representative responded, "It does not matter. Do you, sir, give your word of honor?" Lozada ratified the contract simply by responding in the affirmative and offering the visitor "a measure of cane liquor and cold rolls filled with chopped meat." The inviolability of such niceties should not be overestimated, but they speak to the prominence of shared cultural understandings based in a sense of masculine honor that easily substituted for universalizing legal codes and contracts. One's good character, affirmed through an observable respect for the sanctity of interpersonal relations, formed the basis for mutual trust and did not require the presence of a lawyer. In this manner, parties of distinct social and racial backgrounds entered into agreements with the pretense of resolving or eradicating such markers of distinction.

The involvement of the Catholic Church as a transmitter of moral authority in Jalisco also speaks to the ongoing relevance of supposedly *passé* forms of engagement. Contrary to the assumption that it was a monolithic body taking a reactive stance against liberal initiatives from the moment of independence in 1821, the hierarchy in Guadalajara recognized its privileged position and sought to shape the secularizing tide of the Age of Revolutions as committed citizens of the Republic, at least until midcentury. Rural priests, a much less privileged subset of the church with a stark awareness of local needs, were more varied in their relationship with temporal authorities. One of the ways in which religious authorities in Guadalajara attempted to steady themselves against the pull of anticorporate liberalism was to expand their presence in Tepic in the early 1850s, traveling through the Sierra de Álica and inquiring about local religious needs. If anything, they hoped to maintain and even expand the moral authority of the church by engaging with an increasingly restless flock.[5]

2.5. POPULAR GROUPS: PUZZLES, SANTA ANNA MEMORY CARDS, AND BASEBALL

Puzzles

In newspapers and on cards, word puzzles formed brain teasers that were popular with families as a form of board game. One typical [difficult to follow] puzzle of the period is the following:

Entusiasmo produzcalegría	I produce excitement and joy
El mundo entero me prodiga aprecio	The whole world bestows on me appreciation
El que no me ame debe ser un necio	He who does not love me must be quite foolish
O acaso los sentidos perderia.	Or maybe has lost his senses.
Tres silabas	Three syllables [in Spanish]
dirian con bizarria,	would say with bravery,

Que formarán mi nombre a poco precio	That at a low price would place my name
Si dos letras suprimes el desprecio	If two letters you delete, the contempt
De alguien merece la hembra que saldria	of someone who deserves that female would result
O alguna piedra tu verias [potosa?]	Or some porous rock you would see
Cuyo piedra será de algun agrado,	of which the stone will be of some liking
O una deidad sin duda fabulosa	or an undoubtedly fabulous deity
[Apagrama?] esta diosa y has hallado	[anagram] this goddess you have found
De cierta ocupacion bien fastidiosa	of certain quite boring trade
El tambien fastidioso veralado [venerado]	the also tedious winged being [revered being]

Answer: Music⁶ [in Spanish, Mu-si-ca; and deleting two letters becomes musa, that is a Muse; a girl can serve as a muse, there is the rock Jabel Musa across from Gibraltar, or the goddess, the muse, Euterpe of music. As a near anagram, Suma or Sum for sums or arithmetic, a tedious occupation, doing sums.]

Santa Anna memory cards

In 1816 imported playing cards were taxed at thirty reales per dozen packs. As a precaution, locally produced packs were stamped on the two of swords, and imported ones on the two of coins. On June 27, 1842, tax was imposed on playing cards by General Antonio López de Santa Anna. The treasury would control the manufacture and sale of playing cards through the tobacconists. Auditable accounts were required.

This memory game was meant to teach history by events in the life of Antonio López de Santa Anna, the most dominant political figure in Mexico in the nineteenth century. The cards cover the period from 1822 to 1855, beginning with his rebellion against Iturbide and ending with his leaving Mexico in 1855. The images include one of Santa Anna at the Battle of San Jacinto in Texas in 1836 (Santa-Anna derrotado en S. Jacinto 1836) and seven from the Mexican-American War. The Mexican-American War sequence starts with his return to Mexico in 1846 and goes through the Battles of Angostura, Cerro Gordo, and finally, his retreat from Mexico City in 1847. Unlike some publications relating to Santa Anna, these cards are fairly straightforward and without bias.

In memory games such as this one, all the cards are spread out and laid face down in random order. By turns, each player turns two cards face up. If they match, the player keeps the cards. If they do not match they are

Deck of Santa Anna memory cards.
Copyright 2000–2015 by Dorothy Sloan-Rare Books Inc. Used with permission.

returned face down in their original place. The other player then takes a turn. Alternating play proceeds until all the matching pairs have been discovered. The player with more cards at the end wins. The entire set of memory cards is located on the publisher's webpage for this book.

Baseball

Abner Doubleday, who grew up in Cooperstown, New York, was credited for many years as the person who in 1839 developed the game of baseball. His home community was chosen for Major League Baseball's Hall of Fame. He attended West Point, graduated in 1842 with a commission in the artillery, and served in the US-Mexican War. The baseball legend, apparently a tale invented by the baseball team owners to eliminate any association with the British game of rounders, has been embellished by other accounts as well.

"Baseball during US occupation of Mexico City," from *Terry's Guide to Mexico*

When the local guide is nonplussed to find something to interest the visitor he will point out . . . the spot where the American soldiers under *Scott* and *Worth* [italics are in source unless otherwise indicated] played baseball in 1847 with the wooden leg[a] captured (by the Fourth Illinois regiment) from General *Santa Anna*.

The scrimmage in which the bombastic and irascible *Santa Anna* lost his real leg smacks of the burlesque. The ten years' war for Independence keyed the Mexicans to such a fighting pitch that civil wars seemed almost necessary to drain their martial enthusiasm. In one of these family disagreements (sacking of the *Parian* [market] at Mexico City in 1828) certain French subjects got between the firing-lines, and France preferred a claim of $600,000 against the *Bustamante* government. One item in this claim, $60,000, was demanded by a French pastry-cook (*Pastelero*) for pies alleged to have been stolen and eaten by the *revolucionarios*. This claim became known derisively as the *reclamación de los pasteles*—the pie claim. The French ultimatum of March 21, 1838, was followed by a French squadron (in Oct.) under *Bazoche*, which captured the fortress of *San Juan de Ulua* (Nov. 25) and occupied Vera Cruz (Dec. 5). A landing party under the *Prince de Joinville* attacked the city early one morning while *Santa Anna* slept, and as the sailors were entering their boats after a repulse, the drowsy general rushed after them, and in the squabble was shot in the leg—which was amputated in a

---

[a] The leg is now in Memorial Hall at Springfield, Ill. (U.S.A.). The leg purchased and worn later by the discomfited general is in the Morelia Museum. His real leg was torn from its tomb at Mexico City (in 1863) and dragged with a cord through the street, midst insults albeit it was later secured and buried.

crude way, and later removed from its resting place at *Manga de Clavo* and deposited (under a fine monument) midst imposing ceremonies at Mexico City. To prevent further hostilities a treaty was concluded (March 1839) and Mexico paid $600,000 in full.[7]

ADDITIONAL READING

Pablo Piccato, *The Tyranny of Opinion: Honor in the Construction of the Mexican Public Sphere*. Durham, NC: Duke University Press, 2010, 83–93 (especially).

Leer en español

Díaz, Lilia. "El liberalismo militante." In *Historia general de México: Versión 2000*, by Ignacio Bernal, 583–63. Mexico City: El Colegio de México, 2000.

NOTES

1. Source: https://scholarship.rice.edu/jsp/xml/1911/20697/3/aa00005tr.tei.html.

2. In *A Companion to Mexican History and Culture*, ed. William H. Beezley (Malden, MA: Wiley-Blackwell, 2011), 251–61. Reprinted by permission of Wiley Global.

3. Luis de Pablo Hammeken, "Don Giovanni en El Palenque: El tenor Manuel García y la prensa de la Ciudad de México, 1827–1828," *Historia Mexicana* 61, 1 (Julio-Septiembre 2011), 258, n. 58, citing Andrés Lira, "La creación del Distrito Federal," in *La República Federal Mexicana, gestación y nacimiento*, ed. Octavio Hernández (Mexico City: Navarro, 1974), 7: 91–103.

4. https://tarltonapps.law.utexas.edu/constitutions/mexican1824/t1s1, https://tarltonapps.law.utexas.edu/constitutions/mexican1824/t2s1, https://tarltonapps.law.utexas.edu/constitutions/mexican1824/t3s5.

The above links are from "Federal Constitution of the United Mexican States (1824)," Tarlton Law Library, University of Texas at Austin.

5. Zachary Brittsan, *Popular Politics and Rebellion in Mexico* (Nashville, TN: Vanderbilt University Press, 2015), xiv–xv, 176, with a quotation from Ireneo Paz, *Manuel Lozada: El Tigre de Álica* (1885; Mexico City: Factoria Ediciones, 2000), 3–4. Citation refers to the Factoria Ediciones edition. Reprinted by permission of Vanderbilt University Press.

6. Unidentified newspaper clipping, Biblioteca Lerdo de Tejada

7. James Norman, *Terry's Guide to Mexico* (Garden City, NY: Doubleday & Company, Inc., 1965), 306.

CHAPTER 3

The Liberal Era, 1848–1862

Competing political and social events emerged out of the struggles—especially the devastating loss of territory in the US-Mexican War—of the early national era. The defeat at the hands of the United States intensified major confrontations between liberal and conservative forces with military coups and political disruptions that continued through the wars of the Reform. The wars defined the Liberal regime with its new constitution and the threats of excommunication from the Pope. The Liberal regime eventually resulted in the French intervention. Documents in this chapter highlight the political troubles of the era: the Treaty of Guadalupe Hidalgo that ended the US-Mexican War, and resulted in the new Constitution, of 1857 (3.1); Liberal precepts about society (3.2), and the Pope's reaction to them (3.3); civil and church conflicts that often centered on issues of the treatment of the dead (3.4); and a general explanation of events that resulted in the Liberal regime, with changes that included a mandatory civil marriage ceremony based on the new Constitution (3.5).These documents and the suggested readings demonstrate that popular forces played a vital role in shaping Mexico's fate in the 1850s and 1860s.

3.1. POLITICS: THE TREATY OF GUADALUPE HIDALGO

By the Louisiana Purchase, Texas had become a part of the United States; but in 1819 it had been ceded to Spain in the negotiations for Florida. Two years later Mexico, including Texas, had become independent, and the United States made two unsuccessful attempts to purchase Texas from Mexico. The settlement of Texas by immigrants from the United States finally led to the secession of Texas and its annexation by the United States, with the result that the Mexican War broke out in May 1846. It was closed by the Treaty of Guadalupe Hidalgo, by which the

United States gained not only Texas but New Mexico and Upper California. The treaty had an immediate impact on US-Mexican relations and life in both countries, and its effects remain salient. Neither Mexico nor the United States would be the nations they are today without the political and social changes generated by its provisions and they merit close reflection.

Treaty with Mexico (February 2, 1848)

TREATY OF PEACE, FRIENDSHIP, LIMITS, AND SETTLEMENT BETWEEN THE UNITED STATES OF AMERICA AND THE UNITED MEXICAN STATES CONCLUDED AT GUADALUPE HIDALGO, FEBRUARY 2, 1848; RATIFICATION ADVISED BY SENATE, WITH AMENDMENTS, MARCH 10, 1848; RATIFIED BY PRESIDENT, MARCH 16, 1848; RATIFICATIONS EXCHANGED AT QUERETARO, MAY 30, 1848; PROCLAIMED, JULY 4, 1848. IN THE NAME OF ALMIGHTY GOD

The United States of America and the United Mexican States animated by a sincere desire to put an end to the calamities of the war which unhappily exists between the two Republics and to establish Upon a solid basis relations of peace and friendship, which shall confer reciprocal benefits upon the citizens of both, and assure the concord, harmony, and mutual confidence wherein the two people should live, as good neighbors have for that purpose appointed their respective plenipotentiaries, that is to say: The President of the United States has appointed Nicholas P. Trist, a citizen of the United States, and the President of the Mexican Republic has appointed Don Luis Gonzaga Cuevas, Don Bernardo Couto, and Don Miguel Atristain, citizens of the said Republic; Who, after a reciprocal communication of their respective full powers, have, under the protection of Almighty God, the author of peace, arranged, agreed upon, and signed the following:
Treaty of Peace, Friendship, Limits, and Settlement between the United States of America and the Mexican Republic.

ARTICLE I

There shall be firm and universal peace between the United States of America and the Mexican Republic, and between their respective countries, territories, cities, towns, and people, without exception of places or persons.

ARTICLE II

Immediately upon the signature of this treaty, a convention shall be entered into between a commissioner or commissioners appointed by the General-in-chief of the forces of the United States, and such as may be appointed by the Mexican Government, to the end that a provisional suspension of hostilities shall take place, and that, in the places occupied by the said forces, constitutional order may be reestablished, as regards the political, administrative, and judicial branches, so far as this shall be permitted by the circumstances of military occupation.

ARTICLE III

Immediately upon the ratification of the present treaty by the Government of the United States, orders shall be transmitted to the commanders of their land and naval forces, requiring the latter (provided this treaty shall then have been ratified by the Government of the Mexican Republic, and the ratifications exchanged) immediately to desist from blockading any Mexican ports and requiring the former (under the same condition) to commence, at the earliest moment practicable, withdrawing all troops of the United State then in the interior of the Mexican Republic, to points that shall be selected by common agreement, at a distance from the seaports not exceeding thirty leagues; and such evacuation of the interior of the Republic shall be completed with the least possible delay; the Mexican Government hereby binding itself to afford every facility in power for rendering the same convenient to the troops, on their march and in their new positions, and for promoting a good understanding between them and the inhabitants. In like manner orders shall be dispatched to the persons in charge of the custom houses at all ports occupied by the forces of the United States, requiring them (under the same condition) immediately to deliver possession of the same to the persons authorized by the Mexican Government to receive it, together with all bonds and evidences of debt for duties on importations and on exportations, not yet fallen due. Moreover, a faithful and exact account shall be made out, showing the entire amount of all duties on imports and on exports, collected at such custom-houses, or elsewhere in Mexico, by authority of the United States, from and after the day of ratification of this treaty by the Government of the Mexican Republic; and also an account of the cost of collection; and such entire amount, deducting only the cost of collection, shall be delivered to the Mexican Government, at the city of Mexico, within three months after the exchange of ratifications.

The evacuation of the capital of the Mexican Republic by the troops of the United States, in virtue of the above stipulation, shall be completed in one month after the orders there stipulated for shall have been received by the commander of said troops, or sooner if possible.

ARTICLE IV

Immediately after the exchange of ratifications of the present treaty all castles, forts, territories, places, and possessions, which have been taken or occupied by the forces of the United States during the present war, within the limits of the Mexican Republic, as about to be established by the following article, shall be definitely restored to the said Republic, together with all the artillery, arms, apparatus of war, munitions, and other public property, which were in the said castles and forts when captured, and which shall remain there at the time when this treaty shall be duly ratified by the Government of the Mexican Republic. To this end, immediately upon the signature of this treaty, orders shall be despatched to the American officers commanding such castles and forts, securing against the removal or destruction of any such artillery, arms, apparatus of war, munitions, or other public property. The city of Mexico, within the inner line of entrenchments surrounding the said city, is comprehended in the above stipulation, as regards the restoration of artillery, apparatus of war, & c.

The final evacuation of the territory of the Mexican Republic, by the forces of the United States, shall be completed in three months from the said exchange of ratifications, or sooner if possible; the Mexican Government hereby engaging, as in the foregoing article to use all means in its power for facilitating such evacuation, and rendering it convenient to the troops, and for promoting a good understanding between them and the inhabitants.

If, however, the ratification of this treaty by both parties should not take place in time to allow the embarkation of the troops of the United States to be completed before the commencement of the sickly season, at the Mexican ports on the Gulf of Mexico, in such case a friendly arrangement shall be entered into between the General-in-Chief of the said troops and the Mexican Government, whereby healthy and otherwise suitable places, at a distance from the ports not exceeding thirty leagues, shall be designated for the residence of such troops as may not yet have embarked, until the return of the healthy season. And the space of time here referred to as, comprehending the sickly season shall be understood to extend from the first day of May to the first day of November.

All prisoners of war taken on either side, on land or on sea, shall be restored as soon as practicable after the exchange of ratifications of this treaty. It is also agreed that if any Mexicans should now be held as captives by any savage tribe within the limits of the United States, as about to be established by the following article, the Government of the said United States will exact the release of such captives and cause them to be restored to their country.

ARTICLE V

The boundary line between the two Republics shall commence in the Gulf of Mexico, three leagues from land, opposite the mouth of the Rio Grande, otherwise called Rio Bravo del Norte, or Opposite the mouth of its deepest branch, if it should have more than one branch emptying directly into the sea; from thence up the middle of that river, following the deepest channel, where it has more than one, to the point where it strikes the southern boundary of New Mexico; thence, westwardly, along the whole southern boundary of New Mexico (which runs north of the town called Paso) to its western termination; thence, northward, along the western line of New Mexico, until it intersects the first branch of the river Gila; (or if it should not intersect any branch of that river, then to the point on the said line nearest to such branch, and thence in a direct line to the same); thence down the middle of the said branch and of the said river, until it empties into the Rio Colorado; thence across the Rio Colorado, following the division line between Upper and Lower California, to the Pacific Ocean.

The southern and western limits of New Mexico, mentioned in the article, are those laid down in the map entitled "Map of the United Mexican States, as organized and defined by various acts of the Congress of said republic, and constructed according to the best authorities. Revised edition. Published at New York, in 1847, by J. Disturnell," of which map a copy is added to this treaty, bearing the signatures and seals of the undersigned Plenipotentiaries. And, in order to preclude all difficulty in tracing upon the ground the limit separating Upper from Lower California, it is agreed that the said limit shall consist of a straight line drawn from the middle of the Rio Gila, where it unites with the Colorado, to a point on the coast of the Pacific Ocean, distant one marine league due south of the southernmost point of the port of San Diego, according to the plan of said port made in the year 1782 by Don Juan Pantoja, second sailing-master of the Spanish fleet, and published at Madrid in the year 1802, in the atlas to the voyage of the schooners Sutil and Mexicana; of which plan a copy is hereunto added, signed and sealed by the respective Plenipotentiaries.

In order to designate the boundary line with due precision, upon authoritative maps, and to establish upon the ground land-marks which shall show the limits of both republics, as described in the present article, the two Governments shall each appoint a commissioner and a surveyor, who, before the expiration of one year from the date of the exchange of ratifications of this treaty, shall meet at the port of San Diego, and proceed to run and mark the said boundary in its whole course to the mouth of the Rio Bravo del Norte. They shall keep journals and make out plans of their operations; and the result agreed upon by them shall be deemed a part of this treaty, and shall have the same force as if it were inserted therein. The two Governments will amicably agree regarding what may be necessary to these persons, and also as to their respective escorts, should such be necessary.

The boundary line established by this article shall be religiously respected by each of the two republics, and no change shall ever be made therein, except by the express and free consent of both nations, lawfully given by the General Government of each, in conformity with its own constitution.

ARTICLE VI

The vessels and citizens of the United States shall, in all time, have a free and uninterrupted passage by the Gulf of California, and by the river Colorado below its confluence with the Gila, to and from their possessions situated north of the boundary line defined in the preceding article; it being understood that this passage is to be by navigating the Gulf of California and the river Colorado, and not by land, without the express consent of the Mexican Government.

If, by the examinations which may be made, it should be ascertained to be practicable and advantageous to construct a road, canal, or railway, which should in whole or in part run upon the river Gila, or upon its right or its left bank, within the space of one marine league from either margin of the river, the Governments of both republics will form an agreement regarding its construction, in order that it may serve equally for the use and advantage of both countries.

ARTICLE VII

The river Gila, and the part of the Rio Bravo del Norte lying below the southern boundary of New Mexico, being, agreeably to the fifth article, divided in the middle between the two republics, the navigation of the Gila and of the Bravo below said boundary shall be free and common to the vessels and citizens of both countries; and neither shall, without the consent of the other, construct any work that may impede or interrupt, in whole or in part, the exercise of this right; not even for the purpose of favoring new methods of navigation. Nor shall any tax or contribution, under any denomination or title, be levied upon vessels or persons navigating the same or upon merchandise or effects transported thereon, except in the case of landing upon one of their shores. If, for the purpose of making the said rivers navigable, or for maintaining them in such state, it should be necessary or advantageous to establish any tax or contribution, this shall not be done without the consent of both Governments.

The stipulations contained in the present article shall not impair the territorial rights of either republic within its established limits.

ARTICLE VIII

Mexicans now established in territories previously belonging to Mexico, and which remain for the future within the limits of the United States, as defined by the present treaty, shall be free to continue where they now reside, or to remove at any time to the Mexican Republic, retaining the property which they possess in the said territories, or disposing thereof, and removing the proceeds wherever they please, without their being subjected, on this account, to any contribution, tax, or charge whatever.

Those who shall prefer to remain in the said territories may either retain the title and rights of Mexican citizens, or acquire those of citizens of the United States. But they shall be under the obligation to make their election within one year from the date of the exchange of ratifications of this treaty; and those who shall remain in the said territories after the expiration of that year, without having declared their intention to retain the character of Mexicans, shall be considered to have elected to become citizens of the United States.

In the said territories, property of every kind, now belonging to Mexicans not established there, shall be inviolably respected. The present owners, the heirs of these, and all Mexicans who may hereafter acquire said property by contract, shall enjoy with respect to it guarantees equally ample as if the same belonged to citizens of the United States.

ARTICLE IX

The Mexicans who, in the territories aforesaid, shall not preserve the character of citizens of the Mexican Republic, conformably with what is stipulated in the preceding article, shall be incorporated into the Union of the United States and be admitted at the proper time (to be judged of by the Congress of the United States) to the enjoyment of all the rights of citizens of the United States, according to the principles of the Constitution; and in the mean time, shall be maintained and protected in the free enjoyment of their liberty and property, and secured in the free exercise of their religion without restriction.

ARTICLE X

[Stricken out by the United States Amendments]

ARTICLE XI

Considering that a great part of the territories, which, by the present treaty, are to be comprehended for the future within the limits of the United States, is now occupied by savage tribes, who will hereafter be under the exclusive control of the Government of the United States, and whose incursions within the territory of Mexico would be prejudicial in the extreme, it is solemnly agreed that all such incursions shall be forcibly restrained by the Government of the United States whensoever this may be necessary; and that when they cannot be prevented, they shall be punished by the said Government, and satisfaction for the same shall be exacted all in the same way, and with equal diligence and energy, as if the same incursions were meditated or committed within its own territory, against its own citizens.

It shall not be lawful, under any pretext whatever, for any inhabitant of the United States to purchase or acquire any Mexican, or any foreigner residing in Mexico, who may have been captured by Indians inhabiting the territory of either of the two republics; nor to purchase or acquire horses, mules, cattle, or property of any kind, stolen within Mexican territory by such Indians.

And in the event of any person or persons, captured within Mexican territory by Indians, being carried into the territory of the United States, the Government of the latter engages and binds itself, in the most solemn manner, so soon as it shall know of such captives being within its territory, and shall be able so to do, through the faithful exercise of its influence and power, to rescue them and return them to their country, or deliver them to the agent or representative of the Mexican Government. The Mexican authorities will, as far as practicable, give to the Government of the United States notice of such captures; and its agents shall pay the expenses incurred in the maintenance and transmission of the rescued captives; who, in the mean time, shall be treated with the utmost hospitality by the American authorities at the place where they may be. But if the Government of the United States, before receiving such notice from Mexico, should obtain intelligence, through any other channel, of the existence of Mexican captives within its territory, it will proceed forthwith to effect their release and delivery to the Mexican agent, as above stipulated.

For the purpose of giving to these stipulations the fullest possible efficacy, thereby affording the security and redress demanded by their true spirit and intent, the Government of the United States will now and hereafter pass, without unnecessary delay, and always vigilantly enforce, such laws as the nature of the subject may require. And, finally, the sacredness of this obligation shall never be lost sight of by the said Government, when providing for the removal of the Indians from any portion of the said territories, or for its being settled by citizens of the United States; but, on the contrary, special care shall then be taken not to place its Indian occupants under the necessity of seeking new homes, by committing those invasions which the United States have solemnly obliged themselves to restrain.

ARTICLE XII

In consideration of the extension acquired by the boundaries of the United States, as defined in the fifth article of the present treaty, the Government of the United States engages to pay to that of the Mexican Republic the sum of fifteen millions of dollars.

Immediately after the treaty shall have been duly ratified by the Government of the Mexican Republic, the sum of three millions of dollars shall be paid to the said Government by that of the United States, at the city of Mexico, in the gold or silver coin of Mexico. The remaining twelve millions of dollars shall be paid at the same place, and in the same coin, in annual installments of three millions of dollars each, together with interest on the same at the rate of six per centum per annum. This interest shall begin to run upon the whole sum of twelve millions from the day of the ratification of the present treaty by the Mexican Government, and the first of the installments shall be paid at the expiration of one year from the same day. Together with each annual installment, as it falls due, the whole interest accruing on such installment from the beginning shall also be paid.

ARTICLE XIII

The United States engage, moreover, to assume and pay to the claimants all the amounts now due them, and those hereafter to become due, by reason of the claims already liquidated and decided against the Mexican Republic, under the conventions between the two republics severally concluded on the eleventh day of April, eighteen hundred and thirty-nine, and on the thirtieth day of January, eighteen hundred and forty-three; so that the Mexican Republic shall be absolutely exempt, for the future, from all expense whatever on account of the said claims.

ARTICLE XIV

The United States do furthermore discharge the Mexican Republic from all claims of citizens of the United States, not heretofore decided against the Mexican Government, which may have arisen previously to the date of the signature of this treaty; which discharge shall be final and perpetual, whether the said claims be rejected or be allowed by the board of commissioners provided for in the following article, and whatever shall be the total amount of those allowed.

ARTICLE XV

The United States, exonerating Mexico from all demands on account of the claims of their citizens mentioned in the preceding article, and considering them entirely and forever canceled, whatever their amount may be, undertake to make satisfaction for the same, to an amount not exceeding three and one-quarter millions of dollars. To ascertain the validity and amount of those claims, a board of commissioners shall be established by the Government of the United States, whose awards shall be final and conclusive; provided that, in deciding upon the validity of each claim, the board shall be guided and governed by the principles and rules of decision prescribed by the first and fifth articles of the unratified convention, concluded at the city of Mexico on the twentieth day of November, one thousand eight hundred and forty-three; and in no case shall an award be made in favour of any claim not embraced by these principles and rules.

If, in the opinion of the said board of commissioners or of the claimants, any books, records, or documents, in the possession or power of the Government of the Mexican Republic, shall be deemed necessary to the just decision of any claim, the commissioners, or the claimants through them, shall, within such period as Congress may designate, make an application in writing for the same, addressed to the Mexican Minister of Foreign Affairs, to be transmitted by the Secretary of State of the United States; and the Mexican Government engages, at the earliest possible moment after the receipt of such demand, to cause any of the books, records, or documents so specified, which shall be in their possession or power (or authenticated copies or extracts of the same), to be transmitted to the said Secretary of State, who shall immediately deliver them over to the said board of commissioners; provided that no such application shall be made by or at the instance of any claimant, until the facts which it is expected to prove by such books, records, or documents, shall have been stated under oath or affirmation.

ARTICLE XVI

Each of the contracting parties reserves to itself the entire right to fortify whatever point within its territory it may judge proper so to fortify for its security.

ARTICLE XVII

The treaty of amity, commerce, and navigation, concluded at the city of Mexico, on the fifth day of April, A.D. 1831, between the United States of America and the United Mexican States, except the additional article, and except so far as the stipulations of the said treaty may be incompatible with any stipulation contained in the present treaty, is hereby revived for the period of eight years from the day of the exchange of ratifications of this treaty, with the same force and virtue as if incorporated therein; it being understood that each of the contracting parties reserves to itself the right, at any time after the said period of eight years shall have expired, to terminate the same by giving one year's notice of such intention to the other party.

ARTICLE XVIII

All supplies whatever for troops of the United States in Mexico, arriving at ports in the occupation of such troops previous to the final evacuation thereof, although subsequently to the restoration of the custom-houses at such ports, shall be entirely exempt from duties and charges of any kind; the Government of the United States hereby engaging and pledging its faith to establish and vigilantly to enforce, all possible guards for securing the revenue of Mexico, by preventing the importation, under cover of this stipulation, of any articles other than such, both in kind and in quantity, as shall really be wanted for the use and consumption of the forces of the United States during the time they may remain in Mexico. To this end it shall be the duty of all officers and agents of the United States to denounce to the Mexican authorities at the respective ports any attempts at a fraudulent abuse of this stipulation, which they may know of, or may have reason to suspect, and to give to such authorities all the aid in their power with regard thereto; and every such attempt, when duly proved and established by sentence of a competent tribunal. They shall be punished by the confiscation of the property so attempted to be fraudulently introduced.

ARTICLE XIX

With respect to all merchandise, effects, and property whatsoever, imported into ports of Mexico, whilst in the occupation of the forces of the United States, whether by citizens of either republic, or by citizens or subjects of any neutral nation, the following rules shall be observed:

1. All such merchandise, effects, and property, if imported previously to the restoration of the custom-houses to the Mexican authorities, as stipulated for in the third article of this treaty, shall be exempt from confiscation, although the importation of the same be prohibited by the Mexican tariff.
2. The same perfect exemption shall be enjoyed by all such merchandise, effects, and property, imported subsequently to the restoration of the custom-houses, and previously to the sixty days fixed in the following article for the coming into force of the Mexican tariff at such ports respectively; the said merchandise, effects, and property being, however, at the time of their importation, subject to the payment of duties, as provided for in the said following article.
3. All merchandise, effects, and property described in the two rules foregoing shall, during their continuance at the place of importation, and upon their leaving such place for the interior, be exempt from all duty, tax, or imposts of every kind, under whatsoever title or denomination.

Nor shall they be there subject to any charge whatsoever upon the sale thereof. (4) All merchandise, effects, and property, described in the first and second rules, which shall have been removed to any place in the interior, whilst such place was in the occupation of the forces of the United States, shall, during their continuance therein, be exempt from all tax upon the sale or consumption thereof, and from every kind of impost or contribution, under whatsoever title or denomination.

4. But if any merchandise, effects, or property, described in the first and second rules, shall be removed to any place not occupied at the time by the forces of the United States, they shall, upon their introduction into such place, or upon their sale or consumption there, be subject to the same duties which, under the Mexican laws, they would be required to pay in such cases if they had been imported in time of peace, through the maritime custom-houses, and had there paid the duties conformably with the Mexican tariff.
5. The owners of all merchandise, effects, or property, described in the first and second rules, and existing in any port of Mexico, shall have the right to reship the same, exempt from all tax, impost, or contribution whatever.

With respect to the metals, or other property, exported from any Mexican port whilst in the occupation of the forces of the United States, and previously to the restoration of the custom-house at such port, no person shall be required by the Mexican authorities, whether general or state, to pay any tax, duty, or contribution upon any such exportation, or in any manner to account for the same to the said authorities.

ARTICLE XX

Through consideration for the interests of commerce generally, it is agreed, that if less than sixty days should elapse between the date of the signature of this treaty and the restoration of the custom houses, conformably with the stipulation in the third article, in such case all merchandise, effects and property whatsoever, arriving at the Mexican ports after the restoration of the said custom-houses, and previously to the expiration of sixty days after the day of signature of this treaty, shall be admitted to entry; and no other duties shall be levied thereon than the duties established by the tariff found in force at such custom-houses at the time of the restoration of the same. And to all such merchandise, effects, and property, the rules established by the preceding article shall apply.

ARTICLE XXI

If unhappily any disagreement should hereafter arise between the Governments of the two republics, whether with respect to the interpretation of any stipulation in this treaty, or with respect to any other particular concerning the political or commercial relations of the two nations, the said Governments, in the name of those nations, do promise to each other that they will endeavour, in the most sincere and earnest manner, to settle the differences so arising, and to preserve the state of peace and friendship in which the two countries are now placing themselves, using, for this end, mutual representations and pacific negotiations. And if, by these means, they should not be enabled to come to an agreement, a resort shall not, on this account, be had to reprisals, aggression, or hostility of any kind, by the one republic against the other, until the Government of that which deems itself aggrieved shall have maturely considered, in the spirit of peace and good neighbourship, whether it would not be better that such difference should be settled by the arbitration of commissioners appointed on each side, or by that of a friendly nation. And should such course be proposed by either party, it shall be acceded to by the other, unless deemed by it altogether incompatible with the nature of the difference, or the circumstances of the case.

ARTICLE XXII

If (which is not to be expected, and which God forbid) war should unhappily break out between the two republics, they do now, with a view to such calamity, solemnly pledge themselves to each other and to the world to observe the following rules; absolutely where the nature of the subject permits, and as closely as possible in all cases where such absolute observance shall be impossible:

1. The merchants of either republic then residing in the other shall be allowed to remain twelve months (for those dwelling in the interior), and six months (for those dwelling at the seaports) to collect their debts and settle their affairs; during which periods they shall enjoy the same protection, and be on the same footing, in all respects, as the citizens or subjects of the most friendly nations; and, at the expiration thereof, or at any time before, they shall have full liberty to depart, carrying off all their effects without molestation or hindrance, conforming therein to the same laws which the citizens or subjects of the most friendly nations are required to conform to. Upon the entrance of the armies of either nation into the territories of the other, women and children, ecclesiastics, scholars of every faculty, cultivators of the

earth, merchants, artisans, manufacturers, and fishermen, unarmed and inhabiting unfortified towns, villages, or places, and in general all persons whose occupations are for the common subsistence and benefit of mankind, shall be allowed to continue their respective employments, unmolested in their persons. Nor shall their houses or goods be burnt or otherwise destroyed, nor their cattle taken, nor their fields wasted, by the armed force into whose power, by the events of war, they may happen to fall; but if the necessity arise to take anything from them for the use of such armed force, the same shall be paid for at an equitable price. All churches, hospitals, schools, colleges, libraries, and other establishments for charitable and beneficent purposes, shall be respected, and all persons connected with the same protected in the discharge of their duties, and the pursuit of their vocations.

2. In order that the fate of prisoners of war may be alleviated all such practices as those of sending them into distant, inclement or unwholesome districts, or crowding them into close and noxious places, shall be studiously avoided. They shall not be confined in dungeons, prison ships, or prisons; nor be put in irons, or bound or otherwise restrained in the use of their limbs. The officers shall enjoy liberty on their paroles, within convenient districts, and have comfortable quarters; and the common soldiers shall be disposed in cantonments, open and extensive enough for air and exercise and lodged in barracks as roomy and good as are provided by the party in whose power they are for its own troops. But if any office shall break his parole by leaving the district so assigned him, or any other prisoner shall escape from the limits of his cantonment after they shall have been designated to him, such individual, officer, or other prisoner, shall forfeit so much of the benefit of this article as provides for his liberty on parole or in cantonment. And if any officer so breaking his parole or any common soldier so escaping from the limits assigned him, shall afterwards be found in arms previously to his being regularly exchanged, the person so offending shall be dealt with according to the established laws of war. The officers shall be daily furnished, by the party in whose power they are, with as many rations, and of the same articles, as are allowed either in kind or by commutation, to officers of equal rank in its own army; and all others shall be daily furnished with such ration as is allowed to a common soldier in its own service; the value of all which supplies shall, at the close of the war, or at periods to be agreed upon between the respective commanders, be paid by the other party, on a mutual adjustment of accounts for the subsistence of prisoners; and such accounts shall not be mingled with or set off against any others, nor the balance due on them withheld, as a compensation or reprisal for any cause whatever, real or pretended. Each party shall be allowed

to keep a commissary of prisoners, appointed by itself, with every cantonment of prisoners, in possession of the other; which commissary shall see the prisoners as often as he pleases; shall be allowed to receive, exempt from all duties a taxes, and to distribute, whatever comforts may be sent to them by their friends; and shall be free to transmit his reports in open letters to the party by whom he is employed.

And it is declared that neither the pretense that war dissolves all treaties, nor any other whatever, shall be considered as annulling or suspending the solemn covenant contained in this article. On the contrary, the state of war is precisely that for which it is provided; and, during which, its stipulations are to be as sacredly observed as the most acknowledged obligations under the law of nature or nations.

ARTICLE XXIII

This treaty shall be ratified by the President of the United States of America, by and with the advice and consent of the Senate thereof; and by the President of the Mexican Republic, with the previous approbation of its general Congress; and the ratifications shall be exchanged in the City of Washington, or at the seat of Government of Mexico, in four months from the date of the signature hereof, or sooner if practicable.

In faith whereof we, the respective Plenipotentiaries, have signed this treaty of peace, friendship, limits, and settlement, and have hereunto affixed our seals respectively. Done in quintuplicate, at the city of Guadalupe Hidalgo, on the second day of February, in the year of our Lord one thousand eight hundred and forty-eight.

N. P. TRIST
LUIS P. CUEVAS
BERNARDO COUTO
MIGL. ATRISTAIN

Article IX was modified and Article X was stricken by the US Congress. Here are the original articles.

In addition, there is an explanation or agreement of why the articles where [sic] stricken which is known as the protocol of Querétaro.

ARTICLE IX

The Mexicans who, in the territories aforesaid, shall not preserve the character of citizens of the Mexican Republic, conformably with what is stipulated in the preceding Article, shall be incorporated into the Union of the United States, and admitted as soon as possible, according to the principles of the Federal Constitution, to the enjoyment of all the rights of citizens of the United States. In the mean time, they shall be maintained and protected in the enjoyment of their liberty, their property, and the civil rights now vested in them according to the Mexican laws. With respect to political rights, their condition shall be on an equality with that of the inhabitants of the other territories of the United States; and at least equally good as that of the inhabitants of Louisiana and the Floridas, when these provinces, by transfer from the French Republic and the Crown of Spain, became territories of the United States.

The same most ample guaranty shall be enjoyed by all ecclesiastics and religious corporations or communities, as well in the discharge of the offices of their ministry, as in the enjoyment of their property of every kind, whether individual or corporate. This guaranty shall embrace all temples, houses and edifices dedicated to the Roman Catholic worship; as well as all property destined to it's [sic] support, or to that of schools, hospitals and other foundations for charitable or beneficent purposes. No property of this nature shall be considered as having become the property of the American Government, or as subject to be, by it, disposed of or diverted to other uses.

Finally, the relations and communication between the Catholics living in the territories aforesaid, and their respective ecclesiastical authorities, shall be open, free and exempt from all hindrance whatever, even although such authorities should reside within the limits of the Mexican Republic, as defined by this treaty; and this freedom shall continue, so long as a new demarcation of ecclesiastical districts shall not have been made, conformably with the laws of the Roman Catholic Church.

THE PROTOCOL OF QUERÉTARO

In the city of Queretaro on the twenty-sixth of the month of May eighteen hundred and forty-eight at a conference between Their Excellencies Nathan Clifford and Ambrose H. Sevier Commissioners of the United States of America, with full powers from their Government to make to the Mexican Republic suitable explanations in regard to the amendments which the Senate and Government of the said United States have made in the treaty of peace, friendship, limits and definitive settlement between the two Republics, signed in Guadalupe Hidalgo, on the second day of February of the present year, and His Excellency Don Luis de la Rosa, Minister of Foreign Affairs of the Republic of Mexico, it was agreed, after adequate conversation respecting the changes alluded to, to record in the present protocol the following explanations which Their aforesaid Excellencies the Commissioners gave in the name of their Government and in fulfillment of the Commission conferred upon them near the Mexican Republic.

First.

The American Government by suppressing the IXth article of the Treaty of Guadalupe and substituting the III article of the Treaty of Louisiana did not intend to diminish in any way what was agreed upon by the aforesaid article IXth in favor of the inhabitants of the territories ceded by Mexico. Its understanding that all of that agreement is contained in the IIId article of the Treaty of Louisiana. In consequence, all the privileges and guarantees, civil, political and religious, which would have been possessed by the inhabitants of the ceded territories, if the IXth article of the Treaty had been retained, will be enjoyed by them without any difference under the article which has been substituted.

Second.

The American Government, by suppressing the Xth article of the Treaty of Guadalupe did not in any way intend to annul the grants of lands made by Mexico in the ceded territories. These grants, notwithstanding the suppression of the article of the Treaty, preserve the legal value which they may possess; and the grantees may cause their legitimate titles to be acknowledged before the American tribunals.

Conformably to the law of the United States, legitimate titles to every description of property personal and real, existing in the ceded territories, are those which were legitimate titles under the Mexican law in California and New Mexico up to the 13th of May 1846, and in Texas up to the 2d March 1836.

Third.

The Government of the United States by suppressing the concluding paragraph of article XIIth of the Treaty, did not intend to deprive the Mexican Republic of the free and unrestrained faculty of ceding, conveying or transferring at any time (as it may judge best) the sum of the twelve [sic] millions of dollars which the same Government of the United States is to deliver in the places designated by the amended article.

And these explanations having been accepted by the Minister of Foreign Affairs of the Mexican Republic, he declared in name of his Government that with the understanding conveyed by them, the same Government would proceed to ratify the Treaty of Guadalupe as modified by the Senate and Government of the United States. In testimony of which their Excellencies the aforesaid Commissioners and the Minister have signed and sealed in quintuplicate the present protocol.

[Seal] A. H. Sevier
[Seal] Nathan Clifford
[Seal] Luis de la Rosa[1]

3.2. POPULAR GROUPS: CHILDREN'S HISTORY BOOK

Mexico's most famous popular artist of the late nineteenth and early twentieth centuries was Guadalupe Posada. In addition to broadsheets and newspaper images, he also drew drawings for book covers. Of these the most famous was the series of short books for children written by Heriberto Frías and originally published in 1901. "The Mexican Child's Library," contained 110 sixteen-page booklets published by the Maucci Brothers in Mexico City. These small books introduced readers to Mexico's history from its pre-Columbian past to the regime of Porfirio Díaz. This text also identifies and situates the figures of Santa Anna and Juárez.[2]

Biblioteca del Niño Mexicano [*The Mexican Child's Library*]
Heriberto Frías, *Ten Years of Darkness or the Tree of Liberty* (1901)

The fatherland was bloody and disheartened after the war against the North Americans that wrenched away more than half of the national territory. But its misfortunes were still far from over—civil war continued flooding the country with blood, and you will see in this story how tyrants again threw total darkness over the people until the sun of the Constitution that was called Juárez arrived and then the sun of Peace and Progress: Porfirio Díaz.

The first months of the year 1848 clouds of deep sadness covered our country. Its fields were deserted wastelands, but finally, Peace had been obtained, certainly quite expensively bought!

Child's history of the dark years in politics.
The Jean Charlot Collection, University of Hawai'i.

The Liberal Era, 1848–1862

The faithful and impartial narrator of the events, as I have proposed to be for you, simple readers, felt calm and grateful pleasure on arriving at this point of the story, because he is going to present before your eyes the picture of a noble, honorable, and dignified administration, and the beginning of another equally pure and lofty, wickedly and unfortunately revoked by the everlasting depraved [persons], in order to crown the most disgraceful and ridiculous dictatorship that until that time the Republic had witnessed.

General José Joaquín de Herrera elected to complete the constitutional term, accompanied by the members of the cabinet and high officials moved back to the capital in the middle of the month of June and he began with great skill, wisdom, and energy to perform the work in the difficult circumstances in which he had been placed.

The economy and the morality that were normal for the government in all its actions, contributed much to what the nation restored, in a short time, although not all of them, of its damages. It contributed a great deal to reach this wellbeing the copious amount of the North American indemnification, that, as you know, came to 15 million pesos and that was invested completely in the most urgent needs of the administration.

General Mariano Arista, who was the Minister of War, dedicated himself with great efficiency to correct the huge number of abuses that plague the Army; proceeded with the payment of the troops, he introduced paymasters and blocked the sources of undercover theft that existed under the system of contracts, gratuities, etc. etc.

Without a doubt, you have heard talk of the well-known cholera disease, although fortunately for a long time, since the time we are going through it has not appeared in our country.

That awful scourge of humanity that from time to time travels across the universe making millions of victims that has its origins in the Orient, unleashed horror and terror over Mexico in the year 1850. There was not a house in which there were not eight, ten, fifteen cadavers . . . the streets were uninhabited, deserted, lonely. . . . Many people were buried alive and others were at the point of it, but being able to escape miraculously such a horrible death! Finally, the devastating scourge ended leaving behind its mark.

At this time, the murder of Juan de Díos Cañedo was verified, the great Liberal and eloquent orator in the Hotel de la Gran Sociedad; crime that, because he is such a notable man and it was verified on Holy Thursday, caused a deep sensation among the inhabitants of the capital and everywhere in the country.

As Cañedo opposed the government, it was believed that this motivated the dagger of the murders, but the government explained it as slander proceeding with the greatest energy in this matter that in the beginning covered political characters, and it [the government] hesitated to execute the murderers, who had no other motive than robbery.

They were hanged in front of the Hotel de la Gran Sociedad from the balconies that had been the theater of their crime, for the satisfaction of the vindictive public a few days after the crime had been committed.

The year of 1850 the elections took place for the chief magistrate of the republic, resulting in the election of General Mariano Arista, who took possession of the presidency in January, 1851, with a legal ending to the previous presidency.

We have attended a period unfortunately extremely short on inner peace and wellbeing. Herrera retired to private life with the veneration and deep respect of his fellow citizens. Sr. Arista, who went to replace him had sufficient qualities in order to carry out with dignity the high position, impeccable honesty and strict honesty. As a soldier, he was a slave to the law, brave in danger, humane, and a gentleman. He continued in the tracks of morality, order, respect for the laws and economy of his predecessors.

Most unfortunately, the hydra of passions again showed its monstrous head.

The reduction and moralization of the army that Sr. Arista pursued with determination since he occupied the Ministry of War and with more tenacity he carried out today as the chief magistrate, were the principal causes because they attracted among those who remained without their posts, multitude of enemies willing to take advantage of the first opportunity for revenge.

The Conservatives, hidden enemies of the president, watched for the first opportunity to make break out a revolution favorable to their views. This finally presented itself, and the pronunciamiento of Guadalajara, led by José María Blancarte, by origin a sombrero maker, extended to the entire country, and had as a result the fall of the honorable government, that had no other idea than the happiness and wellbeing of the country.

That awful revolution that caused the daring of the enemies of the Republic igniting as always the bonfire of rancor and surveillances, envy, ambitions ended finally with the return of—who would believe it—of the man fatal to the country, the eternal and evil General Santa Anna, who lived retired then in a foreign country, after his infamous deeds of the years of his unlucky popularity.

Ah! Cursed, cursed man who gave so many, so many disappointments to the fatherland.

And, do you know little friends, about this famous traitor, this cruel bandit, and this salesman of the national honor who entered into Mexico, the capital of the republic? Know him, in order to insult the abominable name of Antonio López de Santa Anna! . . . He entered as a hero, triumphal, acclaimed by the crowds, by the young people easily deceived by the ambitious who exploited them. He entered my little friends that miserable man who lied about his well deserved exile in the region of Turbaco (Colombia), there in South America; he returned a victorious general, being an ill-fated man. . . .

How many misfortunes were going to rain down again on the country as soon as his dictatorship plunged the Mexican nation into a sea of blood. The Mexican Nero, the bold, ambitious man, began his *government,* or better said his reign or dictatorship by surrounding himself with lavish splendor; he brought men who sold themselves to him; thousands of subjects and shopkeepers; he wanted to have a great farce, imitating the kings of Europe, and in order to pay the millions and millions of pesos that came to the grandest costs for celebrations, banquets, ceremonies, processions, parties, opulent alms, donations, and privileges, the exhausted nation could give him barely half of its income. And, he considered it not much!

That man spent all of the treasury of the country on fiestas and salons, on banquets and lavish orgies!

Meanwhile . . . Ahh! . . . meanwhile how much hunger for bread and knowledge, how much need for Enlightenment did the public have. Santa Anna murdered the people with poverty, confusion, and ignorance, if they had not died on the battlefield. . . . And without the slightest remorse! Greedy for money, the vile satrap then committed the most unspeakable of his crimes: he sold a stub (giron) of the national territory, it was then when skillfully and miserably he confirmed the sale to a foreign enemy of the extensive and rich territories called the Mesilla Valley.

This piece of our territory was sold at the despicable price, which no one in the world, no emperor, nor king, nor pope, could arrange, by a Judas anathematized by history! Curse that Judas that is called Santa Anna!

The People! . . . Ah! The Mexican people had a swift, tremendous wake up call in the middle of their weariness . . . it overwhelmed in an instant all the vileness of the tyranny, all the spinelessness of its outrageous famous citizen . . . and the light came in a flash, the great lightning bolt that was the Plan of Ayutla followed by the revolution that became the biblical war of the Reform, after the stunning Constitution of 1857.

Know this, little friends, that always and everywhere, after an evil man oppresses, humiliates, breaks, torments, and exploits the body of those unfortunates who work for him and give him their blood, sweat, and life, after many years of sorrow, slavery, and misery . . . afterward . . . comes the moment when they wake up, raise up, and see, become enraged and with all the fury of their holy indignation turn against their masters, their tormentors, . . . they attack them, they break them through long and dark combat, and when they triumph, because the triumph has a high and divine right, justice is done! Justice is done and with the great exaltation expands their bloody, shining, and worthy victory.

Do you know who won justice for the people through his battles? An eminent, immortal man, man terrible because of his energetic force in the duty and the calm serenity of love of the mother country. And that man . . . was: Benito Juárez

After the crimes of those self-seeking men that one after another seized the office of the presidency of the Republic, after acts of treason, disgrace, stupidity, revolts, blood, fire came the serene splendor of the man who embodied the Law and Justice.

Honor and Respect always the holy and eminent name for the Mexican . . . venerable and high for all the spirits that are loyal to the expression of the most Republican Man of all time. Love his memory because he is an apostle like the good men who surrounded Christ the Evangelist.

Juárez was going to save the dying body of the nation, giving it new life. Saved by the tenacious and heroic apostle, what would this motherland be like?

Only he was able with a miracle that he, with his great sword, made Peace. The man of peace would regenerate the nation. Would it come soon? No one knew then, no one yet could guess that the man destined to be President was already making the enemies of the nation bite the dust in the most glorious battles, but in that night of confusion, blood, and chaos of disgraceful and dark deeds, the sun was about to dawn soon with a new day.

It was beginning to dawn.

Hosanna

Additional Titles in The Mexican Child's Library

The Sinister Campaign or the Glorious Defeats
Maximilian of Austria or an Ephemeral Empire
The Genius of War in Mexico
The Siege of Querétaro and the Hill of the Bells
The Bajío Volunteers or Heroic Days
Napoleon III's Ambitions
The Three Years War and the Battle of Calpulalpán
Cinco de Mayo and the Siege of Puebla

3.3. CHURCH: POPE PIUS IX REJECTS THE CONSTITUTION OF 1857

The Liberals brought together their political views and plans for the nation in the Constitution of 1857. The Liberals did not specifically state that Mexicans enjoyed freedom of religion, but because there was no statement on the Roman Catholic Church as the official religion, opened the country to other churches. In addition, the Constitution limited a number of Church privileges, such as separate courts, and it closed monasteries. Pope Pius IX responded to the Liberals and their document in the following statement.

The Chamber of Deputies, among the many insults it has heaped on Our Most Holy Religion and upon its Ministers, as well as upon the Vicar of Christ on earth, has proposed a new constitution containing many articles, not a few of which conflict with Divine Religion, its salutary doctrines, its most holy precepts, and with its rights. . . . For the purpose of more easily corrupting manners and propagating the detestable pest of indifference and tearing souls away from our Most Holy Religion, it allows the free exercise of all cults and admits the right of pronouncing in public every kind of thought and opinion. . . . And so that the Faithful who reside there may know and the Catholic World may understand that We energetically reprove everything the Mexican government has done against the Catholic Religion, against its Church, its sacred ministers and pastors and against its laws, rights, and properties, as well as against the authority of the Holy See, we raise our Pontifical Voice in apostolic liberty . . . to condemn, to reprove and declare null and void the said decrees and everything else that the civil authority has done in scorn of ecclesiastical authority and of this Holy See. . . . Pope Pius IX.[3]

3.4. MILITARY AND POLICE: BENITO JUÁREZ ORDERS THE ARREST OF A PRIEST WHO REFUSED LAST RITES TO A DEAD MAYOR

Liberal government officials and the Catholic Church hierarchy battled over the separation of secular and religious activities. The definition of these caused problems as the government took control of cemeteries, for example, made marriage a civil contract, and ordered the registration of births in civil offices. The church regarded these as sacraments and refused to extend them to individuals who accepted the new constitution—as the following document discusses.

Notification to the Bishop of a Priest imprisoned for refusing to administer the sacraments to the mayor, Oaxaca, June 22, 1857
Government of the State of Oaxaca
Most Illustrious Señor Bishop of this Diocese
Illustrious Señor:

The government having evidence that the parish priest of Zaachila, don Andrés Jiménez has denied the sacraments to the deceased mayor of Tavehua, not wanting that he receive them in burial, under the pretext that the said functionary did not retract the oath he made to the political constitution of the republic, and in virtue of the instructions that I have from the supreme government of the nation, I have seen fit to have the aforementioned Sr. Jiménez be taken prisoner in this city and be sent out of the state to a place that his Excellency the President determines.

The government cannot view with indifference actions that, alarming the consciences of the citizens, alter the public order and, deciding to impose obedience to the laws, it is not afraid to do what the good of society demands; if it views with appreciation and favor a priest, who carries out his holy mission of peace and morality, it does not hesitate an instant to punish the insubordinate whose actions preach hatefulness and disorder; because otherwise, it would abandon society to the destructive ravages of the one interested in its ruin.

Sr. Jiménez removed for such motive, I request that V.S.I. within a few days send to Zaachila another priest to take charge of the parish.

I declare to V.S.I. my appreciation and attentive consideration.

God and Liberty.
Oaxaca, June 22, 1857.
Benito Juárez[4]

3.5. FAMILY: EPISTLE OF MELCHOR OCAMPO—THE CIVIL MARRIAGE VOWS

Epistle of Melchor Ocampo—the civil marriage vows

The Liberals—as they determined that in order to govern effectively the government needed accurate statistics on births, deaths, and marriages—created civil registries to record this information. Moreover, the Liberals used the following letter as part of the marriage vows. These statements remained in force for over a century. The marriage commitments can be related to other documents such as "The Perfect Wife" in chapter 1.

On July 23, 1859, D. Benito Juarez, interim president then, issues, at the Port of Veracruz, the "Civil Matrimony Law," which has 31 Articles. In Article 15, as a way of ceremonial formalization, the famous epistle, attributed to Melchor Ocampo, was included; and which reads as follows:

"I declare on behalf of Law and Society that you are united in legitimate matrimony with all rights and privileges granted by law, and with the obligations imposed; and also declare:

That this is the only moral mean to establish a family, to conserve the human species and to make up for the imperfections of an individual who cannot provide for itself to reach mankind's perfection. This doesn't exist in a single person, but in spousal duality. Those married must be and will be sacred to each other, even more than what they are to each self.

The man, whose main sexual attributes are courage and strength, must give and shall always give the woman protection, food, and direction, treating her always as the most delicate, sensible, and finest part of himself, and with magnanimity and generous benevolence that a strong being owes the weak, essentially when this weak delivers to himself, and also when Society has entrusted him.

The woman, whose main attributes are self denial, beauty, compassion, shrewdness and tenderness, must give and shall always give the husband obedience, pleasantness, assistance, comfort, and advice; treating him always with the veneration owed to the person supporting and defending us, and with the delicacy of whom doesn't want to exasperate the abrupt, irritable and harsh part of him, which is of his nature.

One to another are owed and shall always give respect, deference, fidelity, trust, and tenderness; both will take care of what they were expecting from each other by joining together, and that this will not be contradicted by this union. That both shall be prudent and attenuate their faults. You shall never say insults to each other, because insults among the married dishonors the one saying them, and proves the lack of judgment or common sense of election; and much less shall physically mistreat each other, because it is vile and cowardly to use force.

Both shall prepare with the steady, friendly and mutual correction of their defects, up to the supreme judgeship of being family parents, in order to when both become that, your children can find in you good example and good conduct to serve as role models. The doctrine that you inspire in these tender and loved bonds of affection will make your luck to prosper or to be adverse; and the happiness or misfortune of your children will be the parent's reward or punishment, fortune or sadness.

Society blesses, believes, and praises good parents, for the great good they do to it, for giving them good and courteous citizens; and the same properly censures and despises those, that by abandonment, or misgiving affection, or by setting bad example, corrupt the sacred depot that nature trusted them with, for granting them such children.

And last, when Society sees that such said persons did not deserve to be elevated to have the honor to become parents, but merely should have lived subject to guardianship, incapable of conducting themselves with dignity, grieves for establishing with its authority the union of a man and a woman who have failed to be free and to conduct themselves towards good."

This is Ocampo's best-known legacy from 1859, which is known as the epistle on marriage, still read out nowadays by judges presiding over civil weddings in many states.[5]

ADDITIONAL READING

Arnold, Linda. "The U.S. Intervention in Mexico, 1846–1848." In *A Companion to Mexican History and Culture*, ed. William H. Beezley, 262–72. Maldan, MA: John Wiley & Sons, 2011.

Leer en español

Vázquez, Josefina Z., ed. *México al tiempo de su guerra con los Estados Unidos (1846–1848)*. Mexico City: Fondo de Cultura Económica, 1997), 17–46.

NOTES

1. Online at http://mexica.net/guadhida.php. Also see *Treaties and Conventions Concluded between the United States of America and Other Powers since July 4, 1776* (Washington, DC: Government Printing Office, 1871); Yale University's Avalon Project relating to the Treaty of Guadalupe Hidalgo, National Archives and Records Administration, General Records of the United States Record Group 11, National Archives Identifier 299809.

2. Various libraries in Mexico and the United States have partial collections of these booklets, but the complete set in excellent condition only exists, as far as we know, in the Jean Charlot Collection at the University of Hawai'i. We thank the curator of the collection, Bronwen Solyom, for her assistance with this image, Ryan S. James for making the digital photograph, and, above all, John Charlot for permission to use the image from the Charlot Collection.

3. Silvestre Villegas, Revueltas, *Antología de textos. La reforma y el segundo imperio. 1853–1867* (Mexico City: UNAM, 2008).

4. Benito Juárez, *Documentos, discursos y correspondencia: Selección y notas de Jorge L. Tamayo*, 1st electronic ed. (Mexico City: Universidad Autónoma Metropolitana, Unidad Azcapotzalco, 2006). Section 13, p. 1. Also online in "500 años de México en documentos," http://www.biblioteca.tv/artman2/publish/1857_148/Notifica_al_obispo_la_prisi_n_de_un_cura_por_negarse_a_administrar_los_sacramentos_a_un_alcalde.shtml.

5. "Melchor Ocampo," Wikipedia, https://en.wikipedia.org/wiki/Melchor_Ocampo. Also see Melchor Ocampo, *Obras completas*, ed. F. Vázquez (Mexico City: Librería Bauret, 1900–1901), III: 345–47.

CHAPTER 4

The French Intervention, 1862–1876

The Liberal troops battled the French armies that invaded Mexico in 1862. One major battle occurred at Puebla, where the Mexicans won a dramatic victory on Cinco de Mayo (May 5) (4.1). The reinforced French troops soon returned, swept the armies before them, captured Puebla, and continued on to Mexico City, where they occupied the capital and installed Maximilian as emperor. Liberal President Benito Juárez escaped and traveled incessantly with his troops. Until the French took the capital city, Juárez's wife organized concerts to raise money for his war effort. Composer Cenobio Paniagua participated in several of them. He wrote *Catalina de Guisa*, the first national opera after independence. He also composed the opera *Pietro d'Abano* (the Italian philosopher who compiled a book of ritual magic) to commemorate the Cinco de Mayo victory. It premiered on May 5, 1863, one year after the battle in Puebla. The 1867 defeat of the French and the capture of Maximilian resulted in foreign requests for his pardon (4.2). His execution and the return of his body to Europe resulted in legends that he was not shot to death in Mexico (4.3). Popular songs did record his wife's return to Europe (4.4) and the struggles of these years (4.5).

4.1. MILITARY: THE BATTLE OF PUEBLA (CINCO DE MAYO, 1862)
(Choice of documents)

Option 1: Board Game. CINCO DE MAYO: The Battle of Puebla, 1862 (2006)

This BSO game, titled CINCO DE MAYO, presents the battle between French troops planning to install Emperor Maximilian, and Juárez's Republican forces for control of the city of Puebla. The Mexican victory is now a national holiday.

The online advertisement describes the game as follows: The battle itself uses some very interesting, colorful terrain, along with the usual units with the evocative names: 2nd Zouaves, the Fijo de Morelia Battalion, Chasseurs d'Afrique, the Oaxaca Lancers, etc. Special rules cover cavalry lancer charges, square formation, a rather early use of trenches, and artillery ammunition.

Most of the rules and mechanics will be quite familiar to anyone who has played BSO games, but all with a nice period flavor. Playing time for CINCO has averaged 2–3 hours, sometimes less, and the rules are only 9 pages. Play the game at least twice.

Option 2: Video.

The festival reenactment of the Battle of Puebla, which takes place annually in Huejotzingo, Mexico, is available in film footage from 1968 (and other film clips on YouTube). Information on the reenactment is discussed in a variety of publications and websites.[1]

Option 3: Opera.

One opera, Ildegonda *(written by Melesio Morales and debuted in 1866), is available on CD (2007), on MP3 download, and on YouTube. Another opera is Cenobio Paniagua's* Catalina de Guisa *(1859), available on YouTube and discussed in Beá Gonzalez's* The Mapmaker's Opera *(2007), which became an off-Broadway musical. If you select* Catalina de Guisa *and the novel, be certain to look at the website http://mapmakersopera.com/, which includes songs from the musical. Enjoy!*

4.2. POLITICS: VICTOR HUGO'S 1867 LETTER TO BENITO JUÁREZ CONCERNING THE EXECUTION OF MAXIMILIAN

Victor Hugo had an international reputation as one of the greatest of French authors. He wrote romantic fiction, plays, and poetry that attracted large audiences. His publications included such classics as The Hunchback of Notre Dame *and* Les Misérables. *Based on his success as a man of letters, he also claimed a reputation as a public intellectual. As a staunch republican he fled France for Belgium when Napoleon III took power, and then exiled himself to the Channel Islands until 1870 with the collapse of the empire.*

Hauteville House, June 20, 1867
To the President of the Mexican Republic Juárez,
You have equaled John Brown. America today has two heroes, John Brown and you. Because of John Brown, slavery has died and you have won liberty. Mexico has been saved by a Principle and a Man. The principle is the Republic and you are the man.

On the other hand, all the monarchical intentions end in failure. All the usurpations that began in Puebla ended in Querétaro.

Europe, in 1863, threw itself on America. Two monarchies attacked your democracy: one with a Prince, the other with an army, the most veteran of European armies, that had a fleet for support as strong as it was on land; that had for support all the finances of France, receiving unlimited replacements; Victorious in Africa, Crimea, Italy; valiantly fanatic for its flag, that possessed an abundance of horses, ammunition, provisions, and formidable munitions. On the other side, Juárez.

On one side two Empires; on the other, a man. A man, with only one man's fist, an outlaw, chased from village to village, from rancho to rancho, from forest to forest, threatened by odious military courts, attacked in caverns like a fierce beast, hounded in the desert. For generals [he had] some desperados; for troops, some ragged individuals. With neither money, nor food, nor power, nor cannons, and scrubland for cities. Here the usurpation called itself legitimate; their Law called it illegal. The usurpation with the imperial helmet on its head and sword in its hand, was saluted by bishops, and proceeded and followed by powerful legions, The Law, alone and ragged. You, the Law, accepted combat.

The battle of One against All the others has lasted five years. Lacking men, you have used things. The terrible climate has helped you; you have had assistance from your Sun; you have had for defenders the impassable swamps, the streams full of crocodiles, the marshes full of fevers, the dense vegetation, the yellow fever of the tropical lowlands, the salty deserts, the great sands without water or plants, where horses died of hunger and thirst, the large and severe Anahuac plateau, like that of Castile, is defended by its barrenness. The ravines always shaken by the tremors of the volcanoes from Colima to Nevada de Toluca. You have called in the help of your natural barriers: the rugged mountain ranges, the high basalt dikes, and the colossal porphyry rocks. You have waged a giant war and your weapons have been the mountains.

And one day, after five years of smoke, dust, and blindness, the cloud has dissipated and then were seen the two empires fallen to the ground, nothing of the monarchy, none of the soldiers, nothing more than the wicked usurpation in ruins and above this horrifying collapse, one man on his feet, Juárez, and at the side of this man, Liberty.

You have done all of this, Juárez, and it is great, but what remains for you to do is greater still.

Listen, Citizen President of the Mexican Republic.

You have just brought down the Monarchies with Democracy. You have demonstrated to them your power, now show your magnificence. After the flash, show the dawn. Against the Caesarism that murdered, you placed the Republic that let live. Against the Monarchies that usurp and exterminate, you placed a people who rule and are restrained. To the barbarians, show civilization. To Despots, Principles.

Dazzling them, Humble the kings before the people; Defeat them, above all, with your piety. Protecting the enemy will affirm Principle. The grandeur of Principle ignores the enemy. Men do not have a name before principle; men are Mankind. Principle does not recognize anything beyond itself. Man in his supreme stupidity only knows this: human like if inviolable. O venerable impartiality of Truth. How beautiful is the Law without judging, only engaged with the Law.

Right before those who legally deserve death is where the Law must actually forswear it. The magnanimous destruction of the scaffold should be done in front of the culprits.

May he who offends against principles be safeguarded by principle. May he have this joy and this shame. May the violator of the law be sheltered by the law. Stripped of its false immunity, royal immunity, you will place true human immunity. May he be stunned to see that what is sacred is not the same as the emperor's view. May this prince, who did not, learn that there is within him misery, royalty, and man. Never has an opportunity as great as this presented itself. Would they dare to execute [Antoni] Berezowski in the presence of a safe and sound Maximilian? One wanted to kill a king and the other, a nation. Juárez, please take this giant step toward civilization. Juárez, abolish the death penalty across the earth. May the world see this marvelous event: the Republic has its assassin, an emperor; at the moment of crushing him, you recognize that he is man, you release him and say to him: you are one of mankind. Go.

That will be, Juárez, your second victory. The first, defeating the usurpation, is grand; the second, pardoning the usurper, will be sublime. Yes, to those monarchs whose prisons are full, whose scaffolds are rusty murderers, to those kings of pursuing [individuals], exiles, prisoners, and Siberia, to those who have Poland, Ireland, Havana, Crete, to those princes obeyed by judges, to those judges obeyed by hangmen, to those hangmen obeyed by death, to those emperors who so easily order a beheading, show them how you save the head of an emperor!

The law of enlightenment opens above all royal laws that spill blood, and in the most Holy book, in the middle of its supreme page one sees the finger of the Republic placed on God's commandment: Thou Shall Not Kill. These words contain the duty. You will fulfill this duty.

The usurper should be pardoned and the Liberator has not done it, pity. Two years ago, December 2, 1859, I appealed in the name of Democracy, I asked the United States for the life of John Brown. I did not obtain it. Today I ask Mexico for the life of Maximilian. Will I obtain it? Yes. And perhaps at this moment my request has already been fulfilled and Maximilian will owe his life to Juárez. And, the punishment? They will ask, The punishment? here it is: Maximilian lives by the grace of the Republic.

Victor Hugo, Hauteville House, June 20, 1867[2]

4.3. CHURCH

Mexican clerical and European secular reaction to Maximilian's execution came in many forms. Composer Franz Liszt, popular throughout Europe and Mexico, wrote a requiem for Maximilian. This genre reflected popular religion that drew on the Mass and represented the ties between monarchy and the Church.

Listen to Franz Liszt, "Marche funèbre, En mémoire de Maximilian I, Empereur du Mexique" ("Funeral march, In memory of Maximilian I, Emperor of Mexico"), 1883. Années de pèlerinage: III année: 6 - Marche funèbre. En mémoire de Maximilien l'Empereur du Mèxique.

Claudio Colombo, *Dall'album Franz Liszt: Années de pèlerinage*, 4 feb 2011.

4.4. FAMILY: MAXIMILIAN DID NOT DIE; JOHN LAMPERTI, "WHO WAS JUSTO ARMAS?" (2004)

Despite Victor Hugo's appeal to Benito Juárez and similar requests from other world leaders, including Great Britain's Queen Victoria, a firing squad executed Maximilian on the Hill of the Bells, outside Querétaro, June 19, 1867. The body was embalmed and publicly displayed. After a lengthy exchange of diplomatic correspondence, the casket was returned to Europe and buried in the Habsburg Imperial Crypt in Vienna. The execution astonished Europeans. The poet Giosuè Carducci, Italy's first Nobel laureate, described it as the result of the Aztec blood lust typical of Mexicans. Édouard Manet depicted the events in a series of paintings, from 1867 to 1869, called "The Execution of Emperor Maximilian." Franz Liszt, the Hungarian composer, wrote a requiem, entitled "Années de Pélerinage (Years of Pilgrimage), with its sixth movement, the "Marche funebre, En mémoire de Maximilian I, Empereur du Mexique" ("Funeral March, In Memory of Maximilian I, Emperor of Mexico") that was first performed in 1883. An enduring tribute came from the ship carrying the Emperor's body when it arrived in Trieste. The ship's band played "La Paloma," Maximilian's favorite song. The Navy vowed never to play it again onboard any Austrian-Hungarian warship. This tradition is still maintained on all Austrian sailing boats.

Often deaths, including executions, under extraordinary or baffling circumstances, generate numerous urban legends and myths. So it happened in Maximilian's case.

Sr. Ronaldo Déneke, an architect from San Salvador presented the theory in 2007 that Maximilian did not really die, but settled down in San Salvador under the name of Justo Armas. His theory is corroborated by a handful of circumstantial evidence. First and foremost, Juarez similarly to Maximilian was a high-degree freemason, and it features in the secret society's vow not take each other's life, therefore Déneke supposes that the firing squad used blanks. Secondly, the dead body—first seen by relatives months later in a very bad state—was deliberately left to decompose so that it should be returned to Maximilian's family in the most unrecognizable state possible. Not even the closest relatives were to notice that the body lying in the coffin was not Maximilian's. According to official records, the family members who had been requested to identify the deceased—among them Maximilian's mother—did not recognize the dead emperor. As a piece of evidence for his theory, Déneke mentions a visit in the course of which Austrian-Hungarian diplomats visited Armas in connection with the succession at the end of 1916, just before Francis Joseph's death. However, they had to return empty-handed. After this incident, Justo Armas lived for two more decades in the Latin American country, and if he really was Maximilian, he died aged approximately 104. His person is surrounded by a lot of uncertainties. What emerges about Armas from the contemporary local press and records is that he appeared in the country middle-aged, was in possession of a European education, knew the etiquette, had an excellent command of several foreign languages, had first-class connections even as a stranger and in his personal appearance perhaps due to his typical moustache he extremely resembled Maximilian.

In order to prove his assumptions, Déneke requested and was granted permission by Otto, the head of the Habsburg family to disinter Armas' body and conduct genetic experiments on it. Based on the evidence of the examination results, the deceased is identical with one of the members of the Habsburg family (Maximilian, Rudolf or John Salvator archdukes come into question). In any case, it is extremely interesting that the urban legend was not created by posterity, but it was also manifest in the conversations of the members of the contemporary social life. However, the above-listed and construed evidence only circumstantially implies that Justo Armas was identical with Emperor Maximilian. This is not proven by any official or scientific research or examination at present.

Déneke sees the origin of the existing, but probably assumed name in a Spanish euphemism used for execution, *hecho justo por las armas.*

Justo Armas?
John Lamperti Collection.

John Lamperti, "Who Was Justo Armas?" (2004)

Moviegoers who saw "A Beautiful Mind," the Oscar winning film biography of mathematician John Nash, were undoubtedly moved by his struggle with schizophrenia, his eventual recovery and the award of the Nobel Prize in economics in 1994. It was obvious that the support Nash received over the years from his wife Alicia Lardé was vital for his survival.[a] The film never revealed, however, that Alicia was Salvadoran. The book on which the film was based does mention that connection, and includes a few intriguing hints about some members of the Lardé family. Following these clues leads quickly to the intriguing and enigmatic figure of don Justo Armas.

Justo Armas was a real person; that is not in question. He was not born in El Salvador, but appeared in its capital sometime late in the 19th century, already in his middle years. Somehow he quickly gained access to many of the leading families in Salvadoran society—including the Lardés, who were wealthy and well connected, although not counted among "the fourteen." Don Justo had elegant European manners, spoke fluent and educated German plus several other languages, and seemed to possess extensive knowledge of upper class European society and court affairs, especially those of Austria and its neighbors. With these assets, he was able to establish a catering service which supplied food, drink, and serving personnel for

---

[a] Sylvia Nasar, *A Beautiful Mind*. New York: Simon and Schuster, 1998. The biography is dedicated to Alicia Lardé Nash.

many high-level social functions; his services included the use of first class tableware and silver utensils, of which he had a considerable store. In the early years of the 20th century, the participation of don Justo Armas was *de rigueur* at the major social events of San Salvador. In addition to catering, he gave classes in manners and etiquette to young ladies from the leading families. One other curious fact stands out. Don Justo always appeared in society impeccably dressed and groomed—and barefoot.

Who was this remarkable man? Where did he come from, and how did he acquire his unusual talents and position? Two astonishing theories have been seriously proposed; as we will see, one of them, but not the other, appears easy to disprove. Of course it is possible that neither is true. Here are those three alternatives.

1) Justo Armas was the crown prince Rudolf, the only son of Austro-Hungarian emperor Francis Joseph. This, naturally, is quite impossible, since Rudolf died at Mayerling near Vienna in 1889 together with his young lover Baroness Marie Vetsera. The two deaths were officially described as suicides (or perhaps murder and suicide), motivated by the frustrations and hopelessness of their illicit love. Suspicions that the crown prince was the target of a politically motivated assassination plot, however, arose immediately and have persisted. But whatever lay behind the events at Mayerling, if Rudolf did in fact die there he could hardly have become Justo Armas.

It is the Prince Rudolf hypothesis which connects Justo Armas with Alicia Lardé (Mrs. John Nash). One of her uncles, Enrique Lardé (1899–1993), has presented a two-part theory. First, he states that he himself is the natural son of don Justo Armas, and second, he asserts that Justo Armas was in reality Rudolf, who did not die at Mayerling after all. Dr. Lardé has written a short book about the matter, which was published soon after his death through the efforts of his son (also named Enrique).[b] That book is the source—apparently the only source—for the following account.

According to this theory, Crown Prince Rudolf was not murdered at Mayerling but was given the chance to save his life by leaving Europe forever and adopting a different identity. (The Baroness Vetsera also did not die, but instead was confined for life in a Carmelite convent.) Rudolf sailed from Hamburg in a ship owned by his cousin, Archduke Johann Salvator. They arrived safely in La Plata, but the ship went down in a storm while trying to pass through the Straits of Magellan. Everyone was drowned—except Rudolf. While clinging to wreckage, the former crown prince made a vow to the Virgin Mary that he would never again wear shoes (would remain in contact with the earth?) if his life were spared. A small fishing boat picked him up soon afterwards. For nearly ten years Rudolf lived and worked

---

[b] Dr. Enrique Lardé, *The Crown Prince Rudolf: His Mysterious Life After Mayerling*. Pittsburgh: Dorrance Publishing Co., 1994. The passage quoted is on page 3.

among the fishermen and peasants of Argentina, then made his way to El Salvador where he arrived in 1898 under the alias Justo Armas. He lived in San Salvador until his death in 1936.

"In those days," writes Enrique Lardé, "when the Archduke came to El Salvador, the only hotel in the city was the Europa Hotel, whose proprietors were my parents, Don Jorge Lardé and Doña Amelie Arthés de Lardé. The Archduke, who no longer made use of his titles of nobility and now, known as 'Justo Armas,' fell in love with Doña Amelie Arthés de Lardé, and the first and only male child of the Archduke was born. I am that child."

Sr. Lardé goes on to support his claim with circumstantial evidence. He states that the "secret" of Justo Armas's true identity was widely known, or at least suspected. "The Austrian Consul," he says, "who had known [the Archduke Rudolf] amid ancestral opulence in his homeland, recognized him barefoot in El Salvador." He adds that this caused "quite a commotion" in the office! But although "all Salvadoran society of the time" knew the secret, Don Justo himself revealed his identity to only one person. That person was Enrique Lardé's mother, Doña Amelie. Shortly before her death in 1911 she in turn explained to her son that don Justo was his biological father. (Enrique had naturally thought of Jorge Lardé as his father, and so he was, by adoption.) She also told Enrique that don Justo Armas was the

Dr. Enrique Lardé-Arthés.
John Lamperti Collection.

Crown Prince Rudolf of Austria—as don Justo had told her, many years before.

It is understandable that Enrique Lardé believed without reservation all of his mother's end-of-life confession, and there is no apparent reason to doubt that Justo Armas had been her lover and was the father of at least this one of her children. Don Justo may well also have told her, and she herself may have believed, that he was the former crown prince. That second part of the story, however, is a-priori far less credible than the first and requires a much higher standard of proof to be accepted as true.

2) Don Justo Armas was the Emperor Maximilian, the younger brother of Emperor Franz Josef of Austro-Hungary. Of course the world "knows" that this is equally impossible. Maximilian's brief rule in Mexico collapsed in 1867, shortly after Napoleon III withdrew the French troops that had established and maintained him on his throne. The emperor could have abdicated and returned to Europe with the French army, but he chose to stay out of a sense of duty and of obligation to his followers. Maximilian was soon captured by the forces of the Mexican Republic headed by Benito Juárez, and he was tried by court martial, sentenced to death, and executed on the Cerro de las Campanas near Querétaro in 1867. If that is so, the ex-emperor could hardly have reappeared in El Salvador as Justo Armas.

Manet's famous painting "The execution of Maximilian" is an imaginative creation. The artist did not witness the events.

A San Salvador architect, Sr. Rolando Déneke, has been intrigued for years by the mystery of Justo Armas and has devoted time and resources to investigating his origin. Déneke has reportedly built a strong case for the theory that Justo Armas was Maximilian. His work has not been published, although that is promised in the near future. However, a Spanish diplomat assigned for a time to El Salvador met Déneke and learned many details of his investigation. This man, Santiago Miralles Huete, has presented the theory in the form of an entertaining novel entitled *La Tierra Ligera*, recently published in Madrid.[c] That novel is the main source for the following resume of Sr. Déneke's case. An even newer book,[d] an account of Maximilian's imperial career, expounds Déneke's theory but apparently has little additional evidence to offer.

Naturally the first and probably most difficult point to be explained is Maximilian's apparent execution in 1867. The answer given by Déneke (and Miralles) involves the reported fact that Maximilian, Justo Armas, and Benito Júarez were all high-ranking members of the Masonic order. One important law of freemasonry forbids the killing of brother Masons. This law presented Júarez with a painful dilemma: while Maximilian's death

---

[c] Santiago Miralles Huete, *La Tierra Ligera*. Madrid: Ediciones de la Discreta, 2000.
[d] Johann Georg Lughofer, *Des Kaisers neues Leben: Der Fall Maximilian von Mexico*. Vienna: Ueberreuter, 2002.

Maximilian, emperor of Mexico.
John Lamperti Collection.

Édouard Manet's fanciful painting of Maximilian's execution.
Édouard Manet, *L'exécution de Maximilien* (Copenhagen).

appeared to be necessary for reasons of state,[e] he must not kill a fellow Mason. The solution Júarez found[f] was a fake execution, to be followed by the disappearance forever of Maximilian of Austria. To make this scheme workable, Maximilian solemnly swore to use always an assumed name and to never reveal that the former emperor was still alive. His new identity was that of Justo Armas, the strange figure who appeared in Central America a few months after the supposed death of Maximilian. Armas first surfaced in Costa Rica, but within three years made his way to San Salvador where he passed the rest of a long and prosperous life. By this account, Armas would have immigrated to El Salvador early in the 1870s.

---

[e] The situation and the arguments for Maximilian's death are outlined by Jasper Ridley in his book *Maximilian and Juarez* [New York: Ticknor and Fields, 1992], pages 275–276. Ridley expresses no doubt that the execution was carried out.

[f] Proponents of this theory are not clear as to whether Juarez planned the sham execution himself or merely agreed to let Maximilian's escape be organized by others without interference.

Following the supposed execution of the former emperor by firing squad, the embalmed body of Maximilian was sent home to Austria. When the casket was opened, his mother is said to have exclaimed, "This is not my son!" As a lighter touch, it is also reported that after the execution Benito Júarez published an edict announcing that the Archduke Francis Maximilian of Austria had been "hecho justo por las armas," a euphemism for execution. This phrase, the suggestion goes, was the origin of the name "Justo Armas"!

According to the theory, his high standing in the Masonic order was also key to the immediate warm reception given the unknown Justo Armas by members of El Salvador's elite. The nation's vice president and chancellor, don Gregorio Arbizú, received him warmly and found for him a respectable government job. As well as being a Mason, Sr. Arbizú was known for his monarchist sympathies which may have further facilitated their friendship. Soon don Justo was installed in a home of his own where he surrounded himself with "dozens of objects of Maximilian of Hapsburg which an invisible hand had managed to convey from Mexico."

There is more. Briefly, Justo Armas was said to bear a striking resemblance to Maximilian, once differences of age and dress are taken into account. Reportedly, don Justo did declare his identity as the ex-emperor to at least one friend during his years in San Salvador; of course even if he did so that cannot be considered conclusive. A Mexican lady ("La Paloma") who reportedly had been the lover of the emperor during his years on the throne became a nun after his death. As "Sister Trinidad" she worked in a San Salvador hospital and was known to regularly visit don Justo Armas, something very unusual for a woman in her situation. Perhaps the most suggestive piece of evidence, verifiable in part, is the visit in 1914 or 1915 by two emissaries of the Austrian government. These men apparently avoided contacts with Salvadoran government officials and instead persistently sought an interview with a reluctant don Justo. When they finally met, the Austrians reportedly begged him to "return" with them to Austria and assume his "rightful position" there, an offer or request which Armas steadfastly refused. All this, if verified, adds up to a suggestive if not compelling circumstantial case that don Justo Armas was in fact the former Emperor Maximilian of Mexico.

Curiously, this theory is mentioned near the beginning of Dr. Lardé's book in a short section entitled "He was not Maximilian." (A reader new to these questions might well ask, "Whoever said he was?") However, that section offers no real evidence for its (negative) thesis, arguing circumstantially that "Even had he not been shot and had succeeded in escaping from Mexico, as those who invented this story claim, Maximilian would have returned to his own country.... Also, when Don Justo arrived in El Salvador in 1898, he looked the forty years of age he indeed was, and not the sixty-six years of his uncle, the Emperor of Mexico." Dr. Lardé wonders why, if Justo Armas was really Maximilian, he would have spent thirty-one years "in hiding" between "leaving Mexico in 1867" and his "supposed arrival" in El Salvador in 1898. He does, however, mention that there was a "great likeness" between the two and states that "the *kinship* of Don Justo and Maximilian was widely known" (emphasis added). Lardé's conclusion is that "these stories . . . are so absurd that they deserve no refutation"—a dangerous line to take when he himself is presenting a theory at least as improbable as the one he dismisses.

What more could be done to substantiate or disprove Justo Armas's identity with the ex-emperor Maximilian? DNA testing is one obvious possibility. *La Tierra Ligera* and other sources report that such tests have been undertaken, and that the results support a family relationship between don Justo and the Habsburgs. Detailed reporting as to how the testing was done and just what it revealed must await the publication of Sr. Rolando Denéke's studies, by himself or another.

3) **The third possibility, of course, is that don Justo Armas was neither Maximilian nor Rudolf** but someone else. Logically, that covers it; one of the three must be true. However, this third case itself leads to interesting mysteries. Whoever he was, the sudden appearance of this cultivated, German-speaking, barefoot man in San Salvador and his rise to prominence in Salvadoran society is a remarkable phenomenon. Some connection with European nobility is plausible, and it even seems quite possible that don Justo had some relationship with the Habsburg family. But that does not mean he was either Maximilian or Rudolf.

Favoring the "someone else" possibility is the fact that don Justo left a brief testament, in which he sketches his own background and states his age in a manner which totally contradicts both of the "imperial family" theories. Of course if that account is true, the story he reportedly told to his former lover Amelie Arthés cannot be, nor is his self identification as Maximilian to a San Salvador friend. Dr. Lardé reprints the testament in his book, and then tries to demonstrate that in it don Justo did not mean what he said but something quite different (pages 87–92). The explanation is not convincing—although, again, not impossible.

It seems more probable that don Justo did not tell the truth to Doña Amelie when they were intimate. This idea fits the Maximilian hypothesis, for under that theory don Justo would have vowed not to reveal himself but could have considered taking Rudolf's identity a permissible and suitably impressive substitute. Of course if he were "someone else" he might have simply lied. He would not have been the first man who invented for himself a romantic background to impress a lover.

Some of the circumstantial evidence fits equally well with either of the two Habsburg theories. Photographs showing a strong resemblance between Emperor Franz Josef, Maximilian, Rudolf, and Justo Armas support the idea of some family connection. The DNA evidence is said to have confirmed this much, even if it did not establish just what that relationship was. In addition, the visit of the Austrian ambassadors imploring don Justo to return supports the existence of a Habsburg connection but is equally consistent with either theory.

The question of timing, though, should be decisive in distinguishing between them. If it can be shown that don Justo Armas arrived in San Salvador earlier than 1889, the year of the crown prince's presumed death, that would absolutely eliminate the possibility that he was Rudolf. I have been assured that this is the case, and that there is documentary evidence proving that Justo Armas appeared in 1871.[8] Such a date fits well with the Maximilian hypothesis. On the other hand, that theory implies an unlikely (but not impossible) longevity for don Justo, who would then have had to be 104 years old when he died in 1936.

The San Salvador daily *El Diario de Hoy* published an obituary of don Justo on May 30, 1936. "Anyone who has participated in the social life of El Salvador during the last 60 years," it says, "knows of don Justo Armas," who was the caterer of highest prestige in the capital. "There was a dense mystery around the life of don Justo Armas," the obituary continues, mentioning in particular that he never used shoes or other footwear. There were speculations that he was a bastard son of one of the kings of Europe, says *El Diario*, and the article concludes that "He has taken to the tomb the secret of his unshod feet and of his noble origin." The obituary reiterates that don Justo lived "more than sixty years" in El Salvador, which of course supports his arrival early in the 1870s.

It is a truism that improbable assertions require high standards of proof. While there is sufficient reason to reject the Rudolf theory on the basis of timing, the same cannot be said for the hypothesis that don Justo was Maximilian. On the information publically available so far, including the books of Lardé and Miralles, the verdict must be that the problem remains open. However, obtaining further evidence in the matter would appear to be possible and indeed it may already exist, so perhaps in the near future this fascinating hypothesis will be definitively established. If don Justo Armas' identity as the former emperor Maximilian can be proved, a great many books and history lessons will need to be rewritten.[3]

4.5. POPULAR GROUPS: "ADIÓS, MAMÁ CARLOTA"

The end of the French Intervention and Maximilian's Empire are best represented musically with the song "Adiós, Mamá Carlota," depicting the departure of the

---

[8] Private communication from Salvadoran journalist and author Carlos Caña Dinarte, who says that prominent newcomers were recorded in the Official Gazette. Dr. Lardé, on the other hand, offers no evidence in support of the claimed 1898 arrival date for don Justo which his theory requires.

Empress to seek continuing aid from Napoleon III, who refused, and then from the Pope. Her efforts failed. The song, whose lyrics parody a poem entitled "Adiós, oh patria mía" by Ignacio Rodríguez Galván, was composed by General Vicente Riva Palacio and published in 1866. A version of the song by Alberto Hernández with excellent images is available at https://www.youtube.com/watch?v= KOI4B_SGiuA.

José de J. Nuñez y Domínguez, "The Origin of the Songs 'Mamá Carlota' and 'Adios a Mamá Carlota'" (1927)

Writer José de J. Nuñez y Domínguez wrote the following articles about the song following the death of Empress Carlota in her father's castle in Belgium, January 19, 1927.[4]

"The Origin of the song, 'Mamá Carlota'"

José de J. Nuñez y Domínguez
Translated by Clea Conlon:
No one in recent days writing about Empress Carlota, following her death, has referred to the famous song that common women sang about the wife of Maximilian on her last trip to Europe, and the Republican Army made its marching song.

Our writers have poured the lyricism of elegies with the most tragic tones over the corpse of the unfortunate Archduchess, but they have not recalled the details of the battle song so closely linked to her life, perhaps because it is not significant enough. In this way, Mexico is losing its everyday character and is forgetting its nationalist traditions.

The Liberal soldiers who fought against the Intervention and Empire, like our recent revolutionary forces with "Valentina" and "Adelita," had their own battle song. It was not one of the anonymous compositions immortalized as battle songs as a result of being repeated by balladeers with dusty sandals plucking harps. The song had a progenitor that stressed Mexican lyrics and an illustrious lineage, although the music itself was of plebian origin and even borrowed from a popular folksong that traveled from mouth to mouth during those times.

During the battles of the [War of the] Reform [1858–1861], the dominant song in the Juarista ranks was "Los Cangrejos," or "The Crabs," from the wicked pen of the "the Romantic" author, Guillermo Prieto. The song, "El Chinaco" or "The Commoner," also alternated as the popular song among the "reds" [the Conservatives]. During the Intervention and the Empire, the song, "La Paloma" predominated during the first era. "Mamá Carlota," or "Adiós Mamá Carlota," the author's original title, was composed a little after the Empress's departure in 1866 from Veracruz.

How do you determine the origin of the famous song that has only been performed on the theater stage a few times; a theater that cultivated the end of the world genre by violating the patriotic and noble sentiment that inspired, and now requires, a certain awareness of the present?

Eduardo Ruiz, a notable writer, historicized the events of the French Intervention in his home state published as a posthumous superb novel about Michoacán during this agitated period. He was an eyewitness to a large number of the events and accompanied the main Liberal leaders on their campaigns. He tells about when General Vicente Riva Palacio, who stayed at his house in Huetamo in 1866, while eating with his secretary Verduzco, and several others, including Ruiz, received a letter. The general, who was also a poet, removed his dark glasses, read the contents with rapt attention, folded it again, and, despite the deep expectations of his tablemates, continued eating and topped his meal off with tasty Uruapan coffee without mentioning the contents of the letter he had received.

Preparing to leave the table, the General stood up and ordered his secretary to bring paper and a pen and he began dictating, without hesitation, the well-known song, with the following lyrics. Ruiz, the secretary, and everyone else heard the improvisation with open mouths. . . .

Adiós a Mamá Carlota:

The Cheerful Seaman
With a calm voice sings
And the anchor comes up
With a strange murmur
The ship is at sea
Like a bouncing ball.
Goodbye, Mamá Carlota,
Farewell, my tender love

From the remote beach
I watch with sadness
The stupid nobility
Of the sanctimonious and the traitorous

In the depths of his chest
he now feels his loss;
Goodbye, Mamá Carlota
Farewell, my tender love.
Coming to an end in the Palace, the
Social gatherings, games, dances,
Upsetting the friars
With the powerful Pain.

> The downtrodden mob
> Created a ruckus screaming:
> Goodbye, Mamá Carlota,
> Farewell, my tender love.
> The muffled murmur
> of the sad chamberlains,
> the chaplains and
> the ladies in waiting cry
> The sad beautiful Mestiza
> Sings with broken lyrics,
> Goodbye, Mamá Carlota,
> Farewell, my tender love.
>
> And as long as the common women,
> already singing victory,
> Keep your memory,
> Without fear or resentment
> They say, as the wind
> Strikes your boat,
> Goodbye, Mamá Carlota,
> Farewell, my tender love.

another verse says:

The sad Chucho Hermosa [Jesús Hermosa was a popular poet at Maximilian's Court]
Sings with a broken lyre
Adiós Mamá Carlota
Adiós, my tender love.

"Adiós a Mamá Carlota"

José de J. Nuñez y Domínguez
Translated by Clea Conlon

Several days ago, after publishing a note relating to the "Goodbye Mamá Carlota" (Goodbye, Mom Carlota) and not "Goodbye Carlota's Boobs," as it is usual to say today, I searched for the son of the famous Michoacán writer, Eduardo Ruiz, who left a volume recording his memories of the war of Intervention in the rich land of the Purepecha. At last, I found the engineer Daniel Ruiz Benitez. After our discussion, I had a few picturesque details about the origin of the song that, from the year 'sixty-six of the last century, is repeated everywhere and every time a date or an event recalls the delicate figure of Doña Carlota, on her return to Europe. Eduardo Ruiz, in his *History of the War of Intervention in Michoacán*, left a delightful chapter that tells the story of the famous "Farewell," but his son has a broader, more intimate story of the day Vicente Riva Palacio dictated the verses of "Goodbye, Mamá Carlota." It was an event inspired by the black Uruapan coffee that sat on the table [a metaphor for after-dinner conversation], an affectionate remembrance for those men the rest of their lives.

ALZATI news. [Alzati refers to the popularization of Italian opera dramatizations with masks. The word was adopted in Mexico to indicate masked balls combining the operatic tradition and, in this case in Michoacán, the indigenous masked dances at fiestas.] Riva Palacio had had the idea to publish a small, popular newspaper that he christened with the name of a popular dance. Many of the issues were handwritten, when the press in Huetamo run by Gregorio Perez Jardon, a humble typographer of the Liberal cause, could not do the job. Other issues were printed. The newspaper did not produce a penny for the Liberals. It was a propaganda page of the attacking warriors. Ruiz said that "The Woodpecker" was given away to "anheteros" and "barilleros" [traveling vendors of needles, threads, and buttons who visited towns to sell their small stock] who visited the plaza at Huetamo, and then went on across Michoacán to Morelia and other places. "The Woodpecker," reached the same selling price as a hectare of land (Michoacán land), a peso.

"Goodbye Mamá Carlota," was published for the first time in "The Green Woodpecker" and the verses of Riva Palacio carried with them, the news of Mrs. Maximilian's trip seeking protection from Napoleon III. Before the newspaper arrived in Morelia, the allies of the French Intervention had carefully concealed this information, which put them in a difficult situation [when it became known].

Riva Palacio was trying to reorganize his forces, and to do that, the author of "Monja y casada" [. . . virgen y martir/ Nun and married, virgin and martyr] dispatched his right hand man, who reported to him that that the Empress Carlota had abandoned the country. This was the news that Riva Palacio received and that led to his burlesque poetry, parodied in the just as famous composition "Adios a Mexico" written by Rodriguez Galvan, with which he begins his first four verses.

The song "Adios a Mamá Carlota" was published immediately in "The Woodpecker" in Huetamo under the direction of General Riva Palacio, who, to the very end, was a man of the pen, and who even during war never ceased to show off his talent, pouring out his satire.

Shortly after its publication, "Adios a Mamá Carlota" was sung by the soldiers of the Central Army, who adapted the first music that came to their minds. Once Riva Palacio heard their adaptation, he advised them to choose the tune of "Los Cangrejos" varying the beat; this became the final tune of "Mamá Carlota."

Completing these notes, we record what the historian, Nicholas Rangel, recalled about this popular song: "The Engineer Jesus Galindo y Villa tells about being in Madrid at the Mexican Legation in 1892. At the time the Mexican Eighth Regiment Band directed by Captain Encarnacion Payén, gave a farewell serenade to the Mexican Minister, General Vicente Riva Palacio. He told Galindo y Villa, during a moment when the musicians rested: 'Tell Payén to play slowly 'Mamá Carlota'. Payén faithfully fulfilled the wishes of the general. And at the end of the last note, Riva Palacio exclaimed, 'Poor woman—Fate has been crueler than men themselves'. And moved by the memory of old times and the warmth of a generous and spontaneous feeling of pity, he wiped away a silent tear in the eyes of this illustrious veteran of the Republic."

ADDITIONAL READING

Jan Harold Brunvand, *The Vanishing Hitchhiker: American Urban Legends and Their Meanings*. New York: W. W. Norton & Company; Revised ed. 2003.

Leer en español:

Cecilia Vázquez Ahumada y Margarita Piña Loredo, *La batalla del 5 del mayo en el carnaval de Huejotzingo, espacio de identidad*. Puebla: El Colegio de Pueda, 2012.

NOTES

1. For information on the Huejotzingo celebration, see Cecilia Vázquez Ahumada y Margarita Piña Loredo, *La batalla del 5 del mayo en el carnaval de Huejotzingo, espacio de identidad* (Puebla: El Colegio de Pueda, 2012).
2. Victor Hugo to Benito Juárez, June 20, 1867, Centro de Estudios de la Historia Mexicana, Fundación Carlos Slim. Online at http://www.wikimexico.com/wps/portal/wm/wikimexico/periodos/mexico-independiente/era-liberal/documentos/carta-de-victor-hugo-a-benito-juarez-20-de-junio-de-1867.
3. Online at https://math.dartmouth.edu/~lamperti/Justo_Armas.html.
4. The author C. M. Mayo, who wrote *The Last Prince of the Mexican Empire* (Lakewood, CO: Unbridled Books, 2010), refers to the song and its analysis by José de J. Nuñez y Domínguez, and provides the newspaper articles without dates or newspaper titles. See the author's website: http://cmmayo.com/maximilian-adios-mama-carlota.html. This website contains the two newspaper articles from February 1927, but does not identify the publication or the exact date.

CHAPTER 5

The Porfirian Years, 1876–1911

The period of Porfirio Díaz covered the years from the mid-1870s until 1911. During this time, the nation experienced efforts to achieve Western modernity as Díaz maneuvered among the main networks to reach a general accommodation, ignoring past conflicts. Documents illustrate the nature of changes regarded as progress, including the appearance of Mexicans by the clothing they wore (5.1); they show that such developments often only formed a façade, such as conditions in the army (5.2); and they reveal the Liberal government's policy to connive at church policies (5.3) and festering opposition among the five networks. Nevertheless, social customs, everyday manners among the elites, remained the subject of great attention and training (5.4). Music, especially popular music, achieved great popularity with the development of recording technology (5.5). But strife within the elites and popular unrest eventually combined to bring a violent end to the Porfiriato with revolution.

5.1. POLITICS: HAT LAWS AND PANTS LAWS

Porfirian officials determined that Mexicans would look modern, if nothing else. Clothing laws dictated how people would appear in towns. These documents describe the clothing.

"Sombrero Tax Effective"
"Big Hats Must Go Out of Fashion in Guadalajara Now"
Guadalajara, Jan. 5, 1906.
　The tax on big straw sombreros, imposed by the city council of Guadalajara with a view to forcing the men of the lower class, in this city, to discontinue their use, has become effect.

The regulations have been somewhat changed since their first publication. As they now stand hat brims of ten centimeters (3.9 inches) or less will not be taxed. For each additional ten centimeters in width of brims a tax of $1.00 will be imposed. For example, the tax on a hat with a brim twenty centimeters wide will be $1.00, and on a hat with a brim thirty centimeters wide will be $2.00. The majority of the big hats are made with rounded brims, and for taxation purposes the exact measurement of the straw in the brim, and not the distance that the brim extends from the crown, will be considered.

Julia Newell Jackson, "Mexico City Hat Stores" (1890)

Hat stores are perhaps the most conspicuous on the street; their large windows filled with gorgeous sombreros with high sugar-loaf crowns and an expanse of the brim like a parasol, splendidly trimmed with gold or silver embroiled bindings, and cable-cord and tassels of the same precious metals. They range in price from twenty-five to seventy-five dollars for one! So the Mexican farmer pays as much for his hat as does the Washington belle.[1]

Harriott Wright Sharratt, "The Land of Grandfather's Hat" (1896)

This is truly the land of Grandfather's Hat, because one generation after another succeeds to the treasured headgear. In its holy crown, the wearer carries all the germs collected through long ages, besides some other things—a bottle of pulque, some sandals, or a cold lunch. If he is fortunate to possess two or more sombreros, he piles one on top of the other and travels around like an animated Chinese pagoda.[2]

E. H. Blichfeldt, "Hats in Oaxaca" (1912)

Having left my hat in one of the shops to be cleaned after a dusty ride, I ventured bareheaded among the vendors, public letterwriters, idlers, and passers-by, in search of a boot-black. When I found him, his first impudent, astonishing words were: "Where's your hat, mister? You'd better look out or they'll arrest you and send you to the army."[3]

"Pants Law in Zacatecas" (1868)

The legislature of Zacatecas passed a law requiring the wearing of trousers with a 25 cent fine for those in breech-cloths.[4]

"Mexico City council debates trouser law" (1890)

The ordinance compelling all the male inhabitants of this city to wear trousers is still under consideration by the city council. Although it has been discussed no action has yet been taken regarding it. In order that persons who have never visited Mexico may not be led into error concerning the costumes of the class against which the proposed ordinance is directed it may be well to state that some people here wear white cotton drawers instead of trousers. The object of the ordinance is to have the latter substituted for the former. Similar ordinances have already been enacted and are now in force in several cities of the republic.[5]

"Forced to wear trousers, Mountaineers around
Guanajuato prefer to pay fines" (1908)

Guanajuato: The local treasury will soon be full to overflowing from the numerous fines collected from the sons of mountains who daily endeavor to enter this ancient town clad in cotton drawers. The law is strict in this particular and the police in the suburbs have strict orders to see that no peon enters the town without a pair of ready-made trousers. (It would be interesting to know who, in Guanajuato, owns the largest interest in the local trousers factory.)[6]

5.2. MILITARY AND MILITIA: STEPHEN NEUFELD, "THE SLY MOCKERIES OF MILITARY MEN: CORRIDOS AND POETRY AS CRITICAL VOICE FOR THE PORFIRIAN ARMY"

Enlisted men used songs, called corridos, *and wrote poetry to describe their life in the army and to mock military pretensions. Singing about their comrades and duties they reasserted rough masculinity, anti-foreign sentiments, and racial identity that had been previously stripped away, as they defied Porfirian official narratives.*

The patio of the barracks rang with amateur song most ordinary nights in Mexico's late-nineteenth century. Improvised and regimental instruments accompanied the enthusiastic men and women of the army as they entertained themselves performing *corridos* (folk songs) about life, love, and war. Meanwhile, in small chambers some three stories above, young officers set pen to paper creating verse and poetry as an exercise in cultivation and culture. Quiet reflections of their own were nonetheless interrupted or perhaps inspired by the boisterous tunes that floated up from below. The unique mixtures of these peoples, and their verses, sheds light on the inner worlds of the soldier and his society.

In an era of accelerated change, the military men of President Porfirio Díaz (1876–1911) gave voice to their lived experiences in many ways, some officers writing martial poetry while in the ranks men sang the more common corrido. The lyrics and verses that filled barracks and institutional periodicals offer us a rich glimpse into the formation of *mexicanidad*

(Mexican-ness). In both genres, the military men expressed ideas about the nation's legitimacy and power, its genealogy and future, and the place of masculinity and sentiment in their society. Officers strived to portray themselves as both *hombres de espada* and *hombres de pluma*, men of sword and of quill.[a] They offered their verses as homage gifts (*obsequios*) to their superiors and even, at times, to the wife of the President. As literary amateurs they tried to straddle the modern and traditional, setting a sense of novelty against perceptions of history, while invoking a particular martial worldview that encompassed their idea of Mexico. Like most of their countrymen the military officers also grappled with making sense of new technologies, emerging classes, and increasing globalization, all of which had direct effect on the ways that the army operated and saw itself. Likewise, soldiers in the ranks took to early corrido ballads to speak of their own army life and in lyrical play mocked the pretensions of the army in some not-so-hidden transcripts.[b] They re-imagined their comrades and deeds in ways that defied the regimes' carefully ordered narratives—reinserting rough masculinity, anti-foreign sentiments, and racial identity where they had been previously stripped away. By comparing the expressions of these different echelons an intriguing picture emerges on how the nation was imagined. On one side, the military as an institution officially dedicated its efforts to a project of positivist modernizing and secular order, yet on the other, an alternative vision from within the ranks demonstrated the distance between rhetorical modernity and actual circumstances. The verses in both forms also communicated a degree of shared experiences in their repudiation of foreign elements, and their adherence to expressing *mexicanidad* in the national tongue. The shared language conventions exposed a common vocabulary with a mostly unified imagining of the *patria* (fatherland) invoked in terms of shared historical experience.[c]

Music filled the Porfirian barracks by night. As tunes spilled into streets neighbors recalled decades later how much they enjoyed the army bands.[d] The military bands also frequently performed for the public in arranged

---

[a] On the men of sword and quill see Luis González, "El liberalismo triunfante," in *Historia general de México, Vol. 2*, ed. Daniel Cosío Villegas et al., 6th ed. (México: Colegio de México, 2005), 638–706; Pablo Piccato, *The Tyranny of Opinion: Honor in the Construction of the Mexican Public Sphere* (Durham: Duke University Press, 2010), 4; Robert Martin Alexius, "The Army and Politics in Porfirian Mexico" (Ph.D. diss., Austin: University of Texas at Austin, 1976); Guillermo Prieto, *Lecciones de historia patria: Obras Completas XXVIII* (México: CONACULTA, 1999), 41.

[b] James C. Scott, *Weapons of the Weak: Everyday Forms of Peasant Resistance* (New Haven, Conn.: Yale University Press, 1985).

[c] Sara Castro-Klarén and John Chasteen, *Beyond Imagined Communities: Reading and Writing the Nation in Nineteenth-Century Latin America* (Baltimore: Johns Hopkins University Press, 2003), xvii–xvix.

[d] Interview of Fausto Becerril (by Eugenia Meyer, 1974, Instituto Mora and INAH, Project of Oral History 1/61) recalls listening to the music of the barracks across from Ildefonso, in downtown Mexico City; yet these tunes scarcely received academic interest, for example, only the briefest mention in Robert Stevenson, *Music in Mexico: A Historical Survey* (New York: Thomas Y. Crowell Company, 1952), 162–163.

venues, but they were equally ready to accompany soldiers for less stilted material, chiefly corridos.[e] Whether with instruments or not, men sang in the evenings and free times in garrison or on campaign. Their sad songs of tragedy and betrayal, of bandits and bullfighters, brought the outside world into army life.[f] The music of the lower-classes represented their stylistic taste, and also held deeper social meanings as they channelled rage and hostility into group solidarity.[g] Of course, there were occasional critics: one officer locked his band in a room and shot at their feet as a dance lesson, but his actions were likely due more to alcohol abuse than genuine critique.[h] But the songs that allowed men and women the taste of home gave sufficient reason to sing. They were an acceptable way to express emotions, to vent loneliness, and were an important measure of cultural capital—every unit desired a good singer. And more, in the repertoire certain songs held special appeal as they spoke to military life, and significantly, challenged it through subversive lyrics and subtle mockeries. Poetry built on this expression for a different audience, adding to a set of stories that articulated nation and gender.

Society considered the writing of verses as an essential element of cultural or social capital for men of the non-working classes. That gentlemen of the middle classes, officers or not, would express themselves in poetry in the last years of the nineteenth century is hardly a surprise.[i] In their world of cultivated salon gatherings, poetry was part of an expected modern skill-set. As one example, memoirs of officers such as Victor Salvador Alvarez spoke fondly of literary discussions in family settings and revealed a great breadth of reading materials that had shaped conversations between military men in a context of humor and erudite competition.[j] In contrast to the argument of Luis González, the distinction between men of the sword and men of the pen was never a neat, clear divide, and more of a political fiction of vying rivals for influence over the president.[k] Eschewing narrow political definitions that sorted all of the elite into either José Yves Limantour's *científico* or Bernardo Reyes' *militar* parties, one finds that officers generally represented a group of reasonably educated and literate men with significant interest and knowledge in modern sciences and literature.

---

[e] For example, see official repertoire of 17th Battalion: AGN (General Archive of the Nation), Comandancia Militar del D.F., Caja 323, Personnel File of Cpt. Santiago Avadaño.
[f] Heriberto Frías, *The Battle of Tomochic: Memoirs of a Second Lieutenant*, Trans. Barbara Jamison (New York: Oxford University Press, 2006 [1893]), 39, 114.
[g] E.P. Thompson, *Customs in Common: Studies in Traditional Popular Culture* (New York: The New Press, 1993), 485: speaking of rough music, but also of popular or lower-class music more generally, he points out that it often channels rage and hostility felt towards conditions of life.
[h] AGN, Comandancia Militar del D.F., Caja 95, Personnel File of Cpt. Luis Delgado, 3/2/77: "dar cañonazos a banda."
[i] Piccato, 10, 11.
[j] Victor Salvador Alvarez, *Memorias de Victor Salvador Alvarez, Tiempo Viejo* (México: E.D.I.A.P.S.A, 1940), 74–85.
[k] Luis González, 638–675.

Modern expectations of the officer classes included considerable schooling at the best military colleges of Mexico, or abroad in France, Germany, Britain, and the United States.[l] As a matter of course the students learned mathematics, engineering, and logistics, but they also spent considerable classroom effort mastering languages and history. Guillermo Prieto's *Lecciones de historia patria* was among the many works assigned at the Colegio Militar that sought to instill in them a love of the nation rooted in a historical vision of liberal triumph, punctuated with his verses.[m] And from the ranks of these impressionable youths and from the army in general, great literary talents appeared including authors such as Ignacio Manuel Altimirano and Manuel Payno. The writers also continued to emerge during the Porfirian era as Francisco Luis Urquizo and Heriberto Frías attest.[n] For officers keenly aware of their social position, poetry provided a creative outlet where they could express their caste identity during a period when the army faced no external threat to justify its budget or importance.

The military poem went beyond the task of expressing sentimental masculinity for socially mobile officers and helped construct an imagining of the nation, much as the corrido did for others.[o] Verse was a common feature in military journals and periodicals exchanged internationally with other armies and distributed nationally as required reading for officers. The mandatory nature of this appreciation may have lessened enthusiasm, but it signals a concerted attempt by the military to create a more cultivated or cultured officer class. By engaging in this literary production, Mexicans could give voice to an alternate vision of their nascent nationalism, whether this had been the military's intent or not.

In poem and corrido alike, artists looked to the past to inspire their progress.[p] They sought heroes and meaningful narratives, making history an ally for self-identification. As Matthew Esposito has demonstrated, these decades saw the creation of a state theater built around the deaths and funerals of the old guard of officers who were passing away almost daily.[q] These men would now be eulogized in poetry and monuments as a matter of course, and remembered in songs. As the elderly slipped into history, the

---

[l] Mílada Bazant de Saldaña, et al. *La evolución de la educación militar de México*, 1. ed. (México: Secretaría de la Defensa Nacional, 1997).
[m] Prieto, 21, 27, 206, 448.
[n] For example: Frías, *The Battle of Tomochic*; Francisco Luis Urquizo, *De la vida militar mexicana* (México: Herrero Hermanos Sucesores, 1920).
[o] See Mark S. Phillips, *Society and Sentiment: Genres of Historical Writing in Britain, 1740–1820* (New Jersey: Princeton University Press, 2000) on evocations of sentimentality as a mediation of readers and writers experiences, which highlighted the individual mind and self-recognition, 19, 29; on masculinity in Mexican literature, see Robert McKee Irwin, *Mexican Masculinities* (Minnesota: University of Minnesota Press, 2003), xv–xix, 4, 47–64.
[p] Fritzsche, 4; Phillips, 26–27, 29.
[q] Matthew D. Esposito, "Death and Disorder in Mexico City: The State Funeral of Manuel Romero Rubio," in *Latin American Popular Culture: An Introduction*, ed. William Beezley and Linda Ann Curcio Nagy (Wilmington: Scholarly Resources, 2000), 87–103.

regime sidled nearer to modernity. Their positivist inspired public works and monuments were inaugurated with verses as equally tender as that of any general's funeral cortege. As a national project this expressive ceremonial drive enhanced the apparent legitimacy of the regime and nation, and not coincidentally, featured at its visual and aural forefront the uniformed military men.

Of National Narratives and Legitimate Violence

Governments throughout the nineteenth century had mostly proved unable to instill in the citizenry a strong sense of national belonging or identity, and had not manufactured a genuine consensus about legitimate rule in all corners of the country. For example, bandit stories, according to Frazer, demonstrated the inability at the highest levels of government to control the image and meaning of Mexico that reached foreigners, singers, and the poor.[r] Bandit literature may have failed in this endeavor throughout Latin America due to the nature of its subject and its inherent potential for interpretative use by the marginalized (for example as critique of policing, or in the emergence of folk-hero brigands).[s]

In contrast to what Juan Pablo Dabove calls "the nightmare of the lettered city" officer poets participated in the creation (albeit amateur and halting) of a national counter-discourse, or new hegemony, that sought to define mexicanidad for the dawning century.[t] The patriotic rhetoric and focus of most soldier-poets turned away from the teratological bandit tales and optimistically made the nation into a protagonist. The country became the sympathetic victor rising from troubled beginnings. Considering Mexico's turbulent nineteenth century, this also situated soldiers as those that forged the nation. Since the Porfiriato was relatively less violent, especially in terms of participating in formal wars and not simply putting down local rebellions, it seemed almost necessary for the writers to remind readers and listeners about the importance of military men. And in this vein, commemoration held powerful potentials. At the same time, verse could challenge official ideas of the military's importance. Some songs and poems wrestled with the contradictions between the regime's liberal rhetoric and its practiced ruthless oppression, particularly in the case of executions and massacres.

Tales of betrayal and injustice had particular appeal to the performers and audiences of corridos, and in the earliest years of the Porfiriato some songs directly criticized the perceived tyranny of the new regime. "De los mártires de Veracruz" (Of the Martyrs of Veracruz) depicted the aftermath of

---

[r] Frazer, 2, 97–99, 176–178.
[s] Dabove, 26–336, 210–211; Gilbert Joseph, "On the Trail of Latin American Bandits: A Reexamination of Peasant Resistance," *Latin American Research Review* 25, no. 3 (1990): 7–53.
[t] Dabove, 285.

a small scale naval mutiny in the port at Veracruz that forces under General Luis Terán brutally suppressed in 1879. The corrido, for its part, portrayed the uprising as brave resistance and saw the execution of the participants as nothing less than criminal and arbitrary:

El general Luis Terán,	The General Luis Terán
con inaudita crueldad,	with unprecedented cruelty
por complacer a un tirano	to please a tyrant
ejecutó a unos valientes.	executed some brave men.
Infame gobernador,	Infamous governor,
dizque del deber cumplido,	saying his duty fulfilled,
con un corazón de fiera,	with a heart of iron,
mostrado en esa ocasión,	showed on this occasion,
no tendrá nunca rival.	he would have no rival.

The regime had no match in cruelty perhaps, but the song at least could challenge the legitimacy of the government by mourning the deaths of nine sailors. Why did they need to die?

Su delito fue atacar	Their crime was to attack
a un tirano presidente,	A tyrannical president,
que se mantenía en el puesto	who held his place
odiado de toda gente.	hated by all people.

Newly installed by coup d'état, President Díaz had no patience for resistance, although the corrido doubtlessly exaggerated both his not-yet-established tyranny and the hatred that people felt for him. Opposition to Díaz's reign had taken up arms in other states, and few supported his serving another term as president in 1880 since his revolutionary platform of "no reelection" had not yet been overturned. Nonetheless, as a dashing young war hero of the French Intervention, and a popular figure in states such as Oaxaca, many saw Díaz as a good choice for solving Mexico's instability. Yet the Liberal rhetoric that his government openly claimed in 1879 was quite at odds with the lack of respect for due process and individual rights that the Veracruz incident came to represent:

Juvencio Robles decía:	Juvencio Robles said:
—Esto parece inhumano,	—this seems inhuman,
que se les forme consejo,	they deserve counsel,
como a todo mexicano.	as do all Mexicans.
[But the general replied]:	
—Es inútil objetar,	—It is useless to object,
que al cabo son malhechores,	that in the end, they are all criminals,
los hemos de ajusticiar.	that we should execute.

The president addressed the uprising with a style of ruthless pragmatism he later embodied and obscured. He sent a terse telegraph to the commanding officer, according to the corrido, "que se les mate en caliente" which has been commonly translated by subsequent critics and historians to mean "kill them on the spot," or "kill them in cold blood."[u] This interpretation lacks nuance, as the Military Dictionary of the time defines "matar en caliente" as "to kill in the heat of the action." Notwithstanding the clarity of wanting these men dead, Díaz preferred that the General take no prisoners and thus avoid possibly embarrassing open trials. For the young regime, it would be better if the mutineers died with guns in hand, and be forgotten as combat casualties:

Sin permitirles testar,	Without allowing them to testify,
los sacaron de mañana . . .	they took them out in the morning . . .
Murieron como valientes,	They died as brave men,
sin pedir gracia ninguna.	without asking any forgiveness.

The corrido ends with a more subtle challenge to the regime by asserting that the brave men asked no mercy of anyone and pardons them for their honor and valor, as the secular State would not. After 1879, the tone of most corridos lessened in direct criticism and ceased the outright naming of officials as villains. Likely this reflected the increased stability and power of the regime to quell dissent, as well as at least a grudging acknowledgment of Díaz's accomplishments.

Most officially sanctioned poetry contrasted with this critical stance, building instead on ideals of Order and Progress, the motto of the regime. These poems assumed the positives of technological improvement and its corresponding effect on morality. The military in their view became the vanguard of a nation becoming modernized, secular, and European-like. These poets further defined the army as a separated place where a new caste of men joined together like a great family, with Díaz as father-figure.[v] This vision used a vocabulary of filial duty and servitude to set the military into a place of honor and prestige.

In "El brindis" we see an overt example of how the military as a community or perhaps as a family saw itself.[w] Corporal Fuentes clearly set out in his toast a view of the army and its values. He saluted the tired man on the

---

[u] For examples, Paul Garner, *Porfirio Díaz: Biography of Power* (New York: Longman, 2001), 87; M. Meyer, W. Sherman, and S. Deeds (eds.), *The Course of Mexican History*, 9th ed. (New York: Oxford University Press, 2010), 379; W. Beezley and M. Meyer (eds.), *Oxford History of Mexico* (New York: Oxford University Press, 2010), 404.

[v] This was not particular to Mexico, see also Leo Baudry, *From Chivalry to Terrorism: War and the Changing Nature of Masculinity* (New York: Vintage, 2005), 245.

[w] D. Fuentes, "El brindis de una pieza" (Toast for an Artillery Piece) in *Boletín Militar* Vol. 2 (July 1900), 16.

march, the specialized sharp-shooters, and lauds their endurance under the worst of conditions. Accepting hardship in all circumstances represented the chief ethos of the idealized soldier. The civilian remains soft and pampered, and clumsy, by contrast. But he saves the climax of the toast for the officer classes and military on an institutional level as those who deserve the best, himself included, as his last evocation was addressed to "us, as servants."

After a century of coups and betrayals this trope of responsible servitude held special weight in official writings. Now, the writers argued, Mexico as a modern nation would no longer be plagued by uncivilized military interventions.[x] The army in Fuentes' view earned this praise for having preserved national honor:

Cumplir lo que se ordenó	To comply with what was ordered
Y hacerlo con ligereza	And to do so swiftly
Sin preguntar quién mandó.	Without questioning who commanded.

A long legacy of supposed obedience was connected to a notion of honor, expectations of hierarchy with a thin veneer of culture, and this now tied closely to the assumption of Díaz's legitimacy. The sacrifice and self-abnegation of the military also carried an undercurrent of expectation. If the army was honorable, and the government legitimate, then there could be no question of civilian interference. The poem thus alluded to some long-held assumptions in the army that they deserved separate rights (*fueros*) and impunity.

A stark division therefore appears as the corrido and poem consider the rightful place of the army in a somewhat peaceful society. Where "Mártires" called the regime's legitimacy into question over its treatment of rebels, the toast presumed (a decade later) that total obedience trumped political concerns. The army's role, whether as dissidents or servants, reflected a social and historical dividing point between these officers and the soldiers, one emphasized in verses describing Mexico's pedigree as nation.[7]

5.3. CHURCH: THE CROWNING OF THE VIRGIN

José Domingo Martínez, O.P., to the Master of the Order

Mejico, October 23, 1895

I will say a few words about the coronation [on October 12, 1895]. The ceremony proved most magnificent, with splendor and pomp never seen in Mexico, it proceeded with the sung Tercia [from the Roman Breviary] and

---

[x] Thomas Janvier, "The Mexican Army." *Harper's New Monthly Magazine* (Nov. 1889): 812–827.

the blessing of the crowns. These were two, one of gold with a profusion of precious stones and the other of silver, donated by the faithful. The mass over, the procession was organized, the two crowns carried on a stretcher by priests. The procession of countless priests and Religious of all orders in their habits and 44 bishops with crosiers, miters and great cloaks, led by the Archbishop of Mexico with the deacon, the sub deacon, and assistant priests. Of the 44 Prelates mentioned, 22 came from the Republic of Mexico; the rest had come from outside of Mexico to the celebrations of the coronation. From Spain, only his Excellence the Archbishop of Santiago de Cuba attended.

After the procession, the Archbishops of Mexico and Michoacán went up to a platform provided for the purpose at the level of the miraculous painting of the most holy Virgin, and placed themselves on each side of the holy image, they took the crown of gold and suspended it at the top of the Guadalupan Virgin. At same moment the immense crowd that filled the naves of the basilica, as if moved by some mysterious force, burst into thundering vivas for the Virgin of Guadalupe, accompanying the shouts with a din of applause that moved and delighted all those of us who had the pleasure of witnessing that ovation that came from the believing soul, transported with joy, and filled with love for the sublime patron of the Mexicans. The doors of the basilica were closed and when by the ringing of the bells the faithful who were outside—there were thousands of persons—knew that the act of coronation had been verified, suddenly and mechanically fell to their knees, reciting a prayer that, composed for that solemn moment, had been distributed throughout the Republic. Mexicans and Spaniards are witnesses affirming that never have they seen in these regions a burst of enthusiasm and such a splendid demonstration of Catholic sentiment as this; and as for me, I have only seen something like it in Rome when his Holiness appeared in the basilica of Saint Peter to receive large pilgrimages.

5.4. FAMILY: ETIQUETTE MANUALS

Handbooks describing manners, deportment, grooming, and social encounters circulated widely during the nineteenth century in Western Europe, the United States, and Latin America, including Mexico. Successful volumes were widely translated and published in numerous editions. Unrivaled was Madame Celnart's The Gentleman and Lady's Book of Politeness . . . Dedicated to the Youth of Both Sexes, *originally published in French in 1830 and soon after with translations in Spanish and English. This volume provided instructions on polite behavior, for example, at dances. On the waltz, she commented: "a dance of quite too loose a character, and unmarried ladies should refrain from it altogether, both in public and private; very young married ladies, however, may be allowed to waltz in private balls, if it is very seldom, and with persons of their acquaintance. It is indispensable for them to acquit themselves with dignity and modesty."* Madame Celnart's (Elisabeth Bayle-Mouillard) volume reached the United States in 1833, and was published in Boston.⁹ The book was highly regarded in Mexico. Rob Buffington has described how it fit with other books of manners and etiquette to guide social behavior in Porfirian Mexico. He stated this succinctly as follows:

The most popular of these guides in Porfirian Mexico was the *Manual de urbanidad y buenas maneras* (*Manual of Urbanity and Good Manners*), first published in 1854 by Manuel Antonio Carreño, a prominent Venezuelan statesman, diplomat, and pedagogue, and reprinted regularly throughout Latin America ever since.ʸ For the Porfirian bourgeoisie, Carreño's *Manual de urbanidad* provided essential and exhaustive instruction in proper forms of comportment for men, women, and children at home and in public. Although modeled on aristocratic self-help manuals, unabashed in its religious moralizing, and unconcerned about entrenched social hierarchies, the Manual de urbanidad nonetheless espoused a reformation of traditional manhood predicated on cleanliness, good grooming, moderation, affability, respectability, love of country, and careful attentiveness to the needs and opinions of others, including women, children, and social "inferiors"—an approach that artfully combined longstanding notions of masculine responsibility and authority with modern ideas about self-mastery and citizenship, especially the sublimation of volatile "passions" in all domains of social life. According to Carreño, the fate of civilization itself was at stake. As he explained in the introduction: "Without knowledge and practice of the laws prescribed by morality, there can be no peace, nor order, nor happiness among men; and in vain would we seek to find in another source the true constitutive and preservative principles of society that we propose to study; and the rules that [these laws] teach us about how to conduct ourselves in [society] with the decency and moderation that distinguish the civilized and cultured man."

After decades of political turmoil in Mexico, Porfirian letrados found Carreño's prescription for civilizing unruly male behavior both compelling and useful.ᶻ Bourgeois parents went out of their way to socialize their sons

---

ʸ By 1992 Carreño's *Manual de urbanidad* had gone through forty-seven editions. Elsa Muñiz, *Cuerpo, representación y poder: México en los albores de la reconstrucción nacional, 1920–1934* (Mexico City: Universidad Autónoma Metropolitana, 2002), 29. See also Victor M. Macías-González, "*Hombres de mundo:* la masculinidad, el consume, y los manuales de urbanidad y buenas maneras," in *Orden social e identidad de género. México, siglos XIX y XX*, ed. María Teresa Fernández Aceves, Carmen Ramos Escandón, and Susie Porter, 267–97. (Mexico City: CIESAS/Universidad de Guadalajara, 2006); Valentina Torres Septién, "Manuales de conducta, urbanidad y buenas modales durante el Porfiriato: Notas sobre el comportamiento femenino," in *Modernidad, tradición y alteridad: La Ciudad de México en el cambio del siglo*, ed. Claudia Agostoni and Elisa Speckman, 271–89. (Mexico City: Universidad Nacional Autónoma de México, 2001).

ᶻ Manuel Antonio Carreño, *Manual de urbanidad y buenas maneras* (Mexico City: Librería de la Vda. de Ch. Bouret, 1920), 5.

according to these precepts. And Education Secretary Justo Sierra, one of President Díaz's most prominent and progressive scientific advisors, even incorporated a simplified version of Carreño's precepts into the elementary school curriculum, with each month of the year dedicated to fostering a different aspect of urbanity.[aa] Carreño's introduction makes clear the knowledge of polite behavior and guidebooks to it.[10]

Manual of Refinement and Good Manners
For the Use of Youth of Both Sexes;
In which is found
The Principal Rules of Refinement and Etiquette
That should be followed in Various Social Situations
Preceded by a short treatise about the
Moral Duties of Man
By
Manuel Antonio Carreño

Introduction

Without knowledge and practice of the laws that morality proscribes, there will not be peace, order, nor happiness among men; and in vain may we aspire to find in another source the real constituent and conservative principles of society that we intend to study and the rules that teach us to behave with the decency and moderation that distinguish the cultured and civilized man.

Virtue is the foundation of everything that is good, and the purest origin of the pleasures and interests that we find in the activity of life. So this is the refinement that brings together so many means that man can use to create easy and enjoyable behavior. Sacrificing at every step his preference and the inclinations of others is nothing more than the same virtue, reducing somewhat the austerity of its character by summoning the thanks and covering that allows it to preside over and legitimate social relations and the recreations and pleasures of the world.

Personal dignity, mild and insinuating manners, body grooming that reveal in a man the candor of the soul, the sobriety, temperance, discretion, prudence, forbearance, and the constant citizen, in sum, to please and never displease others, to bring together all the rules of courtesy. Are not many other duties evident that emanate from the knowledge of God, from the great principle of evangelical charity and from the law that leads us to happiness by the road of moral perfection?

[aa] Raquel Barceló, "El muro del silencio: Los jóvenes de la burguesía porfiriana," in *Historia de los jóvenes en México: su presencia en el siglo XX*, ed. José Antonio Pérez Islas and Maritza Urteaga Castro-Pozo, 114–50. (México: Instituto Mexicano de la Juventud/Centro de Investigación y Estudios sobre Juventud/Archivo General de la Nación, 2004).

The virtuous man has to be of necessity kindly and obliging; and it is from goodness and graciousness that are born all the gentle, calm, and benevolent activities that earn us the respect and affection of others, and at the same time give our people, by the habit of gentleness, that delicacy and culture that communicates so much brightness and luster to the intrinsic qualities of the soul.

Men have lived so permeated in all times with the force of this truth that the romans called *humanitas* (humanity, kindness and politeness); and no author, of the many we have consulted, introduces the demands of refinement but as an emanation of moral duties.

"What in society is called courtesy or politeness," says the celebrated Alibert, [*This appears to be a reference to Jean-Louis-Marc Alibert*, Physiologie des passions, ou, Nouvelle doctrine des sentimens moraux *(published in 1826–27 in Paris).*] "is no more than the attentive mode of expressing all the sentiments of benevolence."

Madame Celnart in her interesting work on the rules that should be observed in polite society presents those religious and moral obligations before entering on the exposition of the duties of etiquette, she covers all the formulas and attentions of courtesy in the highly religious and moral sense of benevolence.

In the *introduction* that precedes "The Code of Refinement of Don Manuel Díez de Bonilla" we find the outline of the work in the following principles:

1. Exercise our obligations with the least annoyance to others
2. Respect obligations of others, even when they might be harmful
3. Recognize merit, although it may come from our enemies
4. Do not cause harm to anyone without just cause or legitimate authorization
5. Work for the good of others, even when it sacrifices ours
6. Give up resentments of the moment that will create greater future arguments
7. Sacrifice personal affections for the public interest
8. Achieve the greatest public benefit with the least prejudice to the members of society

Finally, the Count d'Orsay,[11] author of a beautiful treatise about "Etiquette" in which he confines himself to the refinement of the customs of English society, for which he wrote, he believed that everything should be based on virtue and he ended his interesting examples and observations with these notable words, "Nobility is not in birth, nor in the manners, nor in elegance, but in the soul. An elevated sentiment of honor; the constant habit of respect for the subordinate status of others, a firm and sincere devotion for the truth, tact, and duties of civility, expressed in all of life's customs; here are the essential characteristics that distinguish the true gentleman."

Chapter 1 General Principles

1. Call refinement the set of rules that we have to observe in order to communicate dignity, decorum, and elegance to our actions and words, and in order to demonstrate to others the gentility, care, and respect that we owe to them.
2. Refinement is an expression of moral obligations, and as such, its instructions contain everything to preserve the order and good harmony that should reign among men and to strengthen the ties that they use, by means of the pleasant impressions they produce over each other. [*The phrase ends "los unos sobre los otros," which, seems to be a biblical allusion, see Hebrews 10:23, 24.*]
3. The rules of refinement cannot be found in the law codes of nations; nevertheless, no society in which these rules are absolutely unknown could maintain itself. They teach us to be methodical and accurate in the compliance of our social obligations; to direct our behavior so we do not cause anyone humiliation or antipathy, to tolerate the caprices and weaknesses of men; to be attentive, affable, obliging, sacrificing, whenever it is necessary and possible, our pleasures and comforts; to have cleanliness and composure in our person to enhance our own esteem and to deserve it from others; and to acquire, in short, that fine and dedicated touch that makes us able to appreciate all circumstances in society and proceed according to what each one requires.
4. It is clear, therefore, that without more or less perfect observance of these rules, according to the degree of civilization of each country, men could not inspire any kind of love or esteem; there would be no means of cultivating sociability, which is the principle of preservation and advancement of peoples, and the existence of any well-ordered society would therefore be absolutely impossible.
5. Through a careful study of the rules of refinement and by contact with cultivated and well-educated persons, we acquire what we call especially *good manners*, which are nothing more than decency, moderation, and chance in our actions and words, and that care and noble bearing that appear in all our exterior movements, revealing the gentleness of customs and the culture of understanding.
6. *Etiquette* is an essential part of refinement. This name is given to the ceremonial uses, styles and customs that are observed at the meetings of high and serious character in those acts whose solemnity absolutely excludes all degrees of familiarity and liberty. (There is another kind of etiquette that comprises the ceremony prevailing in the courts of rulers, in parliamentary assemblies and in diplomatic circles; but it can be seen that it cannot be the object of this treatise. We will give, nevertheless, in the appropriate places, those of these rules whose knowledge is necessary for every man in society.)

7. By extension, etiquette is equally considered as the set of polite and ceremonial ways we ought to use with everyone in every situation of life. This kind of etiquette conveys to treatment in general, even in the midst of the most intimate familiarity, a certain level of circumspection that does not exclude expansion of sensitivity nor the most affectionate acts and that never admits familiarity without reserve nor relaxing the means of esteem and respect that is the essential base of social relationships.
8. From this it follows that the general rules of etiquette should be observed in all four sections in which are divided our social relationships, namely: the family or the domestic circle; trusted persons; people with whom we have some familiarity; unfamiliar people. (This division that we consider opportune here so that young people better see how general the application of the theory of etiquette has to be, is not indispensable in the course of the work, but rather where it would become embarrassing and certainly would make diffuse the explanations. So, we understand the first two sections of social relations under the general name *persons of trust*, the last two as *persons of etiquette*; being able to determine easily from the same rules the applications that are peculiar to which of the four in particular without prejudice notwithstanding that we indicate them in those places in which we see fit.)
9. Only Etiquette holds high seriousness in actions and words, the good always accompanied by the grace and gentleness that are in every case the luster of education. As for the formalities that the first three sections demand, naturalness and simplicity become gradually mixed in our acts, until they arrived at the height of the dominance that they ought to exercise in the bosom of our very own family.
10. Although poorly understood trust destroys, as we have already said, the esteem and respect that should govern all our social relations, the lack of a discreet naturalness can convert etiquette practices; eminently conservative of these relationships, in a ridiculous affectation that in turn destroys the same harmony that it is called to keep.
11. There is nothing more disgusting than the exaggeration of etiquette, when we ought to devote ourselves to the most cordial outpouring of our feelings; on the other hand, this exaggeration comes to be, as we will see, a rule of behavior for the circumstances in which it is important to us to cut off a relationship, in which we cannot accustom ourselves to it, without moving away from those persons who deserve our friendship.
12. But such is the attraction of politeness and so many are the conveniences resulting from it to society, that we are more willing to tolerate the tiresome conduct of the excessively formal man than

the excesses of the rude man, and the indiscretions and unfortunate remarks that by ignorance annoys us at every turn with acts of unpremeditated and absurd familiarity.
13. Great should be our care in restricting ourselves to the use of the essence of rationally supported familiarity in every level of friendship. With the exception of the family circle in which we were born and that raised us, all relationships ought to begin under the sphere of the strictest etiquette. So that it can become friendship, time and the conformity of the characters, qualities and inclinations are needed. Any excess of familiarity is abusive and typical of the vulgar, and nothing contributes more effectively to relax and even break the bonds of friendship, even though it was born and consolidated under the aegis of a strong and mutual sympathy. (True friendship is a plant that grows slowly and never becomes stronger unless grafted on the trunk of recognized and reciprocal merit. Lord Chesterfield)
14. The laws of courtesy, as they relate to self-respect and personal dignity and the considerations that we ought to show to others, are in force at all time and in all civilized countries of the world. But those that form the formalities of etiquette as such, offer great variety, according to what is admitted in each community to communicate seriousness and tone to the diverse acts of social life. The first, as emanating directly from moral principles, have a fundamental and immutable character; the second do not alter at all the duty we have to be kind and obliging, and they can therefore, as they are in effect, be subject to the nature, preferences and even the whims of each community.[12]

5.5. POPULAR GROUPS: MUSIC AND FOREIGNERS
(Choice of documents)

Option 1. Music: Javier Garibay, "Mexican Cylinders: Of National Identity and Sound Recordings."

Cylinder recording in Mexico first took place in the midst of "El Porfiriato," (1884–1911) [sic] the three and a half decades in which General Porfirio Díaz led the country as president until the start of the Mexican Revolution. His control was encapsulated by the phrase "Pan o palo," or "bread or a beating," meaning one could either accept his rule, or suffer consequences otherwise. Needless to say, this period was tumultuous in the history of Mexico. Although Porfirio Díaz repressed the country's people, often by privatizing communal landholdings, his reign is also remembered as one in which the country experienced serious economic growth, attracting markets and companies from the United States and Europe to invest in Mexico. One of Díaz's strategies to gain the attention of foreign investors was to do so through the promotion of a national identity, based on Mexico's most rural expressions.

It was during this time that major labels such as Edison, Columbia, and Victor began producing the first sound recordings in Mexico. These companies dispatched recording teams throughout the world to capture music of local communities on wax cylinders and discs. In Mexico, these companies (along with smaller labels, Zonophone and Odeon), were actively recording between 1902 and 1910. Due to the turmoil of the Revolution between 1910 and 1920, however, transnational recording operations ceased in Mexico, and would not continue again until 1921. In this short window of time, these major labels set out to record and preserve "cultural expressions that were considered representative [of Mexico]," but in the process, contributed to the establishment of a level of authenticity that overshadowed other genres. The effect of this process was the erasure of many rural genres, and a reproduction through sound of what was deemed authentically Mexican. In short, these companies ultimately bolstered President Díaz's goal to formulate a national identity for Mexico abroad.

Amongst the collection as part of UCSB's [University of California–Santa Barbara] Cylinder Audio Archive are some of the earliest mariachi recordings by Cuarteto Coculense, recordings by Octaviano Yañez, one of the first guitarists ever recorded, an early adaptation of "Jarabe Tapatío" (Mexican Hat Dance), and various other titles that befell the genre of son abajeño, or "son from the lowlands" (Madrid, 96). The repertoire of recordings in this regional category spans in musical instrumentation and vocal styles as well as several genre variants. These recordings reflect a glimpse into Mexican popular music prior to the revolution, and conversely, the agenda of Porfirio Díaz to concentrate a national identity for Mexico to markets in the western world. Nevertheless, the cylinders of this period give us an idea of how much well-known genres from Mexico have evolved during the past century since they were initially recorded.

- Aires Nacionales / Banda. Edison Gold Moulded Record: 18755. 1905.
- Besos y Pesos / Banda de Artilleria. Edison Blue Amberol: 22038. 1909.
- Jarabe Tapatío / R. H. Robinson. Edison Gold Moulded Record: 18508. 1904.
- El Amor es la Vida / Quinteto Jordá. Edison Gold Moulded: 18780. 1905.
- Las Campanitas / Cuarteto Coculense. Edison Amberol: 6070. n.d.
- Una Noche en La Mar / Rita Villa. Edison Gold Moulded Record: 20362. 1911.

- Viva Jalisco! / Banda de Policia de Mexico. Edison Amberol: 6078. 1910.
- Macario Romero / Herrera Robinson y Picazo. Edison Gold Moulded Record: 18638. 1905.
- Quien Sabe? / Banda de Artilleria. Edison Blue Amberol: 22083. 1910.
- Zacatecas Marcha / Banda Española. Columbia Phonograph Co.: 40322. n.d.
- Anita / Octaviano Yañez. Edison Gold Moulded Record: 20102. 1907.13

Option 2. Foreigners in Mexico: "Poldark Mine, the Cornish miner in Mexico."

Cornish miners represented one of the significant groups of foreigners in Mexico. Examine the following websites for information on their experiences and influence in their new home: https://www.cornish-mining.org.uk/delving-deeper/cornish-mining-mexico; http://www.bbc.co.uk/inside-out/content/articles/2008/09/30/south_west_cornish_miners_s14_w3_feature.shtml; and http://projects.exeter.ac.uk/cornishlatin/pachucarealdelmonte.htm

ADDITIONAL READING

"El arte tradicional del Nacimiento." *Artes de México*, 81 (2006). The articles are in both Spanish and English.

Madrid, Alejandro L. *Transnational Encounters: Music and Performance at the U.S.-Mexico Border*. New York: Oxford University Press, 2011.

Leer en español

Soto, Eduardo Contreras. "Aprender a escuchar. La aparición de las grabaciones en la música mexicana." In . . . *y la música se volvió mexicana*. Testimonio Musical de México, no. 51 (Mexico City: Instituto Nacional de Antropología e Historia, 2010), 178–86.

NOTES

1. *A Winter Holiday in Summer Lands* (Chicago: A. C. McClurg and Company, 1890), 149.
2. *Mexican Vistas Seen from Highways and Byways of Travel* (Chicago: Rand McNally & Company, 1896), 72.
3. *A Mexican Journey* (1912; New York: Thomas Y. Crowell Company, 1919), 97.
4. *Two Republics*, November 28, 1868.

5. *Two Republics,* June 1, 1890.

6. *Mexican Herald,* February 11, 1908, quoted in Charles M. Flaudrau, *Viva Mexico!* (Urbana: University of Illinois Press, 1954), 69, nn. 69–70.

7. In *Mexico in Verse: A History of Music, Rhyme, and Power,* ed. Stephen Neufeld and Michael Matthews (Tucson: University of Arizona Press, 2015), 58–68. Reprinted by permission of the University of Arizona Press.

8. José Domingo Martínez, O.P., Rafael José Menéndez, O.P., and Segundo Fernández, O.P., *Cartas y Crónicas de América (1895–1899)* (Salamanca: Editorial San Esteban, 1995), 42–43.

9. The quotation comes from excerpts of the book at Old Sturbridge Village, http://resources.osv.org/explore_learn/document_viewer.php?DocID=1148.

10. Robert M. Buffington, "Men and Modernity in Porfirian Mexico, 1880–1910," *Oxford Research Encyclopedia of Latin American History,* ed. by William H. Beezley. Reprinted by permission of Oxford University Press.

11. Called *the French Dandy,* Count Alfred D'Orsay (1801–1852) was not only one of the early nineteenth century's most popular men, but he has been described as Europe's first modern man in terms of attitude, behavior, and sexuality. He was French, but came from a mixed European aristocratic background. See Willard Connely, *Count D'orsay: The Dandy of Dandies* (London: Cassell and Company, 1952).

12. Robert M. Buffington, "Men and Modernity in Porfirian Mexico, 1880–1910," *Oxford Research Encyclopedia of Latin American History,* ed. by William H. Beezley. Reprinted by permission of Oxford University Press.

13. Online at http://cylinders-stage.library.ucsb.edu/mexico.php.

CHAPTER 6

The Revolution, 1910–1920

Francisco Madero, in his Plan of San Luis Potosí, called for revolution against Porfirio Díaz, to begin on November 20, 1910. Within months, Madero's followers had defeated the federal army in scattered small battles and, in April 1911, in a bigger battle at Ciudad Juárez (6.1). The victory at Juárez was the big bang, bringing revolution to the nation. The insurrectionary and civil war covered roughly the years from 1910 to 1920 with one battle in the capital city (6.2), efforts to ignore revolution and maintain the search for modern life (6.3), a new constitution (6.4) that dictated a new church relationship with society and changes in the landholding patterns, and the recognition of new national identities and revolutionary heroes (6.5). The documents reveal that the Revolution was partially a result of unresolved nineteenth-century conflicts among the major societal networks, and partially a product of new, twentieth-century demands of agrarians and workers. Documents also convey that some Mexicans tried to ignore the Revolution and continue the life they knew. Despite the heavy fighting, almost exclusively in the countryside, except for the Tragic Ten Days in the capital in 1913, many urban residents tried to live normal lives, and businesses attempted to ignore the revolution. During the decade about one out of seven (about 2 million) Mexicans died or fled the country; nevertheless life went on. Investigating the authors, composers, and subjects of the following documents will result in intriguing results and sketches of major insurgents.

6.1. MILITARY: MICHAEL C. MEYER, "THE BATTLE OF CIUDAD JUÁREZ"

The seizure of Ciudad Juárez by the Revolutionary Army and the events that accompanied the seizure constitute one of the most interesting episodes in the military revolt against the Díaz dictatorship. When the peace negotiations broke down on May 6, [1911], seasoned troops of the revolution—the leadership of Pascual Orozco, Pancho Villa, and the Italian filibuster José Garibaldi (grandson of Giuseppe Garibaldi, the famous nineteenth-century Italian soldier of fortune) were on the outskirts of the border city. Although plans for its seizure had been discussed for more than a month, Madero changed his mind, on May 7, and decided that instead of laying siege to the city the army should turn south. The best explanation for this sudden change of plans is that Madero feared that stray shells would fall on El Paso, Texas, and thus possibly occasion United States military intervention in Mexico. Madero expressed his misgivings too late, however. Violating the provisional president's countermand, Orozco ordered the attack the following day.

There are several plausible explanations for the attack. A common version is that on the morning of May 8, 1911, federal soldiers and revolutionaries began to hurl insults at one another across the trenches. The exchange of *vivas* and *mueras* was soon replaced by more vulgar utterances from both sides, utterances that culminated in the exchange of shots and a full-scale battle. A less colorful but probably more accurate explanation is that Orozco simply took the initiative on his own. After the disaster at Casas Grandes, none of the northern *guerrilleros* placed much confidence in Madero as a military tactician or strategist, and Orozco—as events would demonstrate—was not above opposing the provisional president if he felt the latter was in error. The indecisive, dilatory direction of Madero and the revolutionary junta in El Paso had previously denied Orozco this prize; therefore, realizing that he possessed superior manpower and fully cognizant of the strategic value of a port of entry, Orozco probably resolved that the city would not be denied him again.

Orozco began the attack on Ciudad Juárez at ten o'clock in the morning of May 8, 1911. Upon learning of Orozco's insubordination, Madero informed General Navarro that the engagement was completely unauthorized and personally ordered Orozco to suspend the attack. Orozco's reply was evasive: "It is impossible because our men have already captured some enemy positions. It is best to continue." Orozco ordered his troops to advance to the Rio Grande, above and below the positions that had been fortified by General Navarro's federal garrison. By conducting the campaign parallel to the river than by a frontal assault toward the United States border, the rebel commander hoped to avoid the possibility of inadvertently shelling El Paso. By noon of the first day the rebels had captured several key positions along the railroad line and taken a few houses on the outskirts of the city. By mid-afternoon the first line of federal trenches had fallen to the rebels and by nine in the evening Orozco's troops had moved into the city itself.

During the evening of the first day, Madero once again changed his mind and accepted Orozco's decision to attack. Madero demonstrated his tacit approval by demanding that Navarro surrender the city in order to avoid complications with the United States.

Although sporadic fighting continued throughout the night, it was not until dawn of May 9 that the rebels renewed the attack in earnest. Orozco then changed his tactic and deployed his troops between the federal garrison and El Paso, but still along the river: if stray shells were lobbed over the border, the troops of the government would be held accountable. A good description of the military situation during the morning of the second day is recorded in a dispatch from the Mexican consul in El Paso to the Secretaría de Relaciones Exteriores in Mexico City.

> 10:00 A.M. Considerable losses both sides. It is said that more than fifty rebels have been killed and over twice that number have been wounded. Madero is not commanding his troops. The rebels are in control of Avenida Juárez and the federals cannot fire upon them because they are facing the American border.

By noon, the tide had turned in favor of the assaulters. All communications out of Juárez had been cut and great quantities of federal artillery and ammunition had been captured. In the early afternoon of May 10, 1911, General Navarro hoisted a white flag over the remaining federal barracks and turned the city over to the *Ejército Libertador* [Liberating Army].

Navarro's surrender ushered in a period of complete chaos in Ciudad Juárez. As often happens after the disappearance of civil authority, looting, pillaging, and burning became commonplace. Not only did the brigands and shoplifters of the civilian populace put their talents to the test, but also unruly elements within the army relieved themselves of all pent-up inhibitions and restraint. Orozco immediately issued strict orders to his men to guard stores and houses and to prevent looting, and with thirty-six hours unmitigated anarchy had given way to effective military government. Then, informed that groups of bandits were looting and pillaging in the countryside, Orozco named Lic. Martín Castillos as a special agent of the Revolutionary Army and charged him with ferreting out the bandits and bring them to justice.[1]

6.2. POLITICS: JAVIER MALPICA, "LA DECENA TRÁGICA" (2013)

The "ten tragic days" refers to events leading to the arrest of President Francisco Madero and, ultimately, his assassination.[2]

It was early in the morning on the 9th of February of 1913 when the first bullets fired were heard. A group of conspirators were attacking the Na-

The *décena trágica*, the "tragic ten days" in Mexico City.
Cover image of *Nueva Biblioteca del Niño Mexicano*.

tional Palace. The Presidential Guard was taken by surprise. Someone was trying to take power. Fortunately, President Madero happened to not be there, safely tucked away in the Castle of Chapultepec. But who could be leading this insurrection? Who dared to take power away from the man who had brought democracy to the country?

There were many that were likely responsible for this coup. At the beginning of 1913, the word "popular" was not a word one could use to describe Francisco Madero. Not even two years into his presidency, and already one could say that rabid tigers had more friends than he did. Barely months ago people had voted for him to take the country on a path towards prosperity based on justice and peace. The truth is, trying to fix a country that was more disorderly than a teenager's closet wasn't easy. After everything, this was a kind of disorder that carried with it thirty years of injustice and inequality. It wasn't easy to help the poor without the rich protesting, nor was it easy to please landowners without marginalizing peasants. As a result, people began to feel disillusioned with his presidency. This disenchantment was soon reflected in the many insults and mockeries made of President Madero. Even the newspapers made fun of him and for almost everything: for being educated, for being a good husband, for respecting people, for being an optimist, even for being a vegetarian. As was expected, it didn't take long before this popular discontent was expressed in strikes, intrigue, and, finally, in a coup.

In the early hours of the morning of that 9th of February, when the rebels took the National Palace, General Lauro Villar, military commander of the plaza, was not among them. They would, however, count on the strength of sixty men. And even though there was still doubt over who was behind this attack, no one was surprised by the attack. Many had been convinced that almost any other candidate would have been better than Madero. This wasn't the first time that an armed group had tried to overthrow the president. Months before, a military man named Félix Diaz, who was also the nephew of dictator Porfirio Díaz, and a general by the name of Bernardo Reyes had taken up arms against the legitimate government, convinced that they were destined to occupy the presidential seat. Fortunately for Madero, the two rebels were defeated and jailed before they could carry out their plans. It was Madero, faithful to his convictions and to his respect for human rights, who decided to pardon the violators. He did not execute them, which was the custom at the time when men sent rebels blindfolded before a firing squad at the slightest provocation. And though you may not believe it, many thought Madero should have done it and maybe they weren't wrong . . . now you'll see why.

On the 9th of February, after having repelled the first attack, for a brief moment the soldiers that were defending the palace believed that all was lost. They were wrong. A new group had arrived. Now, things were clearer.

An army of rebels led by Manuel Mondragon had just relieved generals Felix Diaz and Bernardo Reyes from their command posts.

The Reyes group was approaching the palace, confident that it was now under the control of the rebels. This decided their fate. When they attempted to take the palace, they were repelled by the troops loyal to Madero. General Reyes was killed right in the Zócalo.

Meanwhile, Madero decided to abandon the Castle and return to the National Palace. It was a very brave decision, but a bit hasty because, as you can imagine, he was not in danger at the Castle. But Madero was confident that events were in his favor. During his trip to the Palace, many came out into the streets to support him. It was true too that many in the crowd were cheering for Felix Diaz to be their future president. Madero did not manage to reach the palace. He became caught in a crossfire and tried to hide. When he learned that General Lauro Villar was wounded, Madero decided to name Victoriano Huerta as General of the Plaza, in whom he had blind confidence.

The reinforcements from the army loyal to Madero quickly forced the rebels to flee and to entrench themselves but a few hundred meters away in the Ciudadela, where the army had a large quantity of arms and munitions (the arms factory was there too). Under the orders of Díaz and Mondragon, the rebels now had enough resources to continue their insurrection. They did not delay in launching projectiles at the National Palace. Another crossfire ensued in which hundreds of families were trapped. Mexico City has been converted into a terrible war zone.

In the following days, Mexico City experienced one of its worst nightmares in memory. The fighting endured for 10 days. Hundreds had died, military and civilians. This period had been dubbed La Decena Trágica (The Tragic 10 Days), 10 days that became a tragedy. It was not just because of the fiery battle between rebels and defenders of the legal government, which resulted in hundreds dead, untold numbers of wounded, and many destroyed buildings. It was also tragic because it was a period in which democracy was decimated.

In that period, Madero enlisted his best military men, like General Felipe Angeles, to finish with the rebels. Perhaps these men might have been able to suppress the insurrection were it not for one act of infamy that was slowly crystallizing and for which the president had no idea—one of the great acts of treason in recent memory.

Victoriano Huerta, the elected commander chosen by the government to defend it, having found an opportunity for himself to become president, not only forged a pact with the rebels, but he also provided the rebels with food and water and initiated false attacks. He made Madero believe that he was trying to effectively destroy the army of Felix Díaz. At some point, Madero's brother, Gustavo (who was also a delegate in the legislature), found out that the general had colluded with the rebels and planned to overthrow the legitimate government. Madero's brother had unmasked Huerta, the man who had sworn an oath to the President he wanted to overthrow. Madero distrusted his brother, placing confidence in his elected commander. This, as you can imagine, would be a grave mistake. It would not be long before the definitive betrayal took place.

The pressure on Madero soon became unbearable, since he not only was facing the problem of not being able to defeat the rebels, but he also found himself in a difficult situation with the diverse political and diplomatic groups that were pressuring him to resign in order to avoid more bloodshed. The Congress also asked him to leave his post. The president, faithful to his principles, rejected the calls for resignation, saying stoically that he'd rather die than renounce his legitimate right to the presidency. It looked like it was only a question of days. A new traitor emerged: General Aureliano Blanquet, supposedly loyal to Madero, defected to Huerta's side. Without suspecting a thing, the president was arrested by Blanquet. The presidential guard could do nothing against this surprising action. Furious, Madero slapped the general, calling him a traitor. The military man didn't seem to care, who cynically responded: "Yes, I am a traitor."

While this was happening, the greatest traitor of all, Huerta, was celebrating his imminent ascendancy to the presidency and he met Madero's brother in a restaurant, where he asked him to disarm. Madero's brother, without suspecting a thing, fell to the mercy of the rebels who promptly placed him under arrest and took him to the Ciudadela, where he was the victim of horrible torture shortly before he was murdered.

Without wasting time, Huerta, along with Felix Diaz, organized a meeting with the American ambassador and foreign diplomats at the US Embassy. The ambassador was a supporter of the oligarchy and someone who despised Madero for his democratic ideas, which went against US interests. Huerta signed the Embassy Pact with the ambassador, where he was able to negotiate the imprisonment of Madero in exchange for him being recognized as the provisional President. As provisional president, Huerta would be obliged to convene new elections in which Felix Diaz would be guaranteed to be elected.

Imagine what Madero must have felt as he sat in solitude and seclusion after having learned of Huerta's treason. It should have been then, in the throes of his grief, that he should have resigned, along with vice-president Jose Maria Pino Suárez, on the condition that he agree to live in exile.

And though the battle in the capital had finished along with those 10 days of terror, there was still missing that definitive blow against Madero. Huerta was not going to allow the exile of the ex president. He refused to listen to the petitions of the Spanish and Cuban governments. If Huerta was unwilling to listen to these pleas from foreign governments, the United

States ambassador was equally stubborn, who refused to hear the petition from Madero's wife to intercede on behalf of her husband and free him from prison.

Madero and Pino Suárez never saw the light of day again. Or the light of the moon, for that matter. The final betrayal was carried out. Madero's supposed exile never happened. Not even jail for Madero figured into Huerta's plans. The night of the 22nd of February of 1913, while the ex government officials were supposedly being transported to the Lecumberri jail from the National Palace where they had been imprisoned, Huerta and Pino Suárez were executed. Later it was said that they had attempted to flee and it was necessary that they be executed.

The next day, people gathered with candles and cried for their fallen leader. It was too late. The man who had a dream, a dream of a country that worked for the common good, had been drowned in a river of blood.

Victoriano Huerta, the traitor, assumed the presidency. Ambition and the thirst for power had defeated democracy . . . but not for long. A new revolution was about to begin.

(Translation by Juan Diego Marroquin)

Corrido: "Cuartelazo. La Decena Trágica," by las Hermanas Mendoza.[3]

Año de mil novecientos,	In the year nineteen hundred,
de mil novecientos trece,	In nineteen hundred thirteen,
ya mataron a Madero	They killed Madero
y nada que aparece.	And nothing was as it appeared.
Fue llegando Félix Díaz,	Félix Díaz arrived,
con orden militar:	with a military order:
Aquí renuncia usted	Either you resign
o lo mando a fusilar.	or I'll have you killed.
Respondió el señor Madero,	Madero answered,
en su silla presidencial	from his presidential chair
primero me asesinan	You'll have to kill me first
que hacerme renunciar.	before you make me resign.
A las dos de la mañana	At two in the morning
fue el primer cañonazo,	was the first cannon,
y estaban las tropas listas	And the troops were ready
para dar el cuartelazo.	To start the coup d'etat.
Tocaban los clarines,	The bugles played,
sonaban los tambores	The drums were sounding,
las ametralladoras dando	The machine guns
vueltas en los fortines.	sounding in the forts.

Otro día por la mañana,	One day in the morning,
las mujeres llorando,	Women were crying
al ver la ciudadela	To see the citadel
que la estaban bombardeando.	That had been bombed.
Los días muy tranquilos,	The very calm days,
las noches muy serenas,	The very serene nights,
al otro día por la mañana,	One day in the morning,
las calles de muertos llenas.	The streets filled with the dead.
Vuela, vuela, palomita,	Fly, fly, little dove,
párate en aquel romero,	Stop in that rosemary bush,
ándale, avísale a Carranza	Hurry, tell Carranza
que mataron a Madero.	that Madero was killed.
Año de mil novecientos,	In the year nineteen hundred,
de mil novecientos trece,	In nineteen hundred thirteen,
ya mataron a Madero	They killed Madero
y nada que aparece.	And nothing was as it appeared.
Vuela, vuela, palomita,	Fly, fly, little dove,
párate en aquel romero,	Stop in that rosemary bush,
ándale, avísale a Carranza	Hurry, tell Carranza
que mataron a Madero.	that Madero was killed.

Look at one of the YouTube documentaries on the Decena Trágica (if you cannot understand the Spanish, the images are useful) or look at its Google Street View page.

Also listen to the corrido "La Decena Trágica," originally recorded in the United States because of the fighting in Mexico City and the countryside.[4]

6.3. CHURCH: RELIGIOUS PROVISION AND LAND PROVISION OF THE CONSTITUTION OF 1917

Article 130: Religious provision

The Federal Authorities shall have the power to exercise in matters of religious worship and outward ecclesiastical forms the intervention required by law. All other officials shall act as auxiliaries to the Federal authorities.

The Congress cannot enact laws establishing or prohibiting any religion.

Marriage is a civil contract. This and other acts relating to the civil status of persons are within the exclusive jurisdiction of civil officials and authorities, in the manner prescribed by law, and they shall have the force and validity given them by the said laws.

A simple promise to tell the truth and to comply with obligations contracted subjects the promiser, in the event of a breach, to the penalties prescribed by law.

The law does not recognize any juridical personality in the religious groups known as churches.

Ministers of religious creeds shall be considered as persons exercising a profession, and they shall be directly subject to the laws enacted on such matters.

The State Legislatures shall have the exclusive power to determine the maximum number of ministers of denominations according to the needs of each locality.

Only a Mexican by birth may be a minister of any religious denomination in Mexico.

The ministers of religious denominations shall never, in a public or private meeting constituting an assembly, nor in acts of the denomination or religious propaganda, criticize the fundamental laws of the country, the authorities in particular or the Government in general; they shall have no active nor passive vote, nor the right to associate for political purposes.

In order to dedicate new places of worship open to the public, it is necessary to obtain permission from the Secretariat of Gobernación, upon the recommendation previously obtained of the Government of the State concerned. Every place of worship must have a person in charge of it who is responsible to the authorities for compliance with the laws on religious worship within the said building and for the objects which belong to the denomination.

The caretaker of each place of public worship, together with ten other residents of the locality, shall immediately advise the municipal authorities who are in charge of the said place of worship. The outgoing minister accompanied by the incoming minister and ten residents of the locality, shall give notice of each change. The municipal authorities, under penalty of dismissal and fine, not to exceed 1,000 pesos for each violation, shall be responsible for compliance with this provision; under the same penalty, they shall keep a register of the places of worship and another of the caretakers of the same. The municipal authorities, through the Governor of the State, shall give notice to the Secretariat of Gobernación of each permission to open to public use a new place of worship, or of a change of caretakers. Donations in the form of movable objects shall be kept in the interior of church buildings.

Under no condition shall studies carried on in institutions devoted to the professional training of ministers of the denominations be given credit or granted any other dispensation or privilege which shall have for its purpose the accrediting of the said studies in official institutions. Any authority violating this provision shall be criminally liable, and the privilege or step referred to shall be null and void, and shall invalidate the professional title for the attainment of which the violation of this provision was incurred.

Periodical publications of a religious nature, whether by reason of their programs, their titles or merely by their general tendencies, shall not comment upon national political affairs, nor publish information regarding the acts of the authorities of the country or of private persons directly related to the functioning of public institutions.

The formation of any kind of political group, the name of which contains any word or indication whatever to any religious belief, is strictly prohibited. Meetings of a political nature shall not be held within places of public worship.

No minister of any religious denomination may inherit, either on his own behalf or through an intermediary, nor otherwise receive, any real property occupied by any association of religious propaganda or religious or charitable purposes. Ministers of denominations are legally incapable of inheriting by will from the ministers of the same denomination or from any private individual to whom they are not related by blood within the fourth degree.

The acquisition by private parties of personal or real property owned by the clergy or by religious organizations shall be governed by Article 27 of this Constitution.

Trials for violation of the preceding provisions shall never be by jury.[5]

Article 27: Land provision

1. Ownership of lands and waters within the boundaries of the national territory is vested originally in the Nation which has had, and has, the right to transmit title thereof to private persons, thereby constituting private property.
2. Expropriations shall only be made for reasons of public utility and by means of indemnification.
3. The Nation shall at all times have the right to impose on private property such limitations as the public interest any demand, as well as the right to regulate the development of natural resources which are susceptible of appropriation, in order to conserve them and ensure an equitable distribution of public wealth. For this purpose necessary measures shall be taken to divide up the large landed estates; to develop small landed holdings; to create new centers of rural population with the lands and waters that are indispensable to them; to encourage agriculture and to prevent the destruction of natural resources and the damages that property may suffer to the detriment of society. Villages, hamlets situated on private property, and communities which lack lands and water, or do not have them in sufficient quantities for the needs of their inhabitants, shall have the right to be provided with

them from adjoining properties, always having due regard for small landed holdings. Therefore, all grants of lands made up the present time under the decree of January 6, 1915, are confirmed. Private property necessary for the achievement of the above-expressed objectives shall be considered as taken for public utility.
4. In the Nation is vested direct ownership of all minerals or substances which in veins, layers, masses or beds constitute deposits whose nature is different from the components of the land, such as minerals from which metals and metalloids used in industry are extracted; beds of precious stones, rock salt and salt lakes formed directly by marine waters; products derived from the decomposition of rocks, when their exploitation requires underground work; phosphates which may be used for fertilizers; solid mineral fuels; petroleum and all solid, liquid, or gaseous hydrocarbons.
5. In the Nation is likewise vested the ownership of the waters of the territorial seas to the extent and in the terms fixed by International Law; waters of lagoons and inlets of the seacoasts; waters of inland lakes of natural formation which are directly connected with flowing waters; the waters of principal rivers or tributaries from the points at which there is a permanent current of water in their beds to their mouths, whether they flow to the sea or cross two or more States; those of intermittent steams whose main branch traverses two or more States; the waters of rivers, streams, or ravines when they serve as the national boundary or that of States; waters extracted from mines; and the river beds and beds and shores of lakes and streams heretofore mentioned to the extent fixed by law. Any other stream of water not included in the above enumeration, shall be considered as an integral part of the private property through which it flows; but the utilization of the water, when its course passes from one property to another, shall be considered of public utility and shall be subject to the provisions prescribed by the States.
6. In the cases to which the two foregoing paragraphs refer, the ownership of the Nation is inalienable and imprescriptible, and only shall concessions be made by the Federal Government to private parties or civil or commercial corporations organized under Mexican law, on condition that regular efforts be made to develop the resources concerned and that the legal requirements be complied with.
7. Legal capacity to acquire ownership of lands and waters of the Nation shall be governed by the following provisions:
    I. Only Mexicans by birth or naturalization and Mexican companies have the right to acquire ownership of lands, waters and their appurtenances or to obtain concessions for the development of mines, waters or mineral fuels in the Mexican Republic.

The State may grant the same right to foreigners, provided they agree before the Secretariat of Foreign Relations to consider themselves as Mexican nationals with respect to such property, and accordingly not to invoked the protection of Governments in regard to the same, under penalty in case of breach, of forfeiture to the Nation of property so acquired. Within a zone of 100 kilometers along the borders and fifty from the seacoasts, no foreigners shall under any conditions acquire direct ownership over lands and waters.

II. Religious associations known as churches, regardless of creed, shall in no case have legal capacity to acquire, hold or administer real property; all such real property or loans as may be present held by the said religious associations, either directly or through an intermediary, shall revert to ownership by the Nation, any person whosoever being authorized to denounce any property so held. Presumptive evidence shall be sufficient to declare the denunciation well founded. Places of public worship are the property of the Nation, as represented by the Federal Government, which shall determine which of them may continue to be devoted to their present purposes. Bishops' residences, rectories, seminaries, asylums, and schools belonging to religious orders, convents, or any other buildings built or designed for the administration, propaganda, or teaching of a religious creed, shall immediately, as of full right, revert to direct ownership by the Nation, to be used exclusively by the Federation of the States, within their respective jurisdictions, for the rendering of services to the public. All places of public worship which are hereafter erected shall be the property of the Nation.

III. Public or private charitable institutions for the needy, for scientific research, the diffusion of knowledge, mutual aid to members, or for any other lawful purpose, shall not acquire more real property than actually needed for their purpose and immediately and directly devoted thereto; but they may acquire, hold, or administer mortgages on real property provided the term thereof does not exceed ten years. Under no circumstances shall institutions of this kind be under the patronage, direction, administration, charge or supervision of religious bodies or communities, or of ministers of any religious denomination or of their dependents, even though the former of the latter shall not be in active service.

IV. Commercial stock companies shall not acquire, hold or administer rural properties. Companies of this kind which may organize to develop any manufacturing, mining, petroleum or other industry not agricultural by nature, shall be able to acquire, hold, or administer lands only in the amount that is strictly necessary for the establishments or adequate to serve the purposes indicated, which the Federal or State Executive shall determine in each case.

V. Civil or commercial companies owned under the form of bonds payable to bearer shall not acquire, hold or administer rural properties. Companies of this kind which may be organized to develop any manufacturing, mining, petroleum or other industry not agricultural by nature, shall be able to acquire, hold, or administer lands only in the amount that is strictly necessary for the establishments or adequate to serve the purposes indicated and which the Federal or State Executive shall determine in each.

VI. Properties held in common by co-owners, hamlets situated on private property, villages, communities, tribes, and other settlements which in fact or by law conserve their communal character, shall have legal capacity to enjoy in common the lands, woods, and waters which belong to them, or which may have been or shall be restored to them in accordance with the law of January 6, 1915, until such time as the manner of making the division of the lands shall be determined by law.

VII. With the exception of the corporations to which clauses III, IV, V and VI refer, no other civil corporation shall own or administer on its own behalf real estate or mortgage loans derived therefrom, with the single exception of buildings destined immediately and directly for the purposes of the institution. The States, the Federal District and the Territories, as well as the municipalities throughout the Republic, shall enjoy full legal capacity to acquire and hold all real estate necessary for the rendering of services to the public.

8. Federal and State laws within their respective jurisdictions shall determine the cases in which the occupation of private property shall be considered of public utility; and in accordance with the said laws the administrative authorities shall make the corresponding declaration. The value which shall be set as compensation for the expropriated property shall be based on the sum recorded as the fiscal value in the tax assessment or collecting offices, whether this value has been declared by the owner or simply accepted by him by implication, as a basis for the payment of his taxes with ten percent added. The increased value which the property in question may have acquired through improvements made subsequent to the date of the fixing of the fiscal value shall be the only matter which shall be subject to expert opinion and to judicial determination. This same procedure shall be followed when objects are concerned whose value is not recorded in the tax offices.

9. All proceedings, findings, resolutions and operations of demarcation, concession, composition, judgment, transaction, alienation, or auction which may have deprived properties held in common by co-owners, hamlets situated on private property, villages, communities, tribes and other settlements which exist since the law of June 25, 1856, of the whole or part of their lands, woods and waters, are declared null and void; and all the findings, resolutions and operations which take place in the future and produce the same effects shall likewise be null and void. Consequently, all the lands, woods, and waters of which the above-mentioned communities have been deprived, shall be restored to them in accordance with the decree of January 6, 1915, which shall remain in effect as a constitutional law. In case the lands, by way of restitution be not legal in the terms of the said decree, which adjudication may have been requested by any of the above-mentioned communities, those lands shall be given to them by way of grant, and they shall in no event fail to receive such as they may need. Only such lands, title to which may have been acquired in the divisions made by virtue of the said law of June 25, 1856, or such as may be held in undisputed ownership for more than ten years are excepted from the provision of nullity, provided their area does not exceed fifty hectares. The excess over this area shall be returned to the community and the owner indemnified for its value. All laws of restitution enacted by virtue of this provision shall be immediately carried into effect by the administrative authorities. Only the members of the community shall have the right to the lands to be divided and the rights to the same lands shall be inalienable while they remain undivided, as well as those held in ownership when the division has been made.
10. The exercise of the rights belonging to the Nation by virtue of the provisions of this article, shall follow judicial procedure; but as part of this procedure and by order of the respective tribunals, which order shall be issued within the maximum period of one month, the administrative authorities shall proceed immediately to the occupation, administration, auction or sale of the lands and waters in question, together with all their appurtenances, and in no case may the acts of said authorities be set aside until a final decision has been handed down.
11. During the next constitutional term, the Congress and the State Legislatures shall enact laws, within their respective jurisdictions, for the purpose of carrying out the division of large landed estates, based on the following principles:
    (a) In each State and Territory there shall be fixed the maximum area of land which any one individual or legally organized company may own.

(b) The excess of the area thus fixed shall be subdivided by the owner within the term set by local law and the subdivisions shall be offered for sale on conditions approved by the governments in accordance with the same laws.
(c) If the owner shall refuse to make the subdivision, this shall be carried out by the local Government by means of expropriation.
(d) The value of the subdivisions shall be paid in annual amounts that amortize principal and interest within a period of not less than twenty years, during which the person acquiring shall not alienate them. The interest rate shall not exceed five percent per annum.
(e) The owner shall be obliged to receive bonds of a special issue to guarantee the payment of the property expropriated. With this end in view, the Congress shall pass a law authorizing the States to issue bonds to meet their agrarian obligations.
(f) Local laws shall provide for the organization of the family patrimony, determining what property shall comprise it, on the basis that it shall be inalienable and not subject to attachment or encumbrance of any kind.
12. All contracts and concessions made by previous governments since the year 1876, which have had as a consequence the monopoly of lands, waters and natural resources of the Nation by a single individual or company are declared subject to revision and the Executive of the Union is authorized to declare them null and void when they seriously prejudice the public interest.[6]

For the revolutionary context of the land provision of the Constitution, watch the movie Viva Zapata! *(1952), starring Marlon Brandon and Anthony Quinn.*

6.4. FAMILY: AMERICAN GROCERY COMPANY IN 1912 SET UP A MODEL ELECTRIC KITCHEN

American Grocery Company in 1912 set up a model electric kitchen to invite customers to see for themselves the advantages of electrical cooking. This new method was claimed to be "the modern way because it is clean, convenient, comparatively cheap and the most hygienic of all methods."

The model kitchen exhibited coffee percolators, teapots, toasters, grills, flat irons, disc stoves, and water heaters, all of which were electrical. This advertisement from El Diario, *July 14, 1912, proposes new methods of cooking and reads:*

To cook by electricity is within everyone's reach given the low costs of electric current offered by CIA MEX DE LUZ Y FUERZA MOTRIZ (Mexican Light

Life continued during the revolution.
Mexican Light & Power Co. advertisement, *El Diario*, July 14, 1912.

& Power Co.). It is now cheaper to use electricity for heat than any other method—WITH ONE CENT OF ELECTRICITY to 10 cents per kilowatt.

You could run:

- An electric grill 6 minutes
- A radiator 8 minutes
- Engine for sewing machine 3 hours
- Electric iron 6 minutes

You could:

- Boil 2 liters of water
- Cook a dish in a pan
- Heat up a stove from 4 to 15 minutes
- Make 4 cups of coffee in an electric coffeemaker

THE BEST ARE THE CHEAPER ONES.

With the objective to make our home electric utensils better known we are going to hold a CULINARY EXHIBITION in the American Grocery Company store window (Ave. 16 de Septiembre 12) beginning Monday July 15. We will clearly demonstrate the economy, cleanness, and simplicity of all of our appliances, teaching how easy it is to prepare all types of dishes.

"We will prepare tea and coffee in electric teapots and coffeemakers. We will toast bread in our new 'Radiant' toasters. We will show our new combination stoves and grills.

Come see the whole new electric kitchen in which we can easily prepare anything from a dish to an entire banquet.

6.5. POPULAR GROUPS: NATIONAL TYPES REFLECTED IN "LA CUCARACHA" AND IN JOHN REED, "THE RISE OF PANCHO VILLA" (1913)

The revolutionaries identified with different groups in society than the previous Porfirian regime. The editors of El Universal, *one of the two most prominent and rival capital city newspapers in 1917 published images of the national types. Consider the following image and compare it to the clothing laws in the Porfirian section.*

The Revolution, 1910–1920 127

El Universal

Recognition of national types also occurred in music, for example, the well-known "La Cucaracha."

"La Cucaracha," corrido of Pancho Villa (n.d.)[7]

Lyrics:
La maldita cucaracha es un animal muy necio
anda metiendo la pata en la guerra y el comercio
Ya murió la cucaracha ya la llevan a enterrar
entre cuatro zopilotes y un ratón de sacristán

La cucaracha, la cucaracha ya no puede caminar
porque no tiene, porque le falta marijuana que fumar
La cucaracha, la cucaracha ya no puede caminar
porque no tiene, porque le falta marijuana que fumar

La maldita cucaracha es un animal muy necio
anda metiendo la pata en la guerra y el comercio
Ya murió la cucaracha ya la llevan a enterrar
entre cuatro zopilotes y un ratón de sacristán

La cucaracha, la cucaracha ya no puede caminar
porque no tiene, porque le faltan las dos patitas de atrás
La cucaracha, la cucaracha ya no puede caminar
porque no tiene, porque le faltan las dos patitas de atrás

Lyrics in Translation:
The damned cockroach is a really annoying animal
It goes around putting its hand in war and business
The cockroach died and they're bringing it to be buried
Between four vultures and a sacristy mouse

The cockroach, the cockroach can no longer walk
because it doesn't have, because it lacks marijuana to smoke
The cockroach, the cockroach can no longer walk
because it doesn't have, because it lacks marijuana to smoke

The damned cockroach is a really annoying animal
It goes around putting its hand in war and business
The cockroach died and they're bringing it to be buried
Between four vultures and a sacristy mouse

The cockroach, the cockroach can no longer walk
because it doesn't have, because it lacks two hind legs
The cockroach, the cockroach can no longer walk
because it doesn't have, because it lacks two hind legs
(*Translation by Claire Perrott*)

"The Rise of Pancho Villa"

For a description of Pancho Villa, examine the following sketch. John Reed wrote the following profile of the revolutionary general Pancho Villa for Metropolitan Magazine *in the fall 1913. The next year, the article became part of Reed's book* Insurgent Mexico. *It placed him in the same category of journalists who visited the revolution as Jack London and Ambrose Bierce.*

It was while Villa was in Chihuahua City, two weeks before the advance on Torreon, that the artillery corps of his army decided to present him with a gold medal for personal heroism on the field.

In the audience hall of the Governor's palace in Chihuahua, a place of ceremonial, great luster chandeliers, heavy crimson portières, and gaudy American wallpaper, there is a throne for the governor.

It is a gilded chair, with lion's claws for arms, placed upon a dais under a canopy of crimson velvet, surmounted by a heavy, gilded, wooden cap, which tapers up to a crown.

The officers of artillery, in smart blue uniforms faced with black velvet and gold, were solidly banked across one end of the audience hall, with flashing new swords and their gilt-braided hats stiffly held under their arms. From the door of that chamber, around the gallery, down the state staircase, across the grandiose inner court of the palace, and out through the imposing gates to the street, stood a double line of soldiers, with their rifles at present arms. Four regimental bands grouped in one wedged in the crowd. The people of the capital were massed in solid thousands on the Plaza de Armas before the palace.

"*Ya viene!*" "Here he comes!" "Viva Villa!" "Viva Madero!" "Villa, the Friend of the Poor!"

The roar began at the back of the crowd and swept like fire in heavy growing crescendo until it seemed to toss thousands of hats above their heads. The band in the courtyard struck up the Mexican national air, and Villa came walking down the street.

He was dressed in an old plain khaki uniform, with several buttons lacking. He hadn't recently shaved, wore no hat, and his hair had not been brushed. He walked a little pigeon-toed, humped over, with his hands in his trousers pockets. As he entered the aisle between the rigid lines of soldiers he seemed slightly embarrassed, and grinned and nodded to a *compadre* here and there in the ranks. At the foot of the grand staircase, Governor Chao and Secretary of State Terrazzas joined him in full-dress uniform. The band threw off all restraint, and, as Villa entered the audience chamber, at a signal from someone in the balcony of the palace, the great throng in the Plaza de Armas uncovered, and all the brilliant crowd of officers in the room saluted stiffly.

It was Napoleonic!

Villa hesitated for a minute, pulling his mustache and looking very uncomfortable, finally gravitated toward the throne, which he tested by shaking the arms, and then sat down, with the Governor on his right and the Secretary of State on his left.

Señor Bauche Alcalde stepped forward, raised his right hand to the exact position which Cicero took when denouncing Catiline, and pronounced a short discourse, indicting Villa for personal bravery on the field on six counts, which he mentioned in florid detail. He was followed by the Chief of Artillery, who said: "The army adores you. We will follow you wherever you lead. You can be what you desire in Mexico." Then three other officers spoke in the high-flung, extravagant periods necessary to Mexican oratory. They called him "The Friend of the Poor," "The Invincible General," "The Inspirer of Courage and Patriotism," "The Hope of the Indian Republic." And through it all Villa slouched on the throne, his mouth hanging open, his little shrewd eyes playing around the room. Once or twice he yawned, but for the most part he seemed to be speculating, with some intense interior amusement, like a small boy in church, what it was all about. He knew, of course, that it was the proper thing, and perhaps felt a slight vanity that all this conventional ceremonial was addressed to him. But it bored him just the same.

Finally, with an impressive gesture, Colonel Servin stepped forward with the small pasteboard box which held the medal. General Chao nudged Villa, who stood up. The officers applauded violently; the crowd outside cheered; the band in the court burst into a triumphant march.

Villa put out both hands eagerly, like a child for a new toy. He could hardly wait to open the box and see what was inside. An expectant hush fell upon everyone, even the crowd in the square. Villa looked at the medal, scratching his head, and, in a reverent silence, said clearly: "This is a hell of a little thing to give a man for all that heroism you are talking about!" And the bubble of Empire was pricked then and there with a great shout of laughter.

They waited for him to speak—to make a conventional address of acceptance. But as he looked around the room at those brilliant, educated men, who said that they would die for Villa, the peon, and meant it, and as he caught sight through the door of the ragged soldiers, who had forgotten their rigidity and were crowding eagerly into the corridor with eyes fixed eagerly on the *compañero* that they loved, he realized something of what the Revolution signified.

Puckering up his face, as he did always when he concentrated intensely, he leaned across the table in front of him and poured out, in a voice so low that people could hardly hear: "There is no word to speak. All I can say is my heart is all to you." Then he nudged Chao and sat down, spitting violently on the floor; and Chao pronounced the classic discourse.

Villa was an outlaw for twenty-two years. When he was only a boy of sixteen, delivering milk in the streets of Chihuahua, he killed a government official and had to take to the mountains. The story is that the official had violated his sister, but it seems probable that Villa killed him on account of his insufferable insolence. That in itself would not have outlawed him long in Mexico, where human life is cheap; but once a refugee he committed the unpardonable crime of stealing cattle from the rich *hacendados*. And from that time to the outbreak of the Madero revolution the Mexican government had a price on his head.

Villa was the son of ignorant peons. He had never been to school. He hadn't the slightest conception of the complexity of civilization, and when he finally came back to it, a mature man of extraordinary native shrewdness, he encountered the twentieth century with the naïve simplicity of a savage.

It is almost impossible to procure accurate information about his career as a bandit. There are accounts of outrages he committed in old files of local newspapers and government reports, but those sources are prejudiced, and his name became so prominent as a bandit that every train robbery and holdup and murder in northern Mexico was attributed to Villa.

But an immense body of popular legend grew up among the peons around his name. There are many traditional songs and ballads celebrating his exploits—you can hear the shepherds singing them around their fires in the mountains at night, repeating verses handed down by their fathers or composing others extemporaneously. For instance, they tell the story of how Villa, fired by the story of the misery of the peons on the Hacienda of Los Alamos, gathered a small army and descended upon the Big House, which he looted, and distributed the spoils among the poor people. He drove off thousands of cattle from the Terrazzas range and ran them across the border. He would suddenly descend upon a prosperous mine and seize the bullion. When he needed corn he captured a granary belonging to some rich man. He recruited almost openly in the villages far removed from the well-traveled roads and railways, organizing the outlaws of the mountains. Many of the present rebel soldiers used to belong to his band and several of the Constitutionalist generals, like Urbina. His range was confined mostly to southern Chihuahua and northern Durango, but it extended from Coahuila right across the Republic to the State of Sinaloa.

His reckless and romantic bravery is the subject of countless poems. They tell, for example, how one of his band named Reza was captured by the *rurales* and bribed to betray Villa. Villa heard of it and sent word into the city of Chihuahua that he was coming for Reza. In broad daylight he entered the city on horseback, took ice cream on the Plaza—the ballad is very explicit on this point—and rode up and down the streets until he found Reza strolling with his sweetheart in the Sunday crowd on the Paseo Bolivar, where he shot him and escaped. In time of famine he fed whole districts, and took care of entire villages evicted by the soldiers under Porfirio Díaz's outrageous land law. Everywhere he was known as The Friend of the Poor. He was the Mexican Robin Hood.

In all these years he learned to trust nobody. Often in his secret journeys across the country with one faithful companion he camped in some desolate spot and dismissed his guide; then, leaving a fire burning, he rode all night to get away from the faithful companion. That is how Villa learned the art of war, and in the field today, when the army comes into camp at night, Villa flings the bridle of his horse to an orderly, takes a serape over his shoulder, and sets out for the hills alone. He never seems to sleep. In the dead of night he will appear somewhere along the line of outposts to see if the sentries are on the job; and in the morning he returns from a totally different direction. No one, not even the most trusted officer of his staff, knows the last of his plans until he is ready for action.

When Madero took the field in 1910, Villa was still an outlaw. Perhaps, as his enemies say, he saw a chance to whitewash himself; perhaps, as seems probable, he was inspired by the Revolution of the peons. Anyway, about three months after they rose in arms, Villa suddenly appeared in El Paso and put himself, his band, his knowledge of the country and all his fortune at the command of Madero. The vast wealth that people said he must have accumulated during his twenty years of robbery turned out to be 363 silver pesos, badly worn. Villa became a Captain in the Maderista army, and as such went to Mexico City with Madero and was made honorary general of the new *rurales*. He was attached to Huerta's army when it was sent north to put down the Orozco Revolution. Villa commanded the garrison of Parral, and defeated Orozco with an inferior force in the only decisive battle of the war.

Huerta put Villa in command of the advance, and let him and the veterans of Madero's army do the dangerous and dirty work while the old line Federal regiments lay back under the protection of their artillery. In Jimenez Huerta suddenly summoned Villa before a court-martial and charged him with insubordination—claiming to have wired an order to Villa in Parral, which order Villa said he never received.

The court-martial lasted fifteen minutes, and Huerta's most powerful future antagonist was sentenced to be shot.

Alfonso Madero, who was on Huerta's staff, stayed the execution, but President Madero, forced to back up the orders of his commander in the field, imprisoned Villa in the penitentiary of the capital.

During all this time Villa never wavered in his loyalty to Madero—an unheard-of thing in Mexican history. For a long time he had passionately wanted an education. Now he wasted no time in regrets or political intrigue. He set himself with all his force to learn to read and write. Villa hadn't the slightest foundation to work upon. He spoke the crude Spanish of the very poor—what is called *pelado*. He knew nothing of the rudiments or philosophy of language; and he started out to learn those first, because he always must know the *why* of things. In nine months he could write a very fair hand and read the newspapers. It is interesting now to see him read, or, rather, hear him, for he has to drone the words aloud like a small child.

Finally, the Madero government connived at his escape from prison, either to save Huerta's face because Villa's friends had demanded an investigation, or because Madero was convinced of his innocence and didn't dare openly to release him.

From that time to the outbreak of the last revolution, Villa lived in El Paso, Texas, and it was from there that he set out, in April, 1913, to conquer Mexico with four companions, three led horses, two pounds of sugar and coffee, and a pound of salt.

There is a little story connected with that. He hadn't money enough to buy horses, nor had any of his companions. But he sent two of them to a local livery stable to rent riding horses every day for a week. They always paid carefully at the end of the ride, so when they asked for eight horses the livery stable man had no hesitation about trusting them with them. Six months later, when Villa came triumphantly into Juarez at the head of an army of four thousand men, the first public act he committed was to send a man with double the price of the horses to the owner of the livery stable.

He recruited in the mountains near San Andres, and so great was his popularity that within one month he had raised an army of three thousand men; in two months he had driven the Federal garrisons all over the State of Chihuahua back into Chihuahua City; in six months he had taken Torreon; and in seven and a half Juarez had fallen to him, Mercado's Federal army had evacuated Chihuahua, and Northern Mexico was almost free.[8]

ADDITIONAL READING

Vanderwood, Paul J. "Response to Revolt: The Counter-Guerrilla Strategy of Porfirio Díaz." *Hispanic American Historical Review* 56, no. 4 (November 1976): 551–579.

No additional reading in Spanish is provided in this section because of the opportunities to listen and to read the documents in Spanish.

NOTES

1. Michael C. Meyer, *Mexican Rebel: Pascual Orozco and the Mexican Revolution, 1910–1915* (Lincoln: University of Nebraska Press, 1967), 29–32. Reprinted by permission of the University of Nebraska Press.

2. Javier Malpica, "La decena trágica," *Nueva Biblioteca del Niño Mexicano*, audiobook (2015). Spanish-speakers can listen to the program.

3. "Corridos of the Revolution," in *The Course of Mexican Music*, by Janet L. Sturman (New York: Routledge, 2016), 193–96; Las Hermanas Mendoza, "Cuartelazo. La Decena Trágica," http://us.ivoox.com/es/cuartelazo-la-decena-tragica-hermanas-mendoza-audios-mp3_rf_1736472_1.html.

4. Sturman, *Music*, 195–203; the corrido "La Decena Trágica" is available online at https://youtu.be/0V-ZTT6_I5Q.

5. E. V. Niemeyer, Jr., *Revolution at Queretaro: The Mexican Constitutional Convention of 1916–1917* (Austin: University of Texas Press,1974), 235–36.

6. Niemeyer, Jr., *Revolution*, 250–62.

7. Daniel E. Sheehy, "Mexico," in *The Garland Handbook of Latin American Music*, ed. Dale A. Olsen and Daniel E. Sheehy (New York: Garland Publishing, Inc. 2000), 164–65. Also see "La cucaracha—revolución mexicana," https://youtube/B_27Hi 1In6o; "La cucaracha—Gipsy Kings," https://www.youtube.com/watch?v=_VILrlx H3io.

8. Sturman, *Music*, 196–201, 209; http://grammar.about.com/od/classicessays/a/reedvilla08.htm/ Reprinted by permission of Richard Nordquist.

CHAPTER 7

The Revolution as Lived Experience, 1920–1936

During the revolutionary years from 1917 to 1934, Mexicans found their daily lives affected by revolutionary promises, programs, and practices made in the Constitution of 1917 or resulting from it. They also witnessed, these events notwithstanding, a continuation of violence that resulted in the assassination of revolutionary leaders (Emiliano Zapata, Venustiano Carranza, Pancho Villa, and Alvaro Obregón), two major insurrections attempting to overthrow the revolutionary regime (the Delahuerta Rebellion and the Cristero War), and a continuation of sporadic fighting in the countryside. This era ended with the exile of former president Plutarco Calles in 1936 and the initiation of major revolutionary programs by Lázaro Cárdenas. In the midst of this disruption, the revolutionary leaders carried out major programs to establish a new national identity (7.1). Everyday religion continued, despite warfare between the government and the church, that focused on foreign-created vogues among some women (7.2). Revolutionary intellectuals and artists joined with like-minded foreigners who came to see the revolution, and together they created new cultural fashions (7.3). The new communications technology, especially radio, changed everyday practices, often to make time for a variety of radio programs, and family practices, such as board games, reflected popular interests and fears (7.4). In the midst of these changes, there was also a new appreciation of the variety of the nation's indigenous cultures (7.5).

7.1. POLITICS: *MEXICANERÍAS—LA CONSTRUCCIÓN DEL MÉXICO TÍPICO*

Following is the transcript of a twenty-seven-minute documentary distributed by the Centro de Investigaciones y Estudios Superiores (CIESAS). The document shows the subtitles of the program (with very slight editing), and the speakers are identified in italics.

Ricardo Pérez Montfort

In the case of Mexico, the revolutionary political project is a remarkable one of social vindication against social and economic injustice, also the rescue of several popular values. People, who emerge from the revolution, are also being redefined. In the Portiriato the conception of these "people" was very elitist and narrow. On the other hand, the revolution redefines its own subject . . . which is these people who are not like the elite, but most of them; children, women, young people, elders, peasants, and the middle class. And in this sense, there is a sort of political reorientation, because, supposedly, the government is meant for all these people, for the masses. Mexican people, these people who are miserable, who are not educated, who are part of the mass, how can they be governed? Well, one ought to know these people, and during the post-revolutionary period, there is an attempt to define them, to ask: what are these people? And it was found people with quite diverse cultural expressions; from the perspective of the post-revolutionary elite these people are a young nation that needs to be educated, therefore this process must bloom from its own values, to redefine these values and then give them back to the people.

There was a time, twenty-five years ago, when I decided, well, actually, I wanted to merge the historical research and the cultural research. Since then I have been more interested in nationalism conceived from a principle of definition, sometimes from self-definition. But also from the principle of a representation from an attempt to synthesize what it is or what it must be.

Alfonso Morales

Well, the necessity of asserting a national identity to assume this warranty of national identity is the state that emerged from the armed struggle, that those representatives, those victorious sectors of the revolution, are also those who establish what is Mexican and what is not, and therefore what is the enemy. The polarities and the conception of what is owned and what is foreign, what is true and what is deceitful, illusory; that Manichean structure of values has been there from the very beginning.

Ricardo Pérez Montfort

And from the tendency to dominate comes this phenomenon of an official culture, a culture controlled by the State, controlled by a group of individuals which are either in the educational field or among the cultural authorities or even among the political authorities. Just because a certain politic[ian] likes a certain song, this song becomes

fashionable. This is the case of "El Corrido de Agrarista" which became the hymn of the Cárdenas Presidency. Another example is "La Bamba" which became the hymn of Miguel Alemán's Presidency already in the 1940s. We have also this phenomenon that remains and finally has been established as a deep symbol of what is truly Mexican, which is the classic image of the charro and the china poblana dancing "El Jarabe Tapatío" or mariachi music to define Mexican music in general.
Ricardo Pérez Escamilla

The mariachi is Hollywood. Did you know that the mariachi did not have trumpets? There were only five elements, yes. Two violins, a guitarrón, a vihuela, and a guitar. It was a music like . . . how can describe it?
José Santos Marmolejo

A little bit of . . . sones and that kind of stuff, but Mister Azcárraga couldn't stand that music. He wanted a show. Sure, now they play very nice, but they don't have the soul we used to have. In 1926, my father was the first mariachi who made a record and he recorded sones. Those were sones, love songs, dedicated to women, dedicated to the land, dedicated to the war, sones, corridos, waltzes. Especially waltz. How beautifully they were played! Minuets, all that was played. Since 1915, my father came every year with his band to work here in Mexico City. The Mariachi music wasn't known, the music sounded strange and it didn't produce enough to make a living, so they had to go back to their homeland, the village of Tecolotlan. He had to leave Mexico City four times.
Ricardo Pérez Montfort

The idea of tourism that was being promoted in Mexico since the '20s was "Let's sell to the tourist a country that can be consumed and bought a part of it. So what would be that part? It had to be something synthetic, something small; it had to be a quick impression. The "Mexican curios," for example, which even became a sort of international fashion during the '20s and the '30s. To have a little Mexican object meant to be fashionable. A little pyramid, a solar calendar, a little charro hat, an Indian under a cactus, an ashtray saying Mexico curio or a calabash bowl from Michoacán, a little sarape, that kind of stuff. All this was promoted by the revolutionary state and this also increased the production of souvenirs, and it was promoted by the media industry, too. It has to appear in postcards, in radio, in movies, etc. and it is going to be a factor in the market, and the tourist will want to buy that, and that is what the tourist will want to see. Here is where the huge success of the folkloric ballet and the mariachi comes from. Those are grab-and-go products. Here you can have a look at Mexico, of the typi-

cal Mexico, I show it to you in a one-hour show and you can have it to go, and also you can buy the costumes, the music, etc.
Pablo Dueñas

Since 1920, with the nationalist movement started by José Vasconcelos at the time he's appointed Minister of Education there's impulse of what will be known as Mexican; and theatrical employers began to hire Mexican authors and they do not import as many foreign works to produce things that people will say, "look we presenting something Mexican." Here comes the unexpected: the Tehuana costume. The Tehuana costume wasn't created in the Isthmus of Tehuantepec nor the song "La Chiapaneca" which is a traditional waltz from the isthmus which we can consider as one of the emblematic songs of those regions; that costume was created by the Arozamena sisters for a play about Chiapas and the song "La Chiapaneca" was composed by their brother, Juan Arozamena, precisely for that play. Those are fundamental pieces that nowadays are part of the suite that we call Mexican music, which identifies us as Mexicans anywhere in the world, along with the songs "Guadalajara," or "El Mariachi," and "Chapala," y Pepe Guizar that were composed in the vaudeville by request.
Ricardo Pérez Montfort

Another very important thing to consider is the external perspective. As in any Revolution, Mexico becomes a magnet for many intellectuals and artists from the whole world who are interested in what's happening in Mexico. They come and see and start making interpretations, and many of them participate actively in the definition of what is Mexican.
Ricardo Pérez Escamilla

I also want to tell you that tourism in Mexico was developed thanks to the Great Mexican artists and intellectuals. Tourism in Mexico was invoked due to our art. And the main promoters were Diego Rivera, Clemente Orozco, Carlos Merida, Gonzalez Camarena, Miguel Covarrubias. We are talking about artists, intellectuals like Manuel Gamio, Alfonso Caso. I have found articles by Gabriela Mistral, who was in Mexico, who spoke about frescoes and popular arts with the intention of summoning tourism. Doctor Atl contributed to promote our popular arts in a big exhibition as well. Fito Best Maugard created a drawing method. So, what I want to tell you is that we find in tourism expressions of a remarkable esthetic richness. We have compositions that truly reveal the essence of Mexico. But there are also totally foolish things. Because there was also feedback.
Ricardo Pérez Montfort

I think that the typical Mexican product presented at the national and international level is the charro singing with his mariachi, not the china but the charra also accompanied by her mariachi, on stage with the braggart, playful dramatizing behavior.

Marisol Limon

In daily life, even Octavio Paz said, "Ahorita." Even I myself every year celebrate the Independence Day here with my friends, and I offer chiles en nogada and colorful papers, and I dress like the priest Hidalgo, not as a charro, but I fit the stereotype. I mean, that amount of patriotism, I do not feel excluded. I love it. All that is part of my idiosyncrasy.

Folkloric Dance actually represents all what our country is; our life. I have had the opportunity to verify all this in field practices in activities we do in the school that made me choose this life, to dedicate my life to folkloric dance.

Ricardo Pérez Montfort

However I think there have been very important reactions of resistance in the homogenizing process to say, "Well, gentlemen, we are not like that, we are like this and like that or there are certain places where people say, "No, we have a different culture." Here in the musical audio library of the INAH, we have music that upon listening you'd say: so what's Mexican about this? It's Mexican because it is created by a Raramuri musician or a Mayan musician but what emotiveness, sensibility, and identity elements does it have?

Ricardo Pérez Montfort

Lately, there are some phenomena that I find fascinating: the reappearance or appearance of the native cultures, but incorporating contemporary elements. Mayan Rock or maybe Hip Hop jarocho. I find very interesting that kind of stuff; I think it is part of the cultural dynamic, in the same way that the Mexican blues . . . or the Mexican Chotises and Mexicanized fox trots existed. I would say that folkloric ballet which usually ends with churros and chinas dancing the "El Jarabe Tapatío" with mariachis in a Mexican party with confetti, jarritos, punch, pots with mole, all that has still a very huge validity as a representation of what is Mexican or better the stereotype of what is Mexican. The structure created around the Mexican folkloric ballet permitted to become a cultural ambassador of the national folkloric dance. This coincidence of political and cultural interests, of representation abroad, of Amalia [Hernandez] had this particularity: she tried to base her creations, as seriously as she could, on research *in situ* about how the dances and the ceremonies occurred. I mean Amalia plunged her feet and her hands in the land; she assisted in the ceremonies, she met the so-called informers to know where this dance came from and then she showed us her version, a third party version, and from that she decorated, let's us, with a particular emphasis in the theatrical elements those dances and those moments of historical, cultural, and political importance to the nation.

Ricardo Pérez Montfort

The media par excellence the movies, the radio, basically tended to condense, to keep using the same elements and to repeat them; they insisted, for instance, on the idea that the revolutionary man was a mix of Indio Fernandez and Pedro Armendariz, so when we think of Pancho Villa, we do no longer think of Pancho Villa, but of Pedro Armendariz; if we think of a soldadera, we no longer think of the soldadera, but Dolores del Rio or Maria Felix. So all of this is presented and consolidated in the movies, which I agree is at the forefront in the construction of this identity. There we can find the mixture of entertainment, nationalism, pedagogy, genuine and fake popular culture, the transition from popular to massive . . . all these threads and interjections among all these constructs, among all these products that ultimately belong to the collective identity matter, all of them have the movies the biggest showcase, before the days of television, of course.

When the cinema came, it started immediately to take up a very special feature, which is the agrarian environment. Nonetheless, later movies, like "Alla en el rancho grande," which had a big impact with Lorenzo Barcelata and Tito Guizar, gave a spectacular inflection to Mexican popular music, as well as the costumes, tequila, the women's dresses, the impact of Mexican machismo in Mexican song and daily life context. All this starts making a cultural establishment that will internationalize Mexico through the movies, making people think that Mexico is just the china poblana, the charro, tequila, and the songs. As well as stubborn and brave macho males. The "must" for the movies is the show and spectacle, and functions based on a structure of movie stars, established genres; a structure that requires many songs for an illiterate audience to make them feel represented in the stereotypes: the peladito, the maid, a variety of trades and to start giving legitimacy to something we know is a fake that is, those charros that have little to do with the agrarian reality. Nowadays what can we say to define the idea of what is Mexican? You would have to ask a poblano living in New York, a Yucateco settled in Mexico City, a Guanajuatense—but not just a 17 year old Guanajuatense, but a ninety-year-old one, too, and you would realize that what we have organized as a narrative or even already declared dead is very much alive.

Ricardo Pérez Montfort

Hence, I think that the official culture, as such, is actually an aberration. The notion often presented at schools about Mexico as one territory with one sort of people with one government, etc. as a big whole heterogeneous thing, is just an aberration. Fortunately, during the last

20, 30 years, recognition has emerged of the multicultural, the multiplicity, etc. which in a way has started to undermine the classic notions of an official culture. I think that stopping a cultural expression is a long, complicated process. No matter how hard the official culture tries to establish hegemony and to dominate the dynamics of cultural creation the constant cultural expression and its effervescence keep producing and producing new expressions, recovering traditions, etc. I believe that if we conceive culture as an entity in constant movement, there's no way to stop the native cultures, even though these cultures are reinventing themselves constantly.

7.2. CHURCH: RELIGION IN EVERYDAY LIFE

In addition to revolutionary issues, Mexicans also faced growing foreign influences brought by records, radio, movies, and news stories. For many, especially men, the most dangerous development was the "flappers," called in Mexico las chicas modernas *(modern girls) who followed the styles and behavior of women who ignored church instructions and etiquette restrictions, to wear short hair and short*

San Antonio saved family from the Charleston.
Champion Folk Art Collection.

skirts and to dance the Charleston. Some concerned about these issues turned to popular religion. An example is this retablo, *a painting on tin placed in a church in thanks of divine help, from Oaxaca City, Oaxaca,*[1] *that reads:*

> Año de 1930 época del Charleston época de amor época en que me enamore de mi novia y me case fuimos muy felices gracias a que heramos [sic] muy devotos de San Antonio. Pero un día mi mujercita se le ocurrió venderlo porque estorbava [sic]—y empezaron los pleitos y las penurias hasta que lo recupere nuevamente y seguimos siendo felices.—Gracias de Usebio Samorano.

> The year 1930, time of the Charleston, time of love, time in which I fell in love and married my girlfriend, we were so happy because we both were very devoted to San Antonio. But one day my little woman came up with the idea to sell it [*the San Antonio painting*] because it hindered [*her activities*]—then our fights and misery began until I got it back, now we remain happy together.— Thank you, from Usebio Samorano.

7.3. MILITARY AND SECURITY: MOBILE HEALTH BRIGADES AND THE NATIONAL CAMPAIGN FOR VACCINATION

Claudia Agostoni, "National Reconstruction and Public Health"

The promotion of the health and well-being of the people represented the principal issue of concern for the revolutionary governments and was regarded as essential for the reconstruction of the nation. The Department of Public Health (DSP), with the federal obligation to ensure the health, the provision of health services and the organization of specific health campaigns throughout the country [*from 1917*] until 1943, planned, organized, implemented and supervised a wide variety of public health programs and health education campaigns in both cities and the countryside. Among the main recipients of those programs, in accordance with the precepts and goals of social justice present in the 1917 Constitution, were children, women, urban and industrial workers and the rural and indigenous populations.

During the initial years of the 1920s, in particular during the presidency of Álvaro Obregón (1920–1924), important measures were implemented to strengthen and extend the activities in matters of disease prevention, hygienic education, medical research and public health practice. In 1921 the DSP organized the first National Week of the Child in Mexico City and hygiene festivals in schools, and published pamphlets, books and articles with information on the adequate nourishment, health care, and disease prevention measures that children required. The revolutionary government's commitment to the vigor and well-being of school aged children gave rise to the creation of the Service of School Hygiene, whereby medical school inspectors assessed the physical, mental, and moral well-being of children, identified dental, visual and skin disorders, and encouraged vaccination, healthy lifestyles and bodily hygiene to school-aged children and their families. One year later, in 1922 the Section of Hygienic Education and Propaganda was established at the DSP under the leadership of physician Alfonso Pruneda. Its main objective was to disseminate and make accessible as widely as possible hygienic and health advice in homes, schools and factories. Among the most relevant topics the following stood out: personal hygiene, healthy food, sexually transmitted diseases, vaccination, pasteurized milk, and exercise. The DSP also began to published the journal *El Mensajero de la Salud* (The Health Messenger) in 1922, that used short stories, poems and recipes to advise the urban and rural populations how to preserve their health and to encourage the adoption of healthy habits and lifestyles.

The importance that public health policies and programs had for the revolutionary government prompted the establishment of the School of Hygiene (Escuela de Salubridad) in Mexico City in 1922, with the purpose of training numerous health professionals, including bacteriologists, medical inspectors, visiting nurses and vaccination agents. These persons, alongside the staff of the Department of Public Health, were entrusted with the obligation to oversee the adequate implementation and day-to-day functioning of health policies and programs. It was also during the early 1920s when several physicians—among them Miguel E. Bustamante—were sent to the most important medical schools in the United States—such as the Johns Hopkins School of Hygiene and Public Health—to update their knowledge of public health administration and so that popular health education, professional training and reorganization of permanent health departments could be implemented.

A new institution in the arena of public health in Mexico, as in other Latin American nations, was the Rockefeller Foundation. In 1920 the Rockefeller Foundation entered the country with the commitment to eradicate yellow fever in collaboration with the DSP throughout the state of Veracruz, a politically critical endeavor due to the 1914 United States invasion and occupation of the port of Veracruz and other diplomatic conflicts with the United States. The partnership between the Rockefeller Foundation and the DSP was encouraged by President Álvaro Obregón, who defined it as a "scientific" and "neutral" collaboration that would restore the public's confidence in the revolutionary government and its health campaigns. The work formally began in 1921, and its implementation relied on the collaboration of local and federal health authorities, on the support of Mexican physicians and of the general public. The endeavor formed part of the campaign to eradicate that disease from the Americas. Two years later, in 1923 when the US diplomatic recognition of Obregon's government took place, the Rockefeller Foundation and the Department of Public Health approved the organization of a campaign to contain hookworm, another endemic disease. Between 1924 and 1928 numerous mobile brigades staffed with United States and Mexican physicians and health personnel examined, treated and assisted the rural communities of the states of Chiapas, Oaxaca, Tabasco and Veracruz, carried out health and hygienic education campaigns and implemented sanitation programs.

Unequal medical services between the city and the country, the spread of avoidable diseases, and the absence of adequately trained medical and technical personnel to assist the people prompted numerous observers in the second half of the 1920s to state that the unhealthy condition in which the vast majority of the nation's population lived was the issue that had to be systematically and efficiently addressed. In 1926, during the presidency of Plutarco Elías Calles (1924–1928), the first sanitary code of the revolutionary era was decreed, and it established that Congress had the authority to promulgate general, mandatory and nationwide laws relative to the health conditions of the nation; that local authorities would have to comply with all health dispositions enacted and that they should aid the federal health authorities at all times. Also, it acknowledged for the first time, that rural health should be pursued systematically, and that health education programs, sanitary services and the practice of physicians, visiting nurses and other sanitary personnel in both urban and rural areas were of the greatest importance. Physician Bernardo Gastélum, director of the DSP from 1924 to 1928, not only expanded health education and public health programs in rural areas, but also implemented numerous campaigns against childhood and sexually transmitted diseases, smallpox, malaria and tuberculosis, and he was particularly concerned with the training of health professionals. In 1927, Gastélum with the support of President Calles, "called upon state governments to work in conjunction with federal authorities to improve the nation's health conditions" and he established the first municipal health units, composed of a doctor, a nurse and a health inspector to address the "local health needs as defined by the 1926 Sanitary Code." Two years later, the municipal health unit of the city of Veracruz under the direction of physician Miguel E. Bustamante was created, whereby the federalization of health services began. This measure also encouraged the creation of the Rural Hygiene Service (1931) under the leadership of Rafael Silva, director of the DSP between 1930 and 1932.

Other important transformations in the arena of public health were the establishment of the federal Industrial Hygiene and Social Prevision unit and the Service of Child Hygiene, both in 1929. The first had to supervise and guarantee the health of workers, the sanitary conditions of factories and other productive establishments, and to promote the hygienic education of all workers. The second was responsible for the protection and promotion of the health and well-being of children, and was entrusted with the obligation to impose all measures required to diminish infant mortality. Nation-wide health campaigns to contain alcoholism (1929), tuberculosis (1929) and leprosy (1930) began, and particular attention went to contain the spread of malaria in Campeche, Sinaloa and Veracruz, and along the central states of Hidalgo, Morelos and Puebla.

An important transformation began in 1933, when the Department of Public Health created the Federal Health Service in the States (Servicio de Sanidad Federal en los Estados) with the purpose to make efforts uniform and systematic and to quantify the work of all sanitary offices and delegations throughout the country. Particular attention was given to the control of communicable diseases, to the provision of basic health infrastructure and to health and hygienic education. One year later, the Law of Coordination and Cooperation of the Health Services of the Republic (Ley de Coordinación y Cooperación de los Servicios Sanitarios de la República) was decreed, and a new health code was issued (Código Sanitario de los

Public health nurse vaccinates a soldier before he joins the vaccination campaign in the countryside.
Photo from the Ministry of Public Health.

Estados Unidos Mexicanos, 1934), whereby rural health stood out as one of the main priorities of the revolutionary government.

Numerous health challenges remained in the countryside. Gastrointestinal conditions, respiratory diseases, epidemic and endemic smallpox and measles, among others, alongside poor sanitation, rampant malnutrition and widespread poverty were the norm. In 1935, when the First National Congress of Rural Hygiene was celebrated in Morelia, Michoacán, its participants—physicians, nurses, politicians and diverse government representatives from different states—emphasized that the spread of contagious diseases, the lack of basic health infrastructure, the widespread presence and practice of unlicensed physicians, and the scant number of licensed physicians in the countryside stood out among the obstacles that hampered all public health initiatives. Thus, it was urgently required to provide basic health infrastructure, to transform direction of the practice of medicine and to modify the predominantly urban scope of public health programs, issues clearly addressed by President Lázaro Cardenas, especially in his six-year plan (1934–1940).[2]

7.4. FAMILY: DOMESTIC RADIO PROGRAMMING AND BOARD GAME LOTERÍA

New Activities of Radio Cultural Programming
El Universal, March 6, 1927.

The subsecretary of public education decided yesterday [March 5, 1927] on new activities of cultural programming by radio. In order to contribute to the campaign against child mortality, the hygienist doctor Isidro Espinosa de los Reyes, chief of the school medical service, was commissioned to give weekly on Wednesday and Friday at the hour we will soon announce talks on food systems for children, from birth to school age.

Also the rules were adopted for convening a contest for English teachers to propose projects of methods to teach the language of Shakespeare on the radio awarding a prize and the class to the teacher that, in the judgment of a jury, proposes the best method.

Finally, teacher Guadalupe R. de Haro was appointed to give a domestic science course on the same network.[3]

LOTTERY GAME

A popular family board game since the late nineteenth century, lotería or lottery, much like bingo, was also played at local carnivals and fairs. Rather than numbers, the cards featured images that often reflected popular attitudes. The "Death Card"

The Mexican Flapper appeared on the Death card, lottery game.
Champion Folk Art Collection.

*shown above expressed a common view of the Chica Moderna. The game cards often served to tell parables and teach parental lessons.*⁴

7.5. POPULAR GROUPS: CULTURAL EFFERVESCENCE

William Spratling, "Figures in a Mexican Renaissance" (1928)

On returning to Mexico, one of the first things I attended to was looking up Diego Rivera. He was working on the last stages of his celebrated murals in the patio of the Ministry of Education, and as my companion and I entered the building he could be seen above, on the third-floor gallery, painting, his huge figure perched high on scaffolding.

"Que tal, Diego!" I called up in my limited Spanish. "Comment ça va, Spratling!" was the smiling response in good French. There followed introductions and interrogations, interrupted by the necessity for inspecting the glowing compositions of the recent panels. So interesting were they, and so powerfully did they demand my attention, that I must needs leave Diego in conversation with my friend—a prominent New York stage-designer, who, I was glad, also spoke perfect French—in order to follow up the amazing series of paintings that had taken place since I had last been there.

These were no formulated decorations, nor were they the abstracted results of a carefully individualized manner. It was sound painting, organic in every sense, and the impulse back of it was that of one who is fired by a great social consciousness and imagination, not merely by what might be "decor" in color. One felt the analysis of the strivings of a nation here.

Above the firmly drawn and powerfully painted figures in the panels ran the "canciones" of the people, their letters blazoned on simply draped ribbons which related the series. In some of this series Rivera had even employed caricature, and there was one where could be seen the capitalists of America dining, with only dollars in their plates, and a stockticker for a side-dish. Rule by the military class in Mexico also came in for its share of derision. One of the murals illustrated the obvious strength of the peasants as producers of food, with the verse "... el dinero sin alimentos no vale nada ..." draped appropriately above.

Returning to Rivera and S., I found my friend with note-book in hand. Diego was giving him formulas for encaustics and rules for applying paint. I caught a remark to the effect that the self-styled modernists would perhaps be better painters were they willing to learn their craft. Diego was explaining he found all this wealth of subjective material around him a means rather than an obstacle in his efforts to create form. I thought to myself that there indeed was a sound and attitude for one who was a painter and a man and, in this case, for one who was in touch with the problems of something greater than himself as an individual.

While we were there, men passed from time to time and frequently stopped for a word with the painter, seeking his opinion about this or that. It was clear that what he had to say carried weight. We left him being interviewed about something that had to do with imperialism, about which he expressed himself smilingly in a few short sentences, brush in hand; and, finally, he turned back with all intentness to the unfinished figures on the wall.

Before identifying himself with the revolution in 1910, Rivera had already studied abroad. His sense of nationalism for Mexico as well as his convictions about what was Mexican in painting doubtless began to crystallize during those months of working for the revolutionary cause and with the Zapatistas in 1910 and 1911. This is mentioned in his own biographical notes.

The years from 1911 to 1921 were spent mostly in France, where the influence of Picasso, and more particularly of Pissarro, both of whom were his good friends, made itself felt. Besides these, there were later influences, and in 1918 we find that he has remarked the importance of Cezanne and Renoir. It was about this period, too, that Rivera found a warm friend in Elie Faure, whose sympathy and reassurance doubtless meant much to the future leader of a modernistic movement in Mexico.

With the revolution of 1921 things began to happen for the cause of the arts in Mexico. It was at this point that Diego Rivera and his contemporaries, including Orozco, Guillermo Ruiz, a sculptor, and the young architect Carlos Obregon, fostered the formation of a sort of corporation of painters on the basis of a workmen's union. It was a great beginning and, though it must be said that the original group has not maintained its unity, much good work has been accomplished.

Rivera himself was commissioned, at stipulated laborer's wages, to execute his decorations for the National Preparatory School, and a year later, in 1923, began the now famous murals in the courts of the Ministry of Education.

This is an instance of what is happening culturally in Mexico to-day. The same sort of constructional vistas are opening up in other directions, and possibly most of all in public education, which department of the government has received more power to do good (in the form of substantial appropriations) than perhaps any other, even including that of war.

Moises Saenz, as subsecretary of education, has shown more untiring effort in the matter of educating the Indian than probably any other individual in the government there to-day. It being the peculiar problem of this administration to bring into class-consciousness and into effective suffrage native Indian Mexico, which forms a good third of the population, rural schools have been not only a crying need but actually the only specific means of bringing farflung communities into contact and making them integral with the nation. Here has been a problem for Calles's administration even greater than that of assimilating the cumbersome military machine.

This subsecretary is at work in many directions. He may be seen in his offices in the Secretaria—where he is a decidedly approachable person and where he keeps long hours—or he is apt to be met almost anywhere in the Republic, from evenings among the intelligentsia in the city to an encounter in some remote pueblocito, or Indian village, in the mountains. Among these people he is accustomed to make extended trips of inspection, and here his visits and talks take on a paternal aspect that amounts to something almost religious—judging from the honors and welcomes that attend his visits among them.

As a Mexican, he is a rather tall man. He has a decidedly pleasant manner, and is never more interesting than when talking about the educational problems of his government. It is easy to see that he is very much in earnest. Moreover, he talks well. He will be remembered in this country for a number of lectures which he has delivered at various universities, and particularly for those at the University of Chicago, which have since been published in a two-volume edition, along with articles by Herbert Priestly and Manuel Gamio. Interviewing him, one notes that he has the hands of an executive, large and well shaped. His features are strong, with a broad forehead and the thoughtful eyes of a scholar. When he smiles, there is revealed expansively a set of gleaming white teeth.

Like most educated Mexicans of administrative position, Doctor Saenz is well aware of what is going on abroad as well as in Mexico in matters of art and literature. He may not be interested in the abstractions of a Brancusi or in the musical ideas of an Antheil. However, it is significant of this "cultural renaissance" which Mexico is experiencing that men as broad in their sympathies as Saenz should be directing the educational policies of the nation.

In the fine old monastery that is now the Biblioteca Nacional in Mexico City, I found many books on the glories of Spain in the New World. Among them, and with its six tall volumes filling a large area of a certain shelf, was the work of Doctor Atl's on "Churches and Convents of Mexico," a richly illustrated and completely annotated study of the old buildings. Also there were the two thick volumes of his "Popular Arts of Mexico," which, I understand, has been out of print for some time. Having had the opportunity to see the "Churches and Convents" in the offices of the *Journal of the American Institute of Architects* in New York, to whom the Mexican Government had given a set, and being particularly interested in these things, I became desirous of an introduction to the man who seemed to know so much about them. He was hard to find, and I had almost decided that he was a mythical character. People would describe him as "Mexico's man of genius," and there were many stories of the variety of activities in which he interested himself. Few, however, seemed to know him personally. Finally, a friend on a newspaper managed it, and I met Atl.

He was living in the old Convento del Merced, in the oldest and most ruinous section of Mexico City. Passing from a busy market outside and entering through the tremendously thick portals into a great patio surrounded by seventeenth-century arcades gave us the sensation of coming into a somewhat vast and forgotten space.

Doctor Atl was in his study, a large vaulted room on the second floor, his back toward the door, and at that moment dictating to a dark-haired stenographer, who had black eyes and that sort of transparency of skin that only Mexicans of a higher class possess. He turned and with a quick movement was on his feet and ready with a hearty *embrazo* and many *felicitaciones* for my friend. He was a man in his late sixties, apparently dressed for an expedition, with whip-cord breeches and jacket of corduroy. His movements were quick and energetic and his face quite animated in talking.

In the ensuing conversation my newspaper friend found little to say, though he attempted now and then to question the doctor about his explorations of the volcanoes. But nothing must interfere with our talk about the business of Spanish architectural influences in Mexico and Latin America. And I listened well to this little man who, beyond doubt, had more knowledge about these things than any one living.

I broached the subject of the "churrigueresque," that byword of the late Spanish baroque which so many, whether students or not, like to apply indiscriminately. Almost all of the seventeenth and early eighteenth century buildings in Mexico (which period there is most fertile in imaginative quality and in vigor of detail) are thus classified. This idea the doctor repudiated thoroughly and with vehemence. "The series of architectural works of the seventeenth century have essentially Mexican characteristics and cannot possibly be confused with those of either Churriguera, Tome, Pedro de Ribera, Miguel de Figueroa, or any of the other Spanish architects of those times. Nothing could be more absurd!" Books were brought forth and comparisons made. They proved conclusively that what he had asserted was correct. Not only that, but in some cases in checking contemporary examples it even seemed that Mexican influence—the influence, that is, of her richly tropic plant forms—had had an even stronger effect on architectural form in Spain than Spain had had on the New World.

Not only has Atl made a twenty-five-year study of architectural Mexico, the results of which, published by the Mexican Government, are comprised in his "Las Eglesias y Conventos Mexicanos," but he is also a painter of note and has been exhibited successfully in Paris years ago. And he is still painting today with the same sense of experiment that invariably marks the true artist. Moreover, he is an indefatigable explorer, and besides being president of a well-known exploration society is regarded as the greatest authority on the Mexican volcanoes—Popocatepetl, Ixtaccihuatl, and Citlaltepetl (Orizaba). In other words, in Doctor Atl I had found a man who was not merely a perennial enthusiast on the subject of the architecture of his own country or an aimless "naturebug," but a man of broad application and a really important authority; also one for whom almost everything in life still holds the excitement of an adventure. On the whole, it was a decidedly worthwhile morning, as far as I was concerned. I was particularly pleased with the visit for the reason that the theories brought out in conversation had merely confirmed my own ideas as to the stimulating qualities of Mexico itself.

Doctor Atl, painter, explorer, and author of "Churches and Convents in Mexico," is known in his country as Mexico's man of genius. Carlos Obregon Santacilia is a young architect, representative of the generation which has come to the front since the revolution of 1921. Diego Rivera, Mexico's great modern painter, friend of Picasso, Pissarro, and Elie Faure, whose murals in the Ministry of Education have won him world-wide recognition, will have his first American exhibition in New York this winter.

A certain sculptural quality and a primitiveness of line that is almost Aztec marks the otherwise simply "modernistic" buildings of the young architect Carlos Obregon. Here is an example of one of the younger men who have come to the front since the revolution of 1921, and who today is recognized as the foremost of Mexico's *ingenieros architectos*. He is a well trained and able architect of about thirty years of age, and in the past four or five years has been responsible for the designing and construction of such buildings as the new Department of Public Health—an enormous group of buildings being erected in Mexico City—the remodelling of the Foreign

Figures in the Mexican Renaissance (Left: Dr. Atl, Carlos Obregón Santacilia, Diego Rivera; Right: José Clemente Orozco, Moises Sáenz, Frances Toor).
William Spratling, "Figures in the Mexican Renaissance," published in *Scribner's Magazine* 85 (January–June 1928).

Relations Office, and the splendid new Bank of Mexico, just completed. While it cannot be denied that these recent structures reflect in some measure ideals already advanced in contemporary French work (due, doubtless, to Obregon's contacts abroad), they are certainly far fresher and more vital forms of building than those to be found in the average State capital of the United States. Furthermore, it must be said that they do suggest a consciousness of what is native to Mexico, and that, after all, is the important thing back of all that is truly traditional.

I had rather begun to think of Jose Clemente Orozco as Mexico's "enfant terrible," judging from the murals and grim caricatures by this painter which I had seen either on the walls of the Preparatoria or published in political periodicals. The opposite was the case.

Going down to where he was painting, I found a quiet, visionary sort of man at work there. He was reticent in manner and even a little too modest about being drawn in pencil. That he was a man who possessed but one arm seemed a fact to which he apparently attached little importance. He even ventured a little joke about himself and ex President Obregon, who is famous for his one arm.

Orozco is well known in Mexico, where his work has more than once formed the bone of contention in bitter controversies. Aside from anything that might be said for or against his paintings, Orozco is indisputably a man of deep convictions and, like Rivera, his convictions extend beyond what relates to merely beauty in design. He is deeply conscious socially, and his pen caricatures are acrid and biting denunciations of bourgeois Mexico—when they are not merely amusing comments on current vulgarisms. Knowing these drawings, it is easy to visualize the unreasoning fear of the unprintable that inspired our good customs agents at the border to confiscate a collection of his drawings that had been arranged for exhibit in a California art gallery. It is easy, too, to understand Orozco's disgust with this sort of shallowness on the part of government officials. It was probably not the first time his drawings; done with such evident sincerity of conception, had been misunderstood.

As a matter of fact, Clemente Orozco is intensely an individualist, and one whose reactions to contemporary existence are not apt to be of the tame and well ordered variety. In this sense the only contemporary with whom he can definitely be compared is perhaps the German, George Grosse, with the exception that Orozco's paintings on the walls of the Preparatoria Nacional reveal constructive ideals of peculiarly far reaching importance.

Frances Toor, the editor of *Mexican Folkways*, is also, like Diego Rivera, "all over the shop" in Mexico—artistically speaking. She is the one American there who has consistently devoted herself toward preserving what is traditionally and indigenously Mexican in art, and not only this but to the cause of the artists as well. Hers is almost entirely a work of co-ordination and research, and at the same time she is thoroughly in touch with all the various movements and maintains a certain relationship between the departments of the government and the intelligentsia. The newspapers in Mexico like to refer to her as "la editora fecunda y sapiente," an appellation which both she and I found vastly amusing.

This "editora" is close to the Indian. She has travelled alone through many remote regions in Mexico for her material, and the results of these trips have occasionally formed priceless chapters in folkloric research. The names of her contributing editors make an impressive list and include such as Manuel Gamio, archaeologist and former educational leader in Mexico; Tata Nacho, the singer and composer; and Carleton Beals, the American writer and authority on things Mexican. Diego Rivera is her art editor.

Through Frances Toor I met many of the literati, including the younger group of poets and writers as well as the editors of the art magazine *Forma*, and Salvador Novo, who, with Xavier Villaurrutia, edits the literary monthly *Ulises*. Among this group could be found people from all branches of the arts, ranging from woodcut illustrators such as Fernando Leal and that other well known wood engraver Diaz de Leon to and including the Minister of Foreign Affairs, Genaro Estrada, who is also a distinguished novelist. Naturally, there are also newspaper people.

Rafael Valle, an editor of the *Excelsior*, and Esperanza Velasquez Bringas, brilliant publicity director for Calles's presidential campaign, and now head of the national libraries, could be seen among them. At the summer school, which has been an important phase of Mexico's intellectual development, most of these people could be found at one time or another, frequently themselves in charge of a special class in literature or archaeology. Their enthusiasm for cultural progress seemed to portend a real awakening for Mexico, and a more than merely social one.

It is the impossibility of separating these artists and writers from their period, from the toil and strivings of the nation, that lends them particular significance. With the promulgation of the agrarian laws and the gradual distribution of land—with the newly found rights of the laborer and the possibility of education for the Indian—new values have been established and the consciousness of these changes has become far-reaching and all-inclusive, providing for the painter not only mental stimulus but a new reason for being. Art in this sense need be no mere propaganda, since it may actually become a part of the fabric where formerly it was only accessory. The changes and social evolution of Italy of the quattrocento certainly provide no stranger background for a Renaissance than do the circumstances of Mexico of to-day with her scene of cultural growth being staged against a background of real primitivism.[5]

Note: Since this article was written, various minor changes have taken place in the Mexican government and among the newer periodicals there.

Indigenous Mexico.
Mexican Tourism Office.

Portraits and photographs of indigenous peoples, especially women in their colorful traje (traditional dress) appeared on stamps, in the newspapers, on calendars, and in advertisements for tourists. Select one of these categories and analyze an image from the many available on the Internet. The image above shows an example.

ADDITIONAL READING

Rochfort, Desmond. "The Sickle, the Serpent, and the Soil: History, Revolution, Nationhood, and Modernity in the Murals of Diego Rivera, José Clemente Orozco, and Dávid Alfaro Sigueiros," in *The Eagle and the Virgin: Nation and Cultural Revolution in Mexico, 1920–1940*, ed. Mary Kay Vaughan and Stephen E. Lewis. Durham, NC: Duke University Press, 2006, 43–57.

Leer en español

Rushkin, Elissa J., and Isabel Arredondo. "Serenata Transnacional por la Paz: Juliet Barrett Rublee and *The Flame of Mexico* [1932]," *Balajú: Revista de Cultura y Comunicación* 1, no. 2 (August–December 2015): 4–29.

NOTES

1. *Retablo* from the Champion Folkart Collection, Tucson, Arizona.
2. In William H. Beezley, ed., *Oxford Research Encyclopedia for Latin America*, online edition (New York: Oxford University Press, 2016). Reprinted by permission of Oxford University Press.

3. *El Universal*, March 6, 1927, 10.
4. The Mexican Flapper appeared on the Death card, in the 1920s lottery game from the Champion Folk Art Collection. Reprinted by permission of the Champion Folk Art Collection. For further discussion, see William H. Beezley, *Mexican National Identity: Memory, Innuendo, and Popular Culture* (Tucson: University of Arizona Press, 2008), 31–51.
5. *Scribner's Magazine* 85 (January–June 1928): 15–22.

CHAPTER 8

The Apogee of the Revolution, 1934–1940

Lázaro Cárdenas pushed the programs of the revolution to new levels during his presidency, 1934 to 1940. His popularity and his knowledge of the needs of the people resulted from his wide-ranging campaign trips that were totally unnecessary for election (given the official party machinery), the party's development of a comprehensive six-year plan, and his policy of allowing free telegrams to his office one afternoon a week. His emphasis included land distribution, worker benefits, educational opportunities, and his term has been called the regime "of drinking water," bringing potable water to small and medium-sized cities across the nation.[1] The character of the administration, described by most commentators as populist, focused on reclaiming the nation's human and natural resources for the nation. Nothing better expressed the president's commitment to redeem the nation's resources then his expropriation of the oil industry (8.1). His wife, Amalia Solórzano, always played a strong supporting role, and she recalled in her memoirs the family's part in the reaction to the oil expropriation (8.2). Cárdenas also promoted the nation's revolutionary programs through diplomatic programs throughout Latin America, especially with the cultural mission, part of the program he called the "Buen Amigo" program, with the Mexican ship, the *Durango* (8.3). The president's commitment to education, young people, and the secularization of society was portrayed in several films, two of which are presented here (8.4). The President was a romantic (he and his wife named the new presidential residence "Los Pinos," after the place in Michoacán where they first met) and consummate family man, supported by his wife and his young son, Cuauhtémoc. As a young man, he liked the mariachi music of his home state, but with his social revolutionary commitment, he chose the corrido "El Agrarista" as the anthem of his administration. The high culture music expression of his regime came in the ballet *La Coronela* written by Waldeen with music by Silvestre Revueltas (8.5).

8.1 POLITICS: CÁRDENAS EXPROPRIATES THE FOREIGN OIL INDUSTRY

President Lázaro Cárdenas, Speech to the Nation, March, 18, 1938

In each and every one of the various attempts of the Executive to arrive at a final solution of the conflict within conciliatory limits, . . . the intransigence of the companies was clearly demonstrated. Their attitude was therefore remediated and their position deliberately taken, so that the Government, in defense of its own dignity, had to resort to application of the Expropriation Act, as there were no means less drastic or decision less severe that might bring about a solution of the problem. . . . It has been repeated ad nauseam that the oil industry has brought additional capital for the development and progress of the country. This assertion is an exaggeration. For many years throughout the major period of their existence, oil companies have enjoyed great privileges for development and expansion, including customs and tax exemptions and innumerable prerogatives; it is these factors of special privilege, together with the prodigious productivity of the oil deposits granted them by the Nation often against public will and law, that represent almost the total amount of this so-called capital. Potential wealth of the Nation, miserably underpaid native labor, tax exemptions, economic privileges, governmental tolerance—these are the factors of the boom of the Mexican oil industry. Let us now examine the social contributions of the companies. In how many of the villages bordering on the oil fields is there a hospital, or school or social center, or a sanitary water supply, or an athletic field, or even an electric plant fed by the millions of cubic meters of natural gas allowed to go to waste? What center of oil production, on the other hand, does not have its company police force for the protection of private, selfish, and often illegal interests? These organizations, whether authorized by the Government or not, are charged with innumerable outrages, abuses, and murders, always on behalf of the companies that employ them. Who is not aware of the irritating discrimination governing construction of the company camps? Comfort for the foreign personnel; misery, drabness, and insalubrity for the Mexicans. Refrigeration and protection against tropical insects for the former; indifference and neglect, medical service and supplies always grudgingly provided, for the latter; lower wages and harder, more exhausting labor for our people. The tolerance which the companies have abused was born, it is true, in the shadow of the ignorance, betrayals, and weakness of the country's rulers; but the mechanism was set in motion by investors lacking in the necessary moral resources to give something in exchange for the wealth they have been exploiting. Another inevitable consequence of the presence of the oil companies, strongly characterized by their anti-social tendencies, and even more harmful than all those already mentioned, has been their persistent and improper intervention in national affairs. The oil companies' support to strong rebel factions against the constituted government in the Huasteca region of Veracruz and in the Isthmus of Tehuantepec during the years 1917 to 1920 is no longer a matter for discussion by anyone. Nor is anyone ignorant of the fact that in later periods and even at the present time, the oil companies have almost openly encouraged the ambitions of elements discontented with the country's government, every time their interests were affected either by taxation or by the modification of their privileges or the withdrawal of the customary tolerance. They have had money, arms, and munitions for rebellion, money for the anti-patriotic press which defends them, money with which to enrich their unconditional defenders. But for the progress of the country, for establishing an economic equilibrium with their workers through a just compensation of labor, for maintaining hygienic conditions in the districts where they themselves operate, or for conserving the vast riches of the natural petroleum gases from destruction, they have neither money, nor financial possibilities, nor the desire to subtract the necessary funds from the volume of their profits. Nor is there money with which to meet a responsibility imposed upon them by judicial verdict, for they rely on their pride and their economic power to shield them from the dignity and sovereignty of a Nation which has generously placed in their hands its vast natural resources and now finds itself unable to obtain the satisfaction of the most elementary obligations by ordinary legal means. As a logical consequence of this brief analysis, it was therefore necessary to adopt a definite and legal measure to end this permanent state of affairs in which the country sees its industrial progress held back by those who hold in their hands the power to erect obstacles as well as the motive power of all activity and who, instead of using it to high and worthy purposes, abuse their economic strength to the point of jeopardizing the very life of a Nation endeavoring to bring about the elevation of its people through its own laws, its own resources, and the free management of its own destinies. With the only solution to this problem thus placed before it, I ask the entire Nation for moral and material support sufficient to carry out so justified, important, and indispensable a decision. . . . It is necessary that all groups of the population be imbued with a full optimism and that each citizen, whether in agricultural, industrial, commercial, transportation, or other pursuits, develop a greater activity from this moment on, in order to create new resources which will reveal that the spirit of our people is capable of saving the nation's economy by the efforts of its own citizens. And, finally, as the fear may arise among the interests now in bitter conflict in the field of international affairs that a deviation of raw materials fundamentally necessary to the struggle in which the most powerful nations are engaged might result from the consummation of this act of national sovereignty and dignity, we wish to state that our petroleum operations will not depart a single inch from the moral solidarity maintained by Mexico with the democratic nations, whom we wish to assure that the expropriation now decreed has as its only purpose the elimination of obstacles erected by groups who do not understand the evolutionary needs of all peoples and who would themselves have no compunction in selling Mexican oil to the highest bidder, without taking into account the consequences of such action to the popular masses and the nations in conflict.[2]

8.2. FAMILY: THE FIRST LADY'S MEMORIES OF THE OIL EXPROPRIATION

Amalia Solórzano de Cárdenas

What can I say about the magnitude of emotion concerning the expropriation of oil? It has been written and talked about so much, there are so many testimonials by people who were involved in this national act. The general [*President Lázaro Cárdenas*] told me, "Cutie, I believe you should call on Women and encourage their participation in this moment in which the presence of all Mexicans is urgently needed. In a national call, work is necessary in the schools and in the families." So a collection was called for to pay the cost of expropriation. This was rather symbolic help, but, how beautiful was the response!

Immediately, we began to have talks to make plans and decided the collection would take place in Bellas Artes. Badges were made with the national symbol that we all proudly wore.

The wives of all the government officials, as well as of trade unions, women's associations, friends, everybody were invited. All the time, we were receiving the people who came; everyone was quick to adapt to the place and in turn formed groups. There has not been a response more beautiful than that. They arrived with animals, chickens and sheep, money, jewelry, wedding rings, baptism medals, distinct objects, miniatures, everything. The presence of the people was unique. It was very exciting, people were very motivated, wanting to help with nothing more than what they were carrying, but they would like to have done more, I don't know that they could have collaborated more. The children gave their piggy banks. I've seen evidence in the Bank of Mexico that children were given a receipt for their contributions. Cuauhtémoc and his friends went to give their little pigs that they had as banks.

These were days of much activity and great satisfaction. The generosity and quality of the people expressed in every form as they responded to this Act that marked forever our economic sovereignty.

The night of March 18, between 11 and 12 at night, the general asked me to wake up Cuauhtémoc and bring him down to the office to take a photograph. Even half asleep and leaning against the furniture, he appeared with his papa, with me, and some of the secretaries and assistants.

Twenty-five years after the expropriation, friends of the General wanted to give him a gift that consisted of a car and a driver. On finding out, he said to Pedro Ledezma, who had headed up the idea: "Give me something that I can give to the people." He first thought of building material to aid a school, creating a kindergarten, but in the end, there was so much that could be done. And, in those days, with the help of my in-laws, there had been opened the first sewing room in Jiquilpan and hence was born the decision to give sewing machines. So this had raised the car up at 350 sewing machines.

These were given to schools and were installed in particular so that poor people, with a desire to learn to sew, would have that opportunity. After classes ended in schools in the evenings, mothers could go to take cutting class and so they could make clothes with ease. Some sewing machines went to Jiquilpan, others to different places and the last ones were delivered in the Mixteca.[3]

8.3. MILITARY: NAVY—THE VOYAGE OF THE *DURANGO*

The Ministry of Foreign Affairs held a farewell banquet on February 27, 1940, in honour of Col. Ignacio Beteta's impending departure for South America as head of an extraordinary three-month-long artistic, military, commercial, and athletic mission of goodwill aboard the Mexican Navy's destroyer, the *Durango*.[a] The special embassy, which visited Chile, Peru, Ecuador, Panama and Colombia, included track and field athletes, tennis stars, a basketball team, boxers, cyclists, swimmers, shooting and fencing experts, an eighteen-member football team, an equal number of acrobatic motorcyclists, *charros* and polo players, twenty horses, eighty-one students each from the Escuela Militar and the Escuela Naval, members of the Orquesta Típica Miguel Lerdo de Tejada as well as several other popular artists, commercial representatives, and a team of journalists.[b] In each port of call, Beteta and the local Mexican diplomats arranged for commercial exhibits, conferences on the history of the Mexican Revolution, military parades, concert series, athletic exhibitions, competitions between Mexican and local athletes, and numerous receptions and diplomatic ceremonies. In Panama and Peru, the proximity of the port to the centres of government

---

[a] "Banquete en honor del Coronel Beteta," *El Universal* (Mexico City), February 28, 1940.
[b] For the list of participants Reyes Spíndola provided to the Chilean government, see AHGE, SRE, Expediente III-415-14 (II), Reyes Spíndola to Cristóbal Sáenz, February 27, 1940.

enabled the members of the mission to stay in one spot for the duration of the visit. In Chile the mission as a whole travelled by train the short distance to Santiago and participated in events in the capital and beyond. And in Ecuador and Colombia many members of the mission remained at port while Beteta and selected participants travelled to the Andean capitals.

At the goodbye luncheon, which was attended by members of the diplomatic corps and officials of the government ministries represented among the special embassy's nearly five hundred members, the goodwill ambassador's brother, Undersecretary of Foreign Affairs Ramón Beteta, wished the Colonel well on behalf of the Ministry. As *El Universal* reported, the objectives of the mission, in addition to extending fraternal greetings to the governments of the region, included the demonstration of the country's industrial and commercial capacity, its advances in the fields of physical and military education, and the beauty of its folklore.[c] The voyage of the *Durango* epitomised the cultural aspects of the *Política del Buen Amigo* the foreign policy pursued in Latin America during the presidency of Lázaro Cárdenas (1934–1940).

SPORTS

Athletics were particularly effective during the *Durango*'s tour, both in generating interest in the mission and goodwill towards Mexico, but also in portraying the youthful vigour of the Revolutionary government and the Mexican nation. The use of athleticism in cultural diplomacy had long been debated among members of the Foreign Service because they were quite risky.[d] One of the difficulties faced by the *Durango* in Panama was that disagreeable incidents had stained Mexican participation in the IV Juegos Centroamericanos held there in February 1938.[e] At the beginning of the games, the Mexican athletes had been the most applauded of all, but their success on the field soon gave the impression that they could not be beaten. The crowd turned against them and became violent, causing the police to intervene in a particularly brutal manner. The rest of the games were marred by negative attitudes towards the Mexican delegation and inflammatory articles about its athletes in the press.[f] Two years later, Minister Rosenzweig and Col. Beteta both worried that these incidents would cause the *Durango* to be met with a lack of enthusiasm in Panama City.[g] Nevertheless, after the special embassy's stay on the isthmus, Rosenzweig concluded that the mis-

---

[c] Ibid.
[d] On reciprocity for the 1939 visit of Peruvian cadets, see AHGE, SRE, III-415-14 (II), Anselmo Mena to Sáenz, January 29, 1940.
[e] AGN, LCR, Expediente 570/31, Beteta to Cárdenas, May 15, 1940.
[f] For details, see AHGE, SRE, Expediente 30-4-3 (VIII), Estrada Cajigal to Hay, "Reseña política de Panamá por los meses de enero y frebrero de 1938," March 10, 1940.
[g] AGN, LCR, Expediente 570/31, Beteta to Cárdenas, May 15, 1940.

sion had actually done much to repair the damage done during the Juegos; the mission had been a real success that would long be remembered by the people of Panama.ʰ

The athletic contingent of the *Durango* also contributed greatly to the success of the mission in Lima, helping it to overcome great odds. More than any of the other countries visited, some resistance to the idea of the special embassy had been evident in Peru. Prior to the *Durango*'s arrival, one conservative weekly warned that Peruvians should not forget that in addition to being athletes, artists, and cadets, the members of the mission were also representatives of the Revolutionary government of Mexico and its "bloody persecution" of the Roman Catholic Church.ⁱ On the one hand, the embassy brought a message of goodwill, while on the other it brought the political ideology it aimed to spread through the demonstration of Mexico's artistic, athletic, and military prowess.ʲ The Cárdenas government and its representatives played a rather delicate role in internal Peruvian politics because of APRA's affinity with the Revolution. In fact, chargé d'affaires Baumbach reported that Víctor Raúl Haya de la Torre had visited him to say that APRA wanted to organise a demonstration of sympathy for Mexico, but he had advised against it.ᵏ Baumbach had intended to organise a procession of all of the members of the *Durango* before Peruvian President Manuel Prado upon the mission's arrival in Lima, but Prado had declined the honour. Baumbach knew that the idea had been refused because the president feared that members of APRA would take the opportunity to demonstrate against the government and in favour of Mexico.ˡ The Peruvian government met the arrival of the *Durango* with trepidation, but both the President and the people were won over by the mission. Prado spontaneously suspended a cabinet meeting so that he could preside over the polo match held between the Mexicans and the Peruvian military's equestrian team at Lima's country club, and later that evening he resolved to decorate Beteta with the Orden Militar Peruana de Ayacucho, a high honour only rarely bestowed upon foreigners.ᵐ The sports contingent of the *Durango* proved very effective in establishing strong links with the pueblos of South America, on some occasions helping the embassy to overcome obstacles to the establishment of closer relations between Mexico and the host nation.

ʰ AHGE, SRE, Expediente III-415-14 (II), Rosenzweig to Hay, "Memorandum Reservado: Anexo al informe de la legación en Panamá sobre la visita hecha a este país por la misión presidida por el Coronel Don Ignacio M. Beteta," June 1940.
ⁱ "La Embajada Mexicana del 'Durango,'" *Verdades* (Lima), April 6, 1940.
ʲ Ibid.
ᵏ AHGE, SRE, Expediente III-415-14 (II), telegram from Baumbach to SRE, April 10, 1940.
ˡ AHGE, SRE, III-415-14 (I), Baumbach to Hay, April 27, 1940.
ᵐ Ibid.; "Magnífica Exhibición de Equitación Hicieron los Jinetes Aztecas y Peruanos," *La Prensa* (Lima), April 27, 1940; "El Embajador Coronel Beteta fué condecorado por el Mandatario de la Nación con la Orden Militar de Ayacucho," *Universal* (Lima), April 27, 1940.

During the *Durango*'s short stop in Callao on the way to Santiago, Jesús E. Ferrer Gamboa (one of the Mexican journalists aboard the special embassy) had given an interview to Lima's *La Prensa* in which he had stated that the Mexican government considered sports the most democratic medium through which to unify disparate peoples, because athletics were not influenced by racial or nationalist prejudices.[n] Nevertheless, as in the rest of Latin America, education specialists, public health advocates, and eugenicists alike championed physical education as a way to improve Mexico's "backward" and predominantly rural population during the Cárdenas era.[o] This project also related to José Vasconcelos's thinking on the raza cósmica, the theory of mestizaje that while turning European theories of race on their head, nevertheless accepted the existence of inferior and superior races and necessitated the assimilation of Mexico's indigenous population into the mestizo nation. The exhibition of Mexican athletes through the voyage of the *Durango* represented the apparently positive results of this nationalist project to the region, and the Latin American press seems to have accepted the image they presented wholeheartedly. *La Crónica* of Lima declared that never before had a delegation so large and bursting with the strength of youth arrived on Peruvian shores.[p] Reports of this tenor reflected Beteta's declarations to the effect that the athletic delegation represented the youth of Mexico's march towards perfection and "racial improvement."[q] When practiced scientifically, he continued, physical education enabled the pursuit of physical perfection, intellectual growth, and the development of moral and spiritual solidarity among its practitioners.[r] *La Crónica* echoed these remarks when it described the athletes as representatives of the youthful Mexican "race," full of optimism and the faith that the physical and spiritual strength gained through sport afforded them.[s] References to the athletes' youthful masculine vigour—and by extension that of the Mexican nation and "race"—abounded in the coverage of the embassy's activities throughout the region.

POPULAR ARTS/FOLKLORE

Perhaps only the Orquesta Típica Miguel Lerdo de Tejada, which sometimes played up to five times per day during the special embassy's visit

---

[n] "Notable Progreso ha Alcanzado en Méjico la Educación Física," *La Prensa*, March 19, 1940.
[o] On the eugenics movement in Mexico, see Nancy Leys Stepan, *"The Hour of Eugenics"*: Race, Gender, and Nation in Latin America (Ithaca: Cornell University Press, 1991).
[p] "Le Delegación Cultural y Deportiva de México partió ayer rumbo al Norte," *La Crónica* (Lima), April 28, 1940.
[q] "El Coronel Ignacio Beteta, presidente de la Embajada de México, nos hizo interesantes declaraciones antes de su partida," *La Crónica*, April 28, 1940.
[r] Ibid.
[s] "Recuentro de la actuación de la Embajada Cultural Deportiva Mexicana en Lima," *La Crónica*, April 29, 1940.

to Chile, created a more popular impression of Mexico than the athletic mission during the *Durango*'s voyage.[t] These "stage-managed displays of 'folklore' were also an implicit response to the racialized assumptions of Mexican backwardness."[u] But, more broadly, they sought to capitalize on the popularity of Mexican music and the appreciation of the country's typical dances and costumes to encourage admiration of Cárdenas's revolutionary government.

The artistic mission was overwhelmingly male—only five women were included: songstress Mercedes Caroza and four others who performed national dances and sang at performances of the Orquesta Típica.[v] Carlos González served as director of the artistic mission.[w] The Orquesta Típica played at nearly every event organised for the mission; dancers performed the *jarabe tapatío* at the Olympic pool in Panama City and in the *barrios populares* of Santiago.[x]

CONCLUSIONS

At the performance of the Orquesta Típica at the Teatro Sucre in Quito, noted pianist and musical critic Juan Pablo Muñoz Sanz stated that the embassy represented three characteristics of the Mexican national personality: art, nationalism, and revolution.[y] Focusing on popular music as an example of how these three dimensions informed each other, he argued that Mexican culture provided a prototype of *americanidad* for Latin America. Goodwill missions such as the *Durango* did much to create the international face of Mexico in the minds of Latin Americans, but they were also open to interpretation.

The *Oxford Dictionary of Critical Theory* defines a floating signifier as one that absorbs rather than emits meaning.[z] In his analysis of Edgar Allan Poe's "Purloined Letter," Jacques Lacan provides a useful example of the concept. "The content of the stolen letter is never known, its value depends on who

---

[t] AGN, LCR, Expediente 570/31, Reyes Spíndola to Cárdenas, May 1, 1940.
[u] Eric Zolov, "Showcasing the 'Land of Tomorrow': Mexico and the 1968 Olympics," *The Americas* 61:2 (October 2004): 159–188. Also see, Amelia M. Kiddle, "Cabaretistas and Indias Bonitas: Gender and Representations of Mexico in the Americas during the Cárdenas Era," *Journal of Latin American Studies* 42:2 (May 2010).
[v] "Mexican Good Will Mission Going to Chile," *La Estrella de Panamá*, March 12, 1940.
[w] AHGE, SRE, Expediente III-415-14 (II), Reyes Spíndola to Cristóbal Sáenz, February 27, 1940.
[x] "Una noche de arte tuvo lugar en la Piscina Olímpica," *La Estrella de Panamá*, May 12, 1940; AGN, LCR, Expediente 570.31, Beteta to Cárdenas, April 3, 1940.
[y] "Discurso pronunciado por el Sr. Juan Pablo Muñoz S. presentando a la orquesta típica mexicana en el Sucre," *El Comercio* (Quito), May 4, 1940. Juan Pablo Muñoz Sanz would later found Ecuador's Orquesta Sinfónica Nacional. Also see his contemporary works, *La música ecuatoriana* (Quito: Universidad Central, 1938); *Nacionalismo y americanismo musical* (Quito: Imprenta del Ministerio del Gobierno, 1938).
[z] "floating signifier," *Oxford Dictionary of Critical Theory*, accessed online 12/4/2013. http://www.oxfordreference.com/view/10.1093/acref/9780199532919.001.0001/acref-9780199532919-e-254.

holds it, whether the nobleman from whom it is stolen, the Minister who steals it, Dupin who retrieves it, or the Prefect of Police who organizes the retrieval. As form without inherent meaning, the letter continues to circulate, to be exchanged, or to float, and the signification or meaning is dependent upon who holds it, as well as the context in which it is found."[aa]

Five hundred Mexican emissaries floated to South America aboard the *Durango*. The ship itself was empty until the Mexican government filled it with motorcyclists, military cadets, and mariachis. The Cárdenas government attempted to fix the *Durango*'s meaning by employing journalists and lecturers to narrate the voyage and explain it to audiences back home and in the South American cities they visited. Nevertheless, the *Durango* represented different things to different constituencies. Conservative Catholics saw it as a Communist invasion, popular audiences saw its performances as a welcome break from the drudgery of everyday life, local athletes saw it as a threat to their masculinity and athletic prowess, workers and students saw it as a confirmation of the Mexican Revolution's relevance to their own struggles, eugenicists saw it as a validation of the vitality of mestizo Latin America. The Cárdenas presidency and indeed, the Mexican Revolution, like the *Durango*, meant different things to different people. Perhaps, like the purloined letter, its actual contents can never be known. [4]

8.4. CHURCH: THE PRESIDENT'S COMMITMENT TO THE SECULARIZATION OF SOCIETY

Watch one of the following films:
The Power and the Glory (based on the Graham Greene novel) *or Eisenstein in Guanajuato.*

8.5. POPULAR GROUPS: A CORRIDO AND A BALLET

Corrido "El Agrarista"

Voy a cantarles señores	I'm going to sing to you sirs
la canción del agrarista,	The song of the agrarian,
les dirá muchas verdades,	It will tell you many truths,
señores capitalistas.	Capitalist gentlemen.
Es el cantar de los pobres,	This is the tune of the poor,
que en el campo trabajamos,	In the fields we work,

[aa] Gordon E. Slethaug, "Floating Signifier," *Encyclopedia of Contemporary Literary Theory*, edited by Irena Rima Makaryk (Toronto: University of Toronto Press, 1993), 547.

los que con tantos sudores	With much sweat
nuestras tierras cultivamos.	Our lands we cultivate.
Don Porfirio y su gobierno,	Porfirio and his government,
formado por dictadores,	Made up of dictators,
nunca oyeron de su pueblo	never listened to the people's
las quejas y los clamores.	complaints and their clamor.
¡Ay... ay... ay... ay!,	¡Ay... ay... ay... ay!,
luchando por nuestro anhelo,	we're fighting for our desires,
murieron muchos hermanos,	many brothers are dying,
guardemos bien su recuerdo.	let's observe their memory.
Esta es la lucha del pobre	This is the fight of the poor
que sin miedo fue a la guerra,	Without fear they went to war,
a pelear sus libertades	To fight for their liberties
y un pedacito de tierra.	and a small piece of land.
Vino el apóstol Madero,	The apostle Madero came,
y al grito de "¡Redención!"	with a clamor of "Redemption!"
todo el pueblo por entero	all of the people
se fue a la revolución.	engaged in the revolution.
Mataron a don Panchito	They have killed Panchito
se subió Huerta al poder;	And Huerta rose to power;
pero el pueblo verdadero	But the true people's
no dio su brazo a torcer.	Arms could not be twisted.
¡Ay... ay... ay... ay!,	¡Ay... ay... ay... ay!,
luchando por nuestro anhelo,	we're fighting for our desires,
murieron muchos hermanos,	many brothers are dying,
guardemos bien su recuerdo.	let's observe their memory.
Pasó Carranza a la historia,	Carranza passed into history,
y el general Obregón	And the general Obregón
nos repartió nuestras tierras	distributed the land
por todita la nación	All over the entire nation
El general Calles, luego,	General Calles, then,
con su fuerte voluntad,	With his great generosity
protegió nuestros derechos	Protected our rights
y nos brindó su amistad.	And offered his friendship.
Y Cardenas hombre recto	Cardenas an upright man
Que rige nuestros destinos	Who governs our destiny
esta en el alma del pueblo	Is the soul of the people
uniendo a los campesinos.	Uniting the agrarians.

¡Ay... ay... ay... ay!,	¡Ay... ay... ay... ay!,
luchando por nuestro anhelo,	we're fighting for our desires,
murieron muchos hermanos,	many brothers are dying,
guardemos bien su recuerdo.	let's observe their memory.[5]

Len Mullenger reviews a recording of Waldeen's *La Coronela*

Waldeen, a U.S. born ballerina who came to Mexico to dance and stayed, choreographed the ballet "La Coronela" (The woman Colonel). The production was disrupted by the death of its composer, Silvestre Revueltas, and the music had to be completed by others for its premiere on November 23, 1940, in Mexico City. The sets were based on the drawings of José Guadalupe Posada. Then the music was lost, and another version was raised in the 1950s by José Limantour and Eduardo Hernández Moncada, which pulled in some material from other Revueltas scores to cover for music that could not be retrieved. A third version was created by Enrique Arturo Diemecke in the 1990s and this was recorded by him for the Mexican Spartacus label in 2000. This recording by Uruguayan conductor Gisèle Ben-Dor leading the Santa Barbara Symphony was made in 1998 and originally appeared on the Koch label; it makes use of the earlier, Limantour/Hernández Moncada score. As Gisèle Ben-Dor's other recordings, the performance is marvelously exciting, retaining a little roughness that is in keeping with Revueltas' own idiom. The ballet is filled out with a hair-raising account of a lesser-known Revueltas piece, "Itinerarios" (1938), which mixes heroic gestures with immeasurably sad ones and may be a personal reflection of the defeat of the Republicans in the Spanish Civil War. Ben-Dor's recording of "Colorines" (1932) is still the only one of this relatively early work in which Stravinskïan neo-classic gestures collide with Revueltas' typically noisy brand of nationalism.[6]

Watch the Waldeen ballet, La Coronela *[Available on video as* La Coronela *(1940) Punto de partida, CONACULTA, 2001], or listen to the symphonic production of it.*

ADDITIONAL READING

Knight, Alan. "Cardenismo: juggernaut or jalopy." *Journal of Latin American Studies* 26 (February 1994): 73–107.

Leer en español

Pérez Montfort, Ricardo. "La expression popular y el 18 de marzo de 1938." In *Estampas de nacionalismo popular mexicano: Diez ensayos sobre cultura popular y nacionalismo*, 2nd ed., 191–218. Mexico City: CIESAS, 2003.

NOTES

1. Luis Aboites, "The Illusion of National Power: Water Infrastructure in Mexican Cities, 1930–1990," in *A Land between Waters: Environmental Histories of Modern Mexico*, ed. Christopher R. Boyer (Tucson: University of Arizona Press, 2012), 223.

2. Online at https://www.youtube.com/watch?v=Vw2iINGwUa4 (16 minutes).

3. Amalia Solórzano de Cárdenas, *Era otra cosa la vida: Iconografía* (Mexico City: Instituto Politécnico Nacional, 2009), 143, 145.

4. Amelia M. Kiddle, *The Latin American Foreign Policy of Mexican President Lazaro Cardenas* (Albuquerque: University of New Mexico Press, 2016). Reprinted by permission of the University of New Mexico Press.

5. For videos of the corrido, see http://www.bing.com/videos/search?q=corrido+%22del+agrarista%22&view=detail&mid=09C2000A0C0CA62AAC9909C2000A0C0CA62AAC99&FORM=VIRE.

6. Silvestre Revueltas, *La Coronela, Itinerarios, Colorines* Santa Barbara Symphony, English Chamber Orchestra, Gisèle Ben-Dor Koch (1998) 3-7421-2, review by Len Mullenger, *Classical Music on the Web*, http://www.musicweb-international.com/classrev/march99/coronela.htm. Reprinted by permission of Len Mullenger, *Classical Music on the Web*. Also review of Silvestre Revueltas, "La Coronela," Santa Barbara Symphony, English Chamber Orchestra (*Colorines*)/Gisèle Ben-Dor, Re-issue of KOCH 3-7421-2H (1998), review by Bob Briggs, Music Web International.

CHAPTER 9

The Second World War, 1940–1945

The United States declared war on the Axis powers (Germany, Italy, and Japan) following what President Franklin D. Roosevelt called "the Day of Infamy," December 7, 1941. Mexico and other Latin American nations also broke diplomatic relations with the Axis countries; Mexico took the next step and declared war May 22, 1942, following German submarine attacks that sank Mexican oil tankers in the Caribbean. An estimated fifteen thousand Mexicans fought in the war in addition to the famous pilots of Squadron 201. A documentary provides an introduction to Mexico's wartime experience (9.1). Shortly after the declaration of war, Mexican officials initiated a program to intern individuals suspected of Axis loyalties, especially Japanese and Mexican-Japanese, some of whom were sent to the United States (9.2). Building hemispheric cooperation against the Axis included the efforts of the Office of the Coordinator of Inter-American Affairs, a US agency. Its director, Nelson Rockefeller, enlisted the assistance of such celebrities as Walt Disney to produce both educational and public health films; probably the most successful and popular brought together Donald Duck with two friends from Mexico and Brazil, called *The Three Caballeros* (9.3). The war initiated dramatic changes in society in terms of women's public roles, growing employment, guest worker experiences, and recreational activities. President Manuel Avila Camacho reduced government and church tensions when he responded to a reporter's question about religion, saying, "I am a believer." Popular, or day-to-day faith remained prominent and stressed the family as the crucial institution (9.4). During the war, Mexicans sent volunteers into battle, helped solve the US manpower shortage in industry, agriculture, and transportation, and provided critical raw materials to the war effort. Civilians in Mexico as in the United States had little in the way of luxuries because of wartime production demands, but music—on the radio, in the movies, and in nightclubs—flourished, and among the most popular groups was Los Panchos (9.5).

9.1 MILITARY: MEXICAN PUBLIC TELEVISION CHANNEL 22, "MEXICO IN WORLD WAR II. AZTEC EAGLES SQUADRON 201," *MEMORIA VIVA*[1]

This documentary, through interviews, provides different perspectives of the experience of World War II in Mexico. For example, it presents popular perspectives on who was responsible for sinking the Mexican ships that led to declaration of war. Some former members of Squadron 201 provide interviews. Of particular interest, the documentary discusses World War II as presented in Mexican and international cinema. Six movie clips contribute to this narrative: Los tres caballeros; Soy puro mexicano; Disney Pluto, The Army Mascot; Joaquín Pardave and Marga López, ¡La guerra apenas empieza!; Pedro Armendariz, ¡Yo estoy con los gringos!; *and* Casablanca.

Narrator

On May 22 of 1942, President Manuel Ávila Camacho declared war against the Axis countries: Germany, Italy and Japan. It was a state of war with all its consequences, but Mexico looked at it from a defensive perspective. In Mexico City, as well as other cities of the Republic, the government performed bombing simulations to train the people about the potential dangers of the war. The people experienced the war by the scarcity of products that were considered basic and strategic for the victory of the democracy. War propaganda, mostly on the radio, exalted the heroism and sacrifice of the Allies, among them the Mexican air force squadron 201. Using the memory of the protagonists and other witnesses, it is possible to interweave the experiences of them all.

Fernando Nava (Squadron 201)

I was studying in six grade at the Benito Juarez elementary school in the Colonia Roma, it was May—I think it was May 23—when suddenly the professor noticed that outside the classroom a news crier shouted that war was declared, that we were at war. I walked to my home that was five blocks away, and the first thing that I found when I opened the door was my dad, a military man—he was an Artillery colonel—and he was with four other assistants listening to the radio . . . I listened and we heard President Manuel Ávila Camacho with a dignified voice and great patriotism said that Mexico was at war to honor our flag and our ships.

Narrator
The declaration of a state of war . . . did not make clear what role Mexico would play in the conflict. Defensive war? Without a quota of blood? To dispel doubts, Avila Camacho sent a new message to the nation. The second transmission was broadcast on radio and connected to loudspeakers in public places he gave on the night of June 3.

Miguel Moreno Arreola (Squadron 201)
Mr. President made the message with a voice really full of anguish, but all in all, I knew it was saturated with a huge patriotism, right? And he said, "Although Mexico was not prepared for a contest of this nature, we would defend ourselves with all honor."

THREE YEARS BEFORE

Narrator
Everything started three years earlier, at 3:15 am on the first day of September 1939. The news agencies in Mexico received an urgent newsflash, preceded by the ringing of bells on the news ticker, "The Nazis had invaded Poland."
Auditorium of the Republic:
"We interrupt this program to inform you that Europe is in a state of war." [*original video*]
World War II was starting.

Joaquín Rivera Melo (Electrician)
So, back then, XEW to announce a news flash used to have a special noise: pi-pi-pi-pi, and said Germany just invaded Poland. That announced the war, of course! Three days later France and England declared war on Germany.
[*Music*]

Narrator
The war, after the initial commotion, became newsworthy. But, we were so far away! Thus, the blood spilled by the soldiers came as news to newspapers and magazines. The fire bombing crackled the news celluloid and the roar of the combat cannon thundered on the speakers of people's radios. Who would then imagine that Mexico would be involved in the conflict? Why should we participate in something that was foreign to us? Certainly . . . life in Mexico continued without major surprises.
[*Music*]

The weeks passed and the radio bellowed more and more news of the German deployment, while the Mexican press echoed the drama. The invasion of Norway and Denmark, the enormous pressure against England. The victories of Rommel's Africa Corps. The sudden fall of France.

[*Scenes from the movie,* Casablanca, *1942*]

Joaquin Rivera Melo (Electrician)
One day, I was walking in Reforma Street; It was about 10 am when an Extra came out: France has just surrendered! By that time, we already acknowledged that the war would last for many years.

Narrator
We had to learn to live with the absurdity of half the world on fire, and hope that someday things will get better.

Alfonso Cuellar Ponce de León (Squadron 201)
Mexico declared the war because their boats were sunk in the Gulf of Mexico. First, *Potrero del Llano,* it was a tremendous shock for the country. Of course, we were in the Second World War history. The thing was that Mexico declared war, and we had to work more intensely. We changed the statues to produce more war materials.

Narrator
Meanwhile, the uncertainty resulted in the lack of grocery products from overseas. . . .
[*Oral Histories*]
Back then, Salvador Novo noted, "Fortunately, neither Saturday nor Sunday did I run out of gasoline, caused by the shortage. I have started to get gasoline at Cantinflas's station and his secretary assured me that Mario's friends could count on every liter that we needed."

Jacobo Morett (Reporter)
So, there were tremendous lines of people with their little canister to go buy the kerosene; or long lines to buy coal or lines for tortillas, because they all were in short supply especially export products. The negative part for us was the war shortages, and the positive part was that we all felt very Mexican.

[*Scenes from the movie,* ¡Yo estoy con los gringos! (I am with the *gringos!*) *with Pedro Armendariz* (1942).]

Joaquín Rivera Melo (Electrician)
Well, it was at that time, there was no TV, but President Manuel Avila Camacho on a radio announced the news: Mexico is at war with the Axis. The axis was Italy, Germany, Fra . . . *[sic]* and Japan.

[Scenes from the movie, ¡La guerra apenas empieza! (c. 1942) with Joaquín Pardave y Marga López. The president announces that the United States was also in war.]

Narrator

And so it was! On Sunday, December 7, 1941, the Japanese attacked Pearl Harbor. XEQ news interrupted the transmission of the bullfight. Then between melodies and announcements from Perfumerías Urania, la Sal de uvas picot, los Almacenes la Francia Marítima or Fosfocreosol, the best tonic for coughs, the radio gave details of the attack that determined the participation of the United States in the war.

[Scenes from the movie, The Army Mascot, with Disney Pluto (1942).]

Mexico became the answer to many of the problems that arose for its northern neighbor. We provide the raw materials and labor.

[Oral Histories]

Jacobo Morett (Journalist)

We were elementary students when they revealed the event, we really had no capacity or were old enough to appreciate its magnitude, and not even its true dimension. However, the euphoria that erupted in the country, the nationalist psychosis was so strong, because it was impossible to escape from it. I really think of what I experienced and what I read, an awareness of integral nationalism awoke.

ADVERTISING BATTLEFIELDS

Narrator

At the end of 1941, because the United States and other countries in the hemisphere had already entered the conflict; the media launched a campaign to prepare the Mexican people, before the nation joined the conflict.

[Scenes from the movie, Soy puro mexicano (1942).]

Jacobo Morett (Journalist)

Mainly XEW and XEB, two radio stations, competed at the highest level in the struggle to win an audience with the news and the desire to create awareness in the population of the importance of the event that had awakening national consciousness.

[Scenes from the movie, Soy puro mexicano (1942).]

Narrator

The Mexican government created incisive slogans. For example, 1942 was "The year of the effort" and hence many radio messages with their patriotic vehemence heated up the national atmosphere. Until early May 1942, Mexico had followed the war through the media. An incident of April 23, 1942, when the Mexican boat *Tamaulipas* was attacked, this situation certainly changed the night of May 13, 1942, when a submarine attacked and sank *Potrero del Llano* a Mexican oil tanker.

Luis Pérez Carballo (Professor)
It was when we heard, What was its name? That the tanker was sunk, they didn't know who was it? It was *el Potrero del Llano*. Nevertheless, they were expecting to confirm why it was sunk.

Narrator
Now, the declaration of war approached. Our northern neighbor, our partner, started the deployment of its forces and diplomatically invited us to join, saying, "We must collaborate in the efforts."

Joaquín Rivera Melo (Electrician)
The official story was that German submarines were the ones who sank the Mexican boats. Of course, because nobody really believed. Because German submarines had more important targets. In 1942, Germany still maintained its prestige and with its hegemony in much of Europe, a large number of Mexicans admired it.

Jacobo Morett (Journalist)
In the end, everyone knew that Mexico was Germany-phobic, and at the beginning of the Second World War of 1939 the people were Germany-phobic too.

Luis Pérez Carballo (Professor)
Many Mexicans felt sympathy for the Germans, because of the way they worked to be someone.

Narrator
Hence, there were rumors that the attacks was the work of the Americans.

Hector Morales Zuniga (Electrician)
Pushed by the circumstances . . . haphazard events, maybe trickery . . . we believed the sinking of three Mexican boats, allegedly caused by a German submarine.

Narrator
The same ones who said that Germany had threatened to invade Mexico if President Avila Camacho dared to break the neutrality.

Joaquín Rivera Melo (Electrician)
There were many interests who favored that Mexico participate in the war; the United States feared that the Germans would land at the Gulf and the Japanese on the Pacific coast.

A DAY BEFORE . . .

Narrator
On 21 May 1942, another boat the *Faja de Oro* was attacked off Cabo Esperanza during its journey between New York and Tampico; seven crewmembers died. The next day Mexico would enter World War II.

MAY 22, 1942: DAY OF THE WAR ANNOUNCEMENT

Official Announcement: Outside of the Chamber of Deputies, a crowd congregates, including state workers who form a fence for the President of the Republic who came to the opening of the special session of Congress. Convened by General Manuel Avila Camacho and according with the decision taken at the First Council of the secretaries of state; in the sense of . . . declaring a state of war against the Axis powers. Military officers, workers, diplomats and senior administration officials, went to the camera in order to hear the transcendent message that the President will deliver to the Congress, on national crisis, caused by the treacherous attack on our ships by submarines of the totalitarian powers. The President has to face the danger, with the backing of a unified people against the aggressor. Again, throughout history, our country has been ready to defend its freedoms when attacked by those with ambitions of domination and power.

Luis Pérez Carballo (Professor)
All across the country, especially in Mexico City, a great—yes—euphoria of courage and patriotism was generated by the attacks on the Mexican tankers. Then the President of the republic announced the news on television [*sic*] that the sinking of the boats was attributed to the Axis.

Gen. Manuel Avila Camacho, Declaration of War
On the thirteenth day of May the attack came, not decided and frank, but muffled unfair and cowardly, between darkness and absolute confidence of impunity. A week later, they attacked repeatedly. Faced with a second aggression in violation of all norms of international law and involved an eagerness for the execution against our country and its free people a bloody outrage. I simply and courageously accept the realities and declare, according to the proposed advice of the secretary of state and heads of autonomous departments, who gathered in this capital on Friday 22 of the present

year, that as of this date there exists a state of war in our country against Germany, Italy and Japan.

[*Scenes from the movie* Azahares para tu boda *(1950).*]

Joaquín Rivera Melo (Electrician)
It was a spectacular news, Mexico was shocked! because it was entering World War II, it was something very serious.

Narrator
The declaration of war was a response to an unusual reality. However, things change quickly. Mexico was living in uncertainty, those violent years gave another physical appearance to our cities and societies. The war changed the world, and Mexico was no exception. Then came obligatory military service and 201 squadron.

Miguel Moreno Arreola (Squadron 201)
By then the squadron pilots' team was already formed. Squadron 201 was its name: Squadron for the Air Force, and 201 for a fighting game.

Narrator
On July 24, 1944, the squadron 201 of the Mexican Air Force went to the United States. The Mexican people curious and proud when they went to say goodbye at Balbuena airfield.

[*Background Music*]

Narrator
At Parak, Squadron 201 hoisted the Mexican flag on May 2, 1945.

Fernando Nava (Squadron 201)
And there, we were told, "This is where you will make your camp." We thought we would find sleeping facilities, but that night we slept on the ground.

Miguel Moreno Arreola (Squadron 201)
The next day we woke early with reveille and we lined up and the flag was raised.

Fernando Nava (Squadron 201)
And, at the center of the camp where we had settled, the national anthem was played.

Miguel Moreno Arreola (Squadron 201)
Someone out there even had a record player.

Fernando Nava (Squadron 201)
And I had a record player, which I had bought on the ship to do some business by renting it. They borrowed it from me and someone—I do not know who—had the record of the Mexican national anthem, so, that day the national anthem was played and the flag was raised.

Miguel Moreno Arreola (Squadron 201)
It was the most exciting thing I have ever felt in my life. The tears! It was very nice! *Pancho Pistolas* is the current logo of the Air Force, that was our logo: *Pancho Pistolas*.
[*Scenes from the movie* Los tres caballeros *(1944).*]

WAR ACTIONS

Fernando Nava (Squadron 201)
War missions, 96; offensive outputs, 786; defensive outings, 6; flight hours in combat mission, 1966.15; flight hours in combat zone, 595; the total flown 2557.15. Thousand pound bombs dropped 957 and 50 caliber cartridges expended 1666.992.

Narrator
On November 18, 1945, the US government sent back to Mexico fighters. Like a chronicle would say: "They returned victorious!"

Miguel Moreno Arreola (201 Squadron)
Well, return arrival in Mexico was beautiful. I was named to carry the flag, but I must tell you, that it was a tremendous thing, so, I could not hold it, I cried like a little child.

Fernando Nava (Squadron 201)
We had accomplished our task with honor, courage, our Patria entrusted us with a mission at the front of the Pacific War. So, after that, it was the end of the squadron.

EPILOGUE

Miguel Moreno Arreola (Squadron 201)
And . . . I think it was a great honor as far as I am concerned, and wish it never happens again, so that we do not have to walk through those things.

Direction: Eduardo Patino Díaz
Script: Fernando Orduña
Research: Rogelio Martínez

Performance: Salvador Camarena
Production Coordinator: Celia Barrientos
Contents Coordinator: Oscar Estrada
Testimonies Coordinator: Juan Jiménez P.

Testimonies:

Jacobo Morett
Joaquín Rivera Melo
Fernando Nava
Miguel Moreno Arreola
Alfonso Cuellar Ponce de León
Héctor Morales Zúñiga
Alfonso Plaza Gonzales
Luis Pérez Carballo

9.2 POLITICS: INTERNMENT OF JAPANESE AND JAPANESE-MEXICANS

With the declaration of war against Germany, Italy, and Japan or the breaking of diplomatic relations with the Axis Powers, the republics in the Americas reached the following agreement:

Those Axis nationals whose liberty threatens the security of the Hemisphere should be interned for the duration of the present conflict in detention camps established by the Government in interior regions of the country, which are removed from vital areas and, which offer special advantage for the ends sought. They may also be detained in custody pending expulsion to another American Republic for detention or internment.[2]

Excerpts from Densho, *"Uprooting Community:* New Book
Examines the WWII Mass Incarceration of Japanese Mexicans"

Selfa A. Chew, in her book, *Uprooting Community*, examined the experience of Japanese Mexicans in the U.S.-Mexico borderlands during World War II. She illuminated U.S.-backed efforts of the Mexican government to detain, deport, and confine its Japanese residents and Japanese-descent citizens. Their narratives challenge the interpretation that Japanese-Mexicans enjoyed the protection of the Mexican government during the war and refute the mistaken idea that Japanese immigrants and their descendants were not subjected to internment in Mexico. Through her research, Chew provided evidence that, despite the principles of racial democracy espoused by the Mexican government, *Japanese Mexicans* were in fact victims of racial prejudice bolstered by the political alliances between the United States and Mexico.³ Excepts provide these insights:

> Indicating the urgency of addressing the status of Japanese Mexicans, President [Manuel] Avila Camacho reported to the nation his government's actions against "the enemy" in his presidential address of 1942. In Avila Camacho's words, Mexico was spun as a heroic people facing open war against Italy, Germany, and Japan "because the entire nation has demonstrated with its attitude that, when the time arrives, each Mexican knows how to be a soldier determined to defend the motherland, by taking the arms or at their place of work; through productivity or through sacrifice (Applause)." The "defense of the motherland" consisted of the expulsion of Japanese Mexicans and their descendants from the borderlands and the coastal zones. *(63–64)*
>
> The small number of Japanese immigrants in Mexico by 1942 may obliterate the deep consequences of their eviction from U.S.- Mexico borderlands on the notions of what constitutes a democratic society and the meaning of citizenship. As is the case with the Japanese American community or any other social group whose civil rights were suspended during World War II, the implications of targeting a racialized sector in times of crisis are enormous if principles of equality and freedom are to be held as permanent and universal. Historians of the Japanese diaspora in Mexico believe that the number of Japanese immigrants in the borderlands ranged between 2,700 and 4,700 in 1942. Regardless of their number, the relocation program left all members of the Japanese Mexican community—including those born in Mexico, naturalized citizens, and the Mexican children and wives of Japanese immigrants—without the protection of the Mexican Constitution. *(66)*

On March 27, 1942, El Paso's newspapers informed their readers that a group of eighty Japanese from Juárez would have to leave the border city. If there were any qualms about their uprooting, the newspapers calmed them down, stating that the Japanese Mexicans had "been offered farming land in the prosperous farming community of Santa Rosalía [*Camargo*], near Chihuahua City, where they will be able to earn a living for the duration of the war." In fact, the displaced Japanese Mexicans did not stay in Santa Rosalía de Camargo or receive farming land. This group of uprooted borderlanders was held captive in Villa Aldama, Chihuahua. Governor Chavez forced them to work for Tomas Valles de Vivar, a wealthy politician and Chihuahua's treasurer.

In April 1942, despite their lack of resources to start a new life somewhere else, entire families took the train south of the state of Chihuahua. When allowed, other men chose to leave their children and spouses in Juarez, since their fates and the length of time they would be away from their usual occupations and means of support were unknown. Japanese Mexicans in Juarez were not the first group to evacuate the borderlands. The Mexican army and police in Baja California had already removed Japanese Mexican communities in January 1942 from the North Pacific area adjacent to the United States. By April, only those Mexican Japanese who could not travel to the interior for reasons validated by the Ministry of the Interior (Secretaria de Gobernacion) remained at home.

When military authorities ordered Jesus Kihara to leave his home in Juarez, he did not bring his family with him to Camargo. His Mexican wife and children would fare better in the company of their friends, and they all hoped the period of internment in a concentration camp would end soon. The haste of his travel did not allow him, or the rest of his travel companions, to carry any but the essential items they would need while away from their homes for an unspecified time. Later, uprooted Japanese Mexicans from Juarez would learn that, without appropriate housing, no amount of clothing would be enough to protect their bodies from the weather they endured for several months in Villa Aldama, Chihuahua.

Kihara's experience is an example of the troubles and tribulations that many Japanese Mexicans had to endure during the relocation program. Kihara and other Japanese Mexican men and women from Juarez arrived in Santa Rosalia de Camargo in the southeast region of the state of Chihuahua at the end of March 1942. Because the Mexican state did not supply the necessary food or clothing for the Japanese Mexican evacuees, the displaced men and women were responsible for acquiring basic supplies to survive during the days they spent in Camargo, a city located approximately seven hundred miles south of Ciudad Juarez. Some Japanese Mexican men managed in only a few days the difficult task of getting a job in the small city to pay for some of their life expenses. Such sources of income disappeared almost immediately, however.

On May 7, Kihara's group from Juarez, in addition to other, elderly Mexican Japanese individuals from Camargo, was forced to enter the city's jail. Chihuahua's governor, Alfredo Chavez, had ordered the incarceration of "nondangerous" civilians in a crowded space for three days "under the strictest surveillance." Even though Chavez admitted the innocence of the Japanese Mexican detained, he ordered their arrest. The group of displaced Japanese Mexicans was then escorted out and north of Santa Rosalia de Camargo to the hacienda property of Tomas Valles de Vivar in Villa Aldama. *(84–86)*

The Japanese in Mexico

In 1940, it was estimated that the population of Japanese nationals in Mexico was approximately 5,145 and Mexicans of Japanese ancestry (Mexican citizens) roughly 13,052 for a total Japanese population within Mexico of 18,197.[4]

[I]n January 1942, the Mexican government in cooperation with US authorities ordered that all Japanese be removed from Baja California, the rest of the West Coast, and into the interior. The evacuation program was carried out over a period of three months with approximately 2,100 Japanese removed from the states of Baja California, Colima, Sonora, Chihuahua, Sinaloa, Veracruz and Nayarit. The Japanese from these regions were evacuated to Mexico City and Guadalajara. The evacuated Japanese had to register with the Dirección General de Investigaciones Políticas y Sociales (IPS) (an agency in Gobernación) and then they were released on parole if they promised not to leave the designated area without permission *(145; 222, n. 25)*.

By May, 1944, Mexico had sent individuals from all three major Axis nations and their satellite countries to the United States for internment. Many others had been repatriated from Mexico to their native land. For example, above and beyond the fifty-three diplomats and their families who were repatriated in early 1942, over 335 Japanese diplomats from throughout Latin America and their families were returned to Japan. These individuals were from Washington, DC, Havana, Cuba, and Mexico City. Before their repatriation, Japanese diplomats from other Latin American countries were initially housed in the Greenbrier Hotel in White Sulphur/Springs, West Virginia, Grove Park Inn in Asheville, North Carolina, and the Assembly Inn in Montreat, North Carolina *(158–59)*.

Mexico sent a total of 84 Japanese to Chrystal City, Texas or to New Mexico for internment *(157)*. By comparison, Peru sent 1,799 Japanese [*in collaboration with the FBI*] for internment to the Unites States. All adult male Japanese in Cuba were incarcerated during the war *(22, n. 4; on Cuba, 221, n. 20)*. Mexico ordered all Axis nationals to evacuate at least 200 km (124 miles) from the coastlines and 100 km (93 miles) from the US-Mexican border *(222, n. 11)*. Other measures taken by the Mexican authorities included canceling all permits for Japanese fishing in Lower California waters, ordering all persons of the Japanese race to leave Lower California, removing Japanese residents in Barra de Navidad and Cahatlan and the Tampico region, putting into effect a program to remove all Japanese residing on the west coast of Mexico, closing all amateur and private experimental radio transmittal stations by presidential decree, authorizing the passage of United States troops through Mexican soil, and granting permission for American naval forces and military planes to use Mexican harbors and bases.

In 1957, the Mexican government paid 700,000 pesos as reparations to the Japanese community in Mexico for their suffering and loss during the war. Japanese business interests matched the Mexican funds and the result was the purchase of land and the establishment of the Mexico Japanese Association located in the Colonial Las Aguilas, Mexico City. The US issued an apology and reparations in 1980 *(222, n. 12; 143; 194)*.

US Government documents on internment of Japanese and Japanese Latin Americans

Chief
Washington Office
AIS

The 28 Japanese who were deported from Bolivia on 18 May for internment in the U.S. were all members of two fanatical and alarming nationalistic and imperialistic groups. Furthermore, almost all of the individuals have close relatives who live in Japan and all were members of the principal Japanese Society of Bolivia. The possibility of fanatical acts by Japanese in Bolivia has been considerably reduced by their removal, since they constituted ready tools for any subversive activities or overt acts of sabotage which might be ordered by the Japanese Government.

A/E Bolivia, Cable No. 1198. 6 June 1944

A-2 War Dept. only

81 Axis subjects were deported from Bolivia on 18 May 1944, 28 of whom had not been approved by the Enemy Alien Control Unit of the Department of Justice. Of these 28 individuals 21 are Japanese. Great concern was expressed by the Department of Justice because the 28 persons were not previously approved for internment in the U.S. by the Department of Justice and it was indicated that they would not accept these persons unless information was forthcoming that they are proper individuals for internment. It is believed that the above is in support of the case for the deportation and internment in the U.S. of the 21 controversial Japanese individuals and that it is information desired primarily by the Enemy Alien Control Unit for approving their internment.

JO ZACH MILLER, III

DECLASSIFIED
Authority NND 750122

14 June 1944.

AIS-SS

SS, Special Intelligence Branch
AIS, Miami Beach, Florida

CHIEF,
WASHINGTON OFFICE,
AIS

now The 28 Japanese who were deported from Bolivia on 18 May for internment in the U. S. were all members of two fanatical and alarmingly nationalistic and imperialistic groups. Furthermore, almost all the individuals have close relatives who live in Japan and all were members of the principal Japanese Society of Bolivia. The possibility of fanatical acts by Japanese in Bolivia has been considerably reduced by their removal, since they constituted ready tools for any subversive activities or overt acts of sabotage which might be ordered by the Japanese Government.

A/E Bolivia, Cable No. 1198, 6 June 1944.

A-2   War Dept. only.

81 Axis subjects were deported from Bolivia on 18 May 1944, 28 of whom had not been approved by the Enemy Alien Control Unit of the Department of Justice. Of these 28 individuals 21 are Japanese. Great concern was expressed by the Department of Justice because the 28 persons were not previously approved for internment in the U. S. by the Department of Justice and it was indicated that they would not accept these persons unless information was forthcoming that they are proper individuals for internment. It is believed that the above is in support of the case for the deportation and internment in the U. S. of the 21 controversial Japanese individuals and that it is information desired primarily by the Enemy Alien Control Unit for approving their internment.

1-2-3-4-5-6-7-8

CONFIDENTIAL

JO ZACH MILLER, III,

EDWARD J. ENNIS
DIRECTOR

Department of Justice
Alien Enemy Control Unit
Washington 25

May 18, 1944

REPLY TO: LG:rt

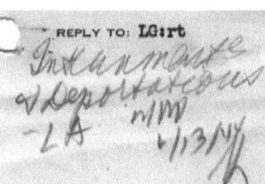

Lieut. Colonel George D. Dorroh
Chief, Visa & Passport Control Branch
Military Intelligence Service
Washington 25, D. C.

Dear Sir:

I have your letter of May 1 requesting certain statistics as to aliens deported to the United States from Latin America for either repatriation or internment.

Our records indicate that 1780 German civilians, 1247 Japanese civilians and 195 Italian civilians have been deported to the United States from the Latin American Republics since December 7, 1941.

Of this number 1216 German civilians, 822 Japanese civilians and 59 Italian civilians were repatriated to their respective countries of origin in the course of various exchanges between the United States and the Axis powers.

With respect to your question titled (c), the number presently interned in the United States, broken down according to the countries from which they were deported, is as follows:

Country	Germans	Italians	Japanese	Misc.	Total
Panama	43	1	1	7	52
Dominican Republic	21	1	1	1	24
Honduras	51	1		3	55
Costa Rica	160	8		2	170
Guatemala	88			4	92
Nicaragua	37	6		4	47
El Salvador	19			2	21
Peru	46	5	471		522
Bolivia	7			1	8
Colombia	24				24
Mexico	1	2	6	3	12
Ecuador	2				2
Haiti	4				4
	503	24	479	27	1033

Japanese internment documents.
United States National Archives and Records Center.

The Axis powers had made careful and intensive preparations for a number of years for political conquest of American republics. South American wealth and natural resources were of special importance to Germany and Japan and both embarked upon a plan of control in South America. When the Nazis began their penetration they found circumstances ideal for their purpose. There were the solid German settlements, the existing German organizations, and a strongly established economic position with roots in the Reich. The Japanese penetration took a course across the Central portion of the continent, which extends from the State of Sao Paulo in Brazil to the plains of Huaral in Peru, thus dividing the South American continent into two sections. A feature of Axis preparation for domination of Latin America was the dispatch to the American republics of a miltitude of trained agents, oftentimes disguised as diplomats, business men, tourists, and cultural and religious missions, etc. These agents served as centers for espionage and propaganda and for stimulation of political dissention and confusion.

By the beginning of World War II the Axis had strongly entrenched themselves in the economic and political life of the Latin American republics and had infiltrated into the military leadership of many of the Armies of Latin America.

Included among the capabilities of Axis organizations and agents in Latin America at the time of the present conflict were:
  (a) Interference with our program to acquire necessary strategic materials.
  (b) Collection of intelligence for submarine operation against Allied shipping.
  (c) Jeopardizing the security of the Panama Canal by assisting any

- 2 -

Of this number no alien deported from Latin America has been either released or paroled from internment except a group of 12 aliens who were brought to the United States from British Honduras at the request of Military Intelligence, and were subsequently released by request of the Secretary of War, after investigation established that they should not have been apprehended originally and deported to this country.

This Department has from time to time granted to certain of these aliens internment at large. This internment at large recognizes their status as internees but permits them to accept employment in certain areas where they can contribute to the relief of the employment shortage. Such aliens are selected only after the most careful consideration of the reports from Latin America, which indicate that in a number of instances the charges against them were either without foundation or were based upon rumor from sources that could not be identified as reliable, and their camp behavior has established that they are not disloyal to the United States. Our records show that 97 Germans, 6 Italians, no Japanese, and 27 aliens of other nationalities have been favored in this respect. Most of the Germans were Jewish refugees from Panama, and that number includes husbands, wives and children.

I believe this information fully answers the inquiries in your letter of May 1.

Very truly yours,

Edward J. Ennis
Director

Japanese internment documents.
United States National Archives and Records Center.

DECLASSIFIED
Authority NND 750122

SECRET

CHECK SLIP
(Informal)
(DO NOT REMOVE FROM THIS PAPER)

HEADQUARTERS AMERICAN INTELLIGENCE COMMAND
MIAMI BEACH, FLORIDA

FILE NO.

NOTE: Use this slip for notes in connection with this paper. All notes will be NUMBERED CONSECUTIVELY, top to bottom. Papers should have attached all records necessary for intelligent action. A line will be drawn the full width of the slip below each note. Both sides of routing slip will be used before additional sheets are added.

SUBJECT: VON OPEL

NO.	DATE	FROM	TO	REMARKS
	27 Apr. 1944	Major GILLESPIE	Chief, SIB thro' Exec., SS	1. There is no record in SS on VON OPEL. The name has been checked under both ways of filing. Evidently this is due to the fact that VON OPEL has never resided in Latin America. There is a card on Federico OPPEL in SS, but this does not appear to be the same man as subject. 2. From newspapers and hearsay it has been learned that Fritz VON OPEL came to the U.S. from Liechtenstein before England entered the war with Germany. He is a member of the VON OPEL family which manufactured small automobiles in Germany and amassed a rather large fortune. Subject renounced his German citizenship probably for tax purposes, became a citizen of Liechtenstein, and, therefore, proceeded to the U.S. At the time the U.S. entered the war, VON OPEL was living at Palm Beach, Fla. When the FBI began rounding up enemy aliens, subject and his wife were arrested and interned in Texas. It is understood that there has been a hearing in Miami within the last 6 months on VON OPEL's petition for release, and that his petition was denied. It is thought that Mrs. VON OPEL was released. 3. Full details on current status of

(USE BOTH SIDES)

See SD Cable 2417, 17 April 1944, from Am. Leg. Bern, to SD

DECLASSIFIED
Authority NND 750122

CONFIDENTIAL

AFH/ncd
27 April 1944

AIS-SS

SS-3953   SS, Special Intelligence Branch
           AIS, Miami Beach, Florida

                                    xxxxxx
AMERICAN UNIT (AIS)
WASHINGTON, D.C.
                                    XX

NECESSARY FOR A STAFF STUDY BEING PREPARED ON THE DEPORTATION AND INTERNMENT SITUATION IS CERTAIN STATISTICAL INFORMATION WHICH IS NOT REVEALED IN FULL BY OUR RECORDS. (FOR MASSENGALE FROM NAYLOR) IF READILY AVAILABLE FROM WASHINGTON SOURCES PLEASE ADVISE THE NUMBER OF GERMAN, ITALIAN, AND JAPANESE CIVILIANS BROUGHT TO THE U.S. FOR INTERNMENT FROM LATIN AMERICA SINCE THE OUTBREAK OF WAR; THE NUMBER OF THESE REPATRIATED IN THE VARIOUS EXCHANGES BETWEEN THE U.S. AND THE AXIS POWERS; AND, BROKEN DOWN ACCORDING TO THE INDIVIDUAL COUNTRIES, THE NUMBER INTERNED AT PRESENT IN THE U.S. ALSO DESIRED IS THE NUMBER OF AXIS NATIONALS WHO HAVE BEEN REPATRIATED ON NEUTRAL SHIPS DIRECT TO EUROPE FROM THE OTHER AMERICAN REPUBLICS, AND THE NUMBER OF AXIS NATIONALS FROM LATIN AMERICA WHO HAVE BEEN RELEASED IN THE U.S. UNDER THE "INTERNMENT AT LARGE" PLAN.

                                                        COX

Copy No. 1-2-3-4
of 4 copies.

CONFIDENTIAL

Japanese internment documents.
United States National Archives and Records Center.

DECLASSIFIED
Authority NND 750122

CONFIDENTIAL

MID/TH
BNM-dh

SX-2842

30 March 1944

SX Special Intelligence Branch
AIC, Miami Beach, Fla.

AIS WASHINGTON   X

SUITCASE OF LEITGEB FOR CURTISS FROM NAYLOR YOUR 1842 HAVE IT SENT TO MID WASHINGTON WHERE MASSENGALE CAN WITH SPECIAL BRANCH WORK IT OVER QUERY WHO IS SUBJECT, WHERE HAS HE BEEN, IS HE INTERNEE OR DEPORTEE WHAT MORE ABOUT HIM CAN YOU FIND OUT OR DO YOU KNOW

COX

1,2,3,4

Copy 2 - Chrono.

CONFIDENTIAL

Japanese internment documents.
United States National Archives and Records Center.

The evacuation of enemy aliens from Latin American countries has been a continuing problem to the U.S. Faced with the fact that many of the American republics have not taken effective steps to curb the freedom of action of dangerous Axis nationals, the U.S. continues to press for the deportation of such enemy aliens to this country for internment.

There are two methods used to safeguard the security of the hemisphere:

1. Internment of dangerous Axis agents.
2. Repatriation.

It is the consensus of opinion that internment must be preferred to repatriation and must constitute the basic security policy respecting dangerous Axis agents and nationals. Repatriation necessarily results in the return to the Axis countries of numerous individuals who possess useful information concerning vital military, political, and economic affairs in the hemisphere, or who may be trained for military service. It is known that certain German nationals who were repatriated disseminate subversive propaganda to Latin America by means of short wave radio; also Germany faces a man-power shortage and could well use repatriated men of military age.

There are two exceptions to the basic policy against repatriations:

1. Recognized program of exchanging officials following declaration of war or severance of diplomatic relations.
2. Exchange of ordinary private persons.

There have been two difficulties with regard to deportations.

1. The reluctance of the Department of Justice to accept for internment Axis nationals who were not dangerous enough to meet the domestic requirements for internment in the U.S.,
2. The statutory regulations and political attitude of a considerable number of American republics which prevented their deporting Axis nationals to the United States for internment.

An attack on the initial difficulty was made by the Department of State with the Department of Justice, which in early 1943 sent two of its officers of the Enemy Control Unit on an extensive trip of those South and Central American republics which were least opposed to sending Axis nationals to the U.S. for internment.

The second of the afore-mentioned difficulties was handled through the medium of the Committee for Political Defense held in Montevideo in May 1943. The committee adopted the resolution which provides for recommendation to the governments of American republics of the need for:

1. The adequate detention of dangerous Axis nationals, and
2. The deportation of such persons to another American republic for detention when adequate local detention facilities are lacking.

In practically all instances it has been necessary for the U.S. to participate with the individual Latin American countries in order to effectively promulgate control of dangerous enemy aliens. This participation has been of two types:

1. In the form of the bilateral oral agreements between our Government and that of a particular American Republic, under dangerous Axis nationals are sent from the Central and South American countries to the U.S. to be interned. This type of control measures has been used successfully in all of the Central American Republics and in Panama, Ecuador, and Peru.
2. Another type of control program in which the U.S. has participated is exemplified in the country of Cuba, where the U.S. is financing the internment program, whereby dangerous aliens are interned on the Isle of Pines.

The majority of the Central and South American countries have cooperated willingly with the U.S. in the control of Axis nationals. However, Argentina, Bolivia, Chile, Paraguay, Uruguay, and Venezuela have refused to take steps against the Axis nationals, while Colombia has only recently agreed to effect control measures against Axis nationals.

Not encouraging to future cooperation from Latin American countries has been the recent action of the Department of Justice in releasing in the United States a number of Axis nationals from Latin America. These released internees were found jobs at standard American wages and were placed in the custody of their employers. When this treatment becomes known to the Latin American countries they will interpret this as a change of policy by the U.S. which they will feel free to imitate. It appears that the advantages thus bestowed on deported persons are of such character as to irritate many informants and democratic sympathizers and will thus subject the American officials to much embarrassing criticism.[5]

9.3. THE MILITARY

Popular Image of Soldier.
The *Picot Song Book* cover.

Army Nursing Unit.
Official Mexican army magazine.

9.4. CHURCH AND FAMILY: FRANCISCO DE PAULA ENTRALA, *BIENAVENTURANZAS*—THE UNOFFICIAL BEATITUDES OF THE FAMILY

1. Happy the family that has discovered that it is not the same striving to make a home, than simply to be preoccupied with building a house.
2. Happy the family that has recognized that it is not the same to talk seriously, putting in its place, merely, telling something that happened.
3. Happy the family that knows that it is not the same to share what one owns than to lend something or, from time to time, "to be charitable."
4. Happy the family that understands that it is not the same to practice religion and its rituals, than to live the faith and that faith is life.
5. Happy the family that learns to practice tolerance when differences arise and to put love above all else; love that everyone believes and practices it above all.
6. Happy the family that confides in its children, honors his elders, and attends to the weak and, little by little, builds a better society.
7. Happy the family that is the seed of new family that will continue on the pilgrimage to love.⁶

9.5 POPULAR GROUPS: *THE THREE CABALLEROS* (1944) AND LOS PANCHOS

Watch the Disney film The Three Caballeros.

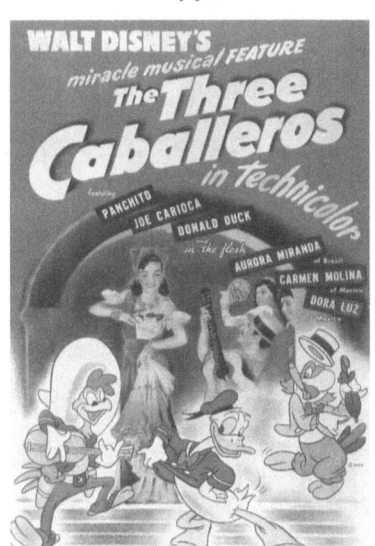

Cover of *The Three Caballeros* film soundtrack.

Los Panchos, established in the 1940s, became an internationally famous trio singing romantic ballads. They quickly sold over a million copies of their records and appeared in over fifty films of the Golden Age. The three original members were Alfredo Gil and Chucho Navarro from Mexico, and Hernando Avilés from Puerto Rico. Gil, in an interview, said they named the group for the three most famous Panchos in Mexican history—Pancho Madero, Pancho Villa, and Pancho Pistolas.

Their early hit songs included "Solamente una vez" and "Perfidia," both of which have intriguing recording histories. Agustín Lara (1897–1970), the famous singing star and composer, wrote "Solamente una vez" (literally, "Only Once," but translated into English as "You Belong to My Heart"), and tenor José Mojica introduced it in the 1941 film Melodías de América. Numerous other bands quickly covered it. The Disney production team retitled it "You Belong to My Heart," with English lyrics (they have no similarity to the original) written by Ray Gilbert and Dora Luz sang it in The Three Caballeros. (Disney used it again in the short, Pluto's Blue Note in 1947.)[7]

The Mexican, Hollywood, and Disney films resulted in numerous copies of the song, and it continued to be recorded for many years. Besides Los Panchos, other Spanish versions included those by Benny Moré, Ignacio Piñeiro, Pedro Vargas, Julio Iglesias, Roberto Carlos, Andrea Bocelli, Chucho Valdés, Plácido Domingo, Nat King Cole, Marty Robbins, Lucho Gatica, Guadalupe Pineda, Roland Shaw & His Orchestra, Luis Miguel, and Cliff Richard and the Shadows. The first English-language covers came from Bing Crosby and the Xavier Cugat orchestra and Elvis Presley, as part of the Million Dollar Quartet.

"Perfidia" (Perfidy), a song of love and faithlessness, was written by Alberto Domínguez (1911–1975), who published it in 1939. Xavier Cugat's recording of it became a hit in 1940. It was followed by an instrumental version, then another with lyrics in English translation by Milton Leeds. Cuban bandleader Desi Arnaz sang the Spanish version in the 1941 film Father Takes a Wife, starring Gloria Swanson. Director Wong Kar-wai used this version in his films Days of Being Wild, In the Mood for Love, and 2046. Many others have recorded "Perfidia," including Xavier Cugat, Hugo Montenegro, Julie London, the Four Aces, Charlie Parker, Laurel Aitken, Bud Roman and the Toppers, Mel Tormé, Olavi Virta, Café Tacuba, Glenn Miller, Nana Mouskouri, King Tubby, Phyllis Dillon, James Last, the Ventures, the Shadows with and without Cliff Richard, Trini Lopez, Linda Ronstadt (in Spanish and English), Nat King Cole, Sara Montiel, Los tres caballeros, and Javier Solís (in Spanish), Lawrence Welk, Luis Miguel, Isaac Delgado, mandolinist Dave Apollon, Olivia Molina, Perez Prado, Freddy Fender, Ibrahim Ferrer, Los Rabanes, Andrea Bocelli, Alfredo Sadel, Ray Conniff, Duke Pachanga, Frank Galan, John Altman, Ben E. King, Café Tacuba, Wilbert Alonzo Cabrera, and many others. An English arrangement of "Perfidia" was also the founding song of the Princeton Nassoons, Princeton University's oldest a cappella group.[8]

Listen to a Spanish- and an English-language version of these two songs.

ADDITIONAL READING

Shale, Richard. "Donald Duck Joins Up: The Walt Disney Studio during World War II." In *Studies in Cinema*, no. 16, ed. Diana M. Kirkpatrick. Ann Arbor: University of Michigan, UMI Research Press, 1982.

Leer en español

Aurrecoechea, Juan Manuel. "Paquete de sorpresas: Disney, México y *Los tres caballeros*." *Universidad de México* (Febrero 2003), 129–33. Online at http://www.revistadelauniversidad.unam.mx/ojs_rum/files/journals/1/articles/15621/public/15621-21019-1-PB.pdf.

NOTES

1. Online at https://www.youtube.com/watch?v=51AqhAvZuBA [2014]. Also see http://wn.com/escuadr%C3%B3n_201.
2. Jerry García, *Looking Like the Enemy: Japanese Mexicans, the Mexican State, and US Hegemony, 1897–1945* (Tucson: University of Arizona Press, 2014), 150. Reprinted by permission of the University of Arizona Press.
3. This article, a blog entry, is online at http://www.densho.org/uprooting-community-new-book-examines-the-wwii-mass-incarceration-of-japanese-mexicans/; its subject is Selfa A. Chew, *Uprooting Community* (Tucson: University of Arizona Press, 2015). Page numbers for excerpts from Chew are in italics. Reprinted by permission of the University of Arizona Press.
4. García, *Looking Like the Enemy*, 221, n. 4. Subsequent citations will be shown as italicized page numbers in text. Also see Correspondence from Edward J. Ennis, Department of Justice, Alien Enemy Control Unit to his agency, Ibid., 223, n. 33; and Major, G.S.C., Assistant military attaché Cantwell C. Brown, "Restrictions on Enemy Aliens in the State of Chiapas. Military Intelligence Division, Mexico City, December 1, 1943," NARA, record group 165, entry 188, box 993, *Records of the War Department General and Special Staffs*. Office of the Director of Intelligence G-2, Subordinate Offices Latin American Branch, 1940–46.
5. Emergency Advisory Committee for Political Defense, "Detention and Expulsion of Dangerous Axis Agents and Nationals, May 21, 1943," NARA, record group 165, *Records of the War Department General and Special Staffs*, Office of the Director of Intelligence G-2, Subordinate Offices Latin American Branch, 1940–46, entry 188, box 990.
6. Francisco de Paula Entrala, *Las Bienaventuranzas (páginas De La Familia): Novala De Costumbres* (1923; Charleston, SC: Nabu Press, 2012), 31, in Spanish. And see http://www.laverdadcatolica.org/F33.htm.
7. Recordings of "You Belong to My Heart" can be located at the Allmusic.com and YouTube websites, and the sheet music on several websites.
8. "Perfidia" recordings can be found on the Allmusic.com YouTube websites. Numerous movies, including *Casablanca*, and novels have featured the song.

CHAPTER 10

The Miracle, 1945–1985

The "Miracle" defined a period of economic growth and political stability following World War II. Standard studies make general references to the Miracle and examine particularly political and economic developments, but few have investigated its precise details. Eric Zolov names the short story "Battles in the Desert" as an excellent introduction to the era. Another possibility is to consider one of two films, *Los olvidados* or *Nosotros los pobres*, that capture post–World War II society. The story and the films offer an introduction to the era and provide information for discussion of popular religion (10.1). Other documents underscore the economic and political forces that helped to propel the nation's and the capital's dramatic growth, with magazine covers serving as murals of society's glitz, glamor, and humor. Magazines such as *Jueves de Excelsior* displayed at kiosks and hawked by vendors reached many more persons than the murals ever did in the decades before (10.2). Other documents emphasize the social and cultural consequences of the Miracle. The economic growth, social improvements, and international reputation of the nation resulted in the decision to have Mexico host the 1968 Olympics, only to witness weeks before the games the disaster of the student demonstrations and the massacre at Tlatelolco (10.3). In about a decade and half, the capital city suffered an additional calamity with the earthquake of 1985 (10.4). Popular culture experienced and registered all these major changes that defined the era (10.5).

10.1. INTRODUCTION TO THE ERA THROUGH SHORT STORY AND FILM

José Emilio Pacheco, "Battles in the Desert" (1987 translation)

The past is a foreign country.
They do things differently there.

—L. P. Hartley, *The Go-Between*

I. The Ancient World

I remember, I don't remember. What year was it? We already had supermarkets, but still no television, only radio: *The Adventures of Charles LaCroix, Tarzan, The Lone Ranger, The Legion of the Dawn Treaders, The Child Professors, Tales from the Streets of Mexico, Panseco, Doctor I.Q., Doctor Lovesick from Her Soul Clinic.*

Paco Malgesto narrated the bullfights; Carlos Albert covered soccer games; Mago Septien was the baseball announcer. The first postwar cars had begun to circulate: Packards, Cadillacs, Buicks, Chryslers, Mercurys, Hudsons, Pontiacs, Dodges, Plymouths, De Sotos. We went to see Errol Flynn and Tyrone Power movies, to matinees featuring an entire film from beginning to end. My favorite was *The Mongo Invasion*. The most popular songs of the day were "Without You," "La Rondalla," "My Little Donkey," "La Mucura," "My Little Love." Once again, an old Puerto Rican bolero could be heard everywhere: "However high the heavens or the skies, / however deep the ocean lies, / nothing in the world from you will keep / my love for you so true and deep."

It was the year of polio: the schools were full of children with orthopedic devices; the year of the foot-and-mouth-disease: tens of thousands of sick cattle were being shot throughout the country; the year of the floods: downtown had once again become a lake, and the people rode in boats through the streets. They say that with the next storm, the sewage system will burst and inundate the capital. So what, my brother answered, we are living up to our ears in shit anyway under Miguel Aleman's regime.

The face of El Señor Presidente was everywhere: immense drawings, idealized portraits, ubiquitous photographs, allegories of progress showing Miguel Aleman as Our Father Who Art in Heaven, laudatory caricatures, monuments. Public adulation, incessant private abuse. As punishment, we had to write in our notebooks a thousand times: I must obey, I must obey my parents and my teachers. They taught us national history, national language, geography of the capital city: the rivers (there were still rivers), the mountains (they were still visible). This was the ancient world. The grown-ups complained about inflation, exchange rates, traffic, immorality, noise, delinquency, overpopulation, beggars, foreigners, corruption, the limitless wealth of the few and the abject misery of almost everyone else.

The newspapers said: This is an anguished moment for the entire world. The specter of final war is hovering on the horizon. The atomic mushroom was the dismal symbol of our times. Nevertheless, there was still hope. Our textbooks confirmed this: Mexico, as can be seen on the map, is shaped like a cornucopia, a horn of plenty. For a still unimaginable 1980, a future of plenitude and universal well-being was predicted, without specifying just how it would be achieved. Clean cities without injustice, poor people, violence, congestion, or garbage. Every family with an ultramodern and aerodynamic (words from that era) house. No one will want for anything. Machines will do all the work. Streets full of trees and fountains, traveled by silent, nonpolluting vehicles that never collide. Paradise on earth. Finally, utopia will have been found.

In the meantime, we modernized and incorporated into our vocabulary terms that had sounded like Chicanoisms when we had first heard them in the Tin Tan movies and then slowly, imperceptibly, had become Mexicanized: *tenquiu, oquei, uasamara, sherap, sorry, uan moment pliis*. We began to eat *hamburguesas, pays, donas, jotdogs, malteadas, aiscrim, margarina, pinutbuter*. Fresh juice drinks of lemon, jamaica, and sage were buried by Coca-Cola. Only the very poor continued to drink *tepache*. Our parents soon got used to drinking *jaibol*, even though at first it had tasted to them like medicine. Tequila is prohibited in my house, I once heard my Uncle Julian say. I serve only whisky to my guests: We must whitewash the taste of Mexicans.

II. Ravages of War

During recess we used to eat those kinds of cream tarts that no longer exist. We played in two gangs: Arabs and Jews. Israel had just been established and there was a war against the Arab League. The children who really were Jews and Arabs only insulted each other or fought when they spoke. Our professor, Bernardo Mondragon, said to them: You were born here. You are as Mexican as your fellow students. Don't pass on the hatred. After all that has happened (the endless massacres, the extermination camps, the atomic bomb, the millions and millions of deaths), the world of tomorrow, the world in which you will grow up and be men, should be a peaceful place, without crime, without vileness. A short laugh rang out from the back row. Mondragon watched us sadly, probably asking himself what will become of us over the years, how many evils and catastrophes are we yet to witness.

The extinguished brilliance of the Ottoman Empire still persisted like the light of a long-dead star. For me, a child of the Roman Quarter, both Jews and Arabs were "Turks." The "Turks" didn't seem as strange as Jim, who was born in San Francisco and spoke two languages without an accent; or Toru, who was brought up in a concentration camp for Japanese; or Peralta and Rosales. They did not pay tuition; they were on scholarship; they lived in the rundown neighborhood called the Doctors Quarter. The Highway of Piety—not yet renamed Cuauhtemoc Avenue—and Urueta Park formed the border line between the Roman Quarter and Doctors.

Little Rome was another town altogether. The Bag Man lurks there. The Great Kidnapper. If you go to Little Rome, my son, they will kidnap you, scratch your eyes out, cut off your hands and your tongue, then throw you out into the streets to beg, and the Bag Man will take everything you get. During the day he is a beggar; at night he is an elegant millionaire, thanks to the exploitation of his victims. The fear of being near Little Rome. The fear of riding the streetcar over the Coyoacán Avenue bridge: only rails and girders. Underneath runs the dirty River of Piety, which sometimes overflows when it rains.

Before the war in the Middle East, our class's main sport revolved around giving Toru a hard time. Slant eyes, Chinaman, ate the shit and away he ran. Watch out, Toro, I'm going to nail you up by the horns. I never joined in with the jeers. I thought about how I would feel if I were the only Mexican in a school in Tokyo; about how Toru must suffer when he sees those movies that portray the Japanese as gesticulating monkeys who died by the thousands. Toru was the best student in the class. He excelled in every subject. Always studying, with a book in his hands. He knew jujitsu. One time he got sick of it and almost tore Dominguez to pieces. He forced him to get down on his hands and knees and beg for forgiveness. Nobody messed with Toru after that. Today he manages a Japanese factory and employs four thousand Mexican slaves.

I am from the Irgun. I will kill you: I am from the Arab League. The battles in the desert began. We called it that because it was a courtyard of red earth—brick and volcanic rock dust—without any plants or trees, just a cement box in the back. It was built over a passageway leading from the house on the corner to the street across the way that was used as an escape route during the times of religious persecution. We thought this underground area was a vestige of some prehistoric era. Nevertheless, the Cristero war was closer to us at that time than our infancy is to us now. This was the religious war against reform in which many members of my mother's family participated as more than just sympathizers. Twenty years later she continued to worship martyrs like Father Pro and Anacleto Gonzalez Flores. No one, on the other hand, remembered the thousands of dead peasants, the agrarian reform advocates, the rural professors, the press gangs.

I did not understand anything: war, any war, seemed to me to be the stuff of which movies are made. Sooner or later the good guys win (who are the good guys?). Fortunately, there had been no wars in Mexico since

General Cardenas squelched the Saturnino Cedillo uprising. This was difficult for my parents to believe, because their childhood, adolescence, and youth were spent against a background of constant battles and executions. But things seemed to be going well that year. Classes were constantly being called off so they could take us to the inaugurations of highways, avenues, sports arenas, dams, hospitals, ministries, enormous buildings.

As a rule, they were nothing more than a pile of rocks. The president inaugurated enormous unfinished monuments to himself. Hours and hours under the sun without so much as a sip of water—hey, Rosales, bring some lemons, they're great to quench your thirst, pass one over here—waiting for Miguel Aleman to arrive. Young, smiling, simpatico, shining, waving from aboard a cattle truck surrounded by his retinue. Applause, confetti, paper streamers, flowers, girls, soldiers (still wearing their French helmets), gunmen, the eternal little old lady who breaks through the military barricade and is photographed with El Señor Presidente as she hands him a bouquet of roses.

I had many friends, but my parents did not like any of them: Jorge because he was the son of a general who fought against the Cristeros; Arturo because his parents were divorced and he was looked after by an aunt who charged people to read their fortunes; Alberto because his widowed mother worked in a travel agency, and a decent woman should never work outside the home. That year Jim and I became friends. During these inaugurations, which had become a natural part of life, Jim would say: Today my father is going to come. And then: Do you see him? He is the one with the sky-blue tie. There he is, standing next to President Aleman. But nobody could distinguish him from all those other heads plastered with linseed oil or cream. But yes, they often published pictures of him. Jim carried the clippings around in his knapsack. Did you see my dad in *El Excelsior*? How strange: you don't look like him at all. Well, they say I look like my mother. I'm going to look like him when I grow up.

III. Ali Baba and the Forty Thieves

It seemed strange for Jim, whose father was an influential businessman and held an important position in the government, to be attending a run-of-the-mill school more appropriate for those of us who lived in the downwardly mobile Roman Quarter than for the son of Miguel Aleman's omnipotent close friend and banking partner. Every time the president blinked, Jim's father made millions: contracts for everything; land in Acapulco; import-export and construction permits; authorization to establish subsidiaries of North American companies in Mexico; stocks in the asbestos industry just when a new law was proclaimed requiring all porches to be lined with carcinogenic asbestos; the reselling of powdered milk destined for free school breakfasts in poor neighborhoods; falsification of vaccinations and medicines; enormous dealings in gold and silver on the black market; large parcels of land bought for pennies an acre just weeks before the announcement of a new round of development projects that would raise the value ten thousand times; a hundred million pesos changed into dollars and deposited in Switzerland the day before the devaluation.

Even less comprehensible was that Jim would live with his mother in an apartment on the third floor near the school rather than in a mansion in Las Lomas, or at least in Polanco. Strange. . . . Not really, the others would say during recess. Jim's mother is that guy's *mistress*. His wife is an old hag who always appears at social events. If you want to see her, just watch where they're giving things away to poor children (ha, ha, my dad says that first they make them poor and then they give them handouts). She's obese and repulsive. She looks like a cross between a parrot and a mammoth. But Jim's mother, on the other hand, is young, beautiful. Some people think she is his sister. And, Ayala chimed in, he isn't the son of that son-of-a-thieving-bastard who's fucking Mexico over anyway. His father is a *gringo* journalist who took his mother with him to San Francisco and then wouldn't marry her. The Señor doesn't treat Jim very well. They say he's got women all over the place. Even movie stars and things like that. Jim's mother is just one of many.

That's not true, I answered. Don't talk like that. How would you like it if they talked about your mothers that way? No one dared say these things directly to Jim but, as if intuiting what they were saying, he insisted: I don't see my dad very much because he's always abroad, working for his country. Sure, whatever you say, Alcaraz replied: "Working for his country"—Ali Baba and the forty thieves. At home they say they're even stealing what isn't there to steal. The whole Aleman government is just a den of thieves. Why don't they buy you a new sweater with the money they steal from the rest of us?

Jim starts to fight and doesn't want to talk to anybody. I cannot imagine what would happen if he found out what they were saying about his mother behind his back (when Jim is present, our classmates limit their attacks to the Señor). Jim has become my friend because I do not judge him. In other words, it is not his fault. Nobody chooses how, when, where, or to whom one is born. We will no longer participate in the recess wars. Today the Jews took over Jerusalem, but tomorrow the Arabs will get their revenge.

After school on Fridays, Jim and I would often go to the Rome, the Royal, the Balmori: movie theaters that no longer exist. Lassie or young Elizabeth Taylor movies. And our favorite was the triple feature we must have seen a thousand times: *Frankenstein, Dracula,* and *The Wolfman.* Or the double feature: *Adventures in Burma* and *God Is My Co-Pilot.* Or even the one Father Perez del Valle loved to show on Sundays in the Club Vanguard: *Goodbye,*

Mr. Chips. It made me as sad as when I saw *Bambi.* I saw that Walt Disney movie when I was three or four, and they had to drag me out of the theater in tears because [the] hunters had killed Bambi's mother. They killed millions of mothers during the war. But I did not know that; I did not cry for them or their children, even though in Movieland—along with Donald Duck, Mickey Mouse, Popeye the Sailorman, Woody the Woodpecker, and Bugs Bunny cartoons—they showed the newsreels: bomb formations falling on cities, cannons, battles, fires, ruins, dead bodies.

IV. A Middle Ground

I had so many brothers and sisters I could never invite Jim over to my house. My mother was always cleaning up after us, cooking, or washing clothes. She would have loved to buy a washing machine, a vacuum cleaner, a blender, a pressure cooker, an electric refrigerator (ours was one of the last existing iceboxes that needed to be loaded with a fresh block of ice every morning). At that time my mother could only see the narrow horizon she had been shown at home. She detested everyone who was not from Jalisco. She thought that all other Mexicans were foreigners and particularly loathed those from the capital. She hated the Roman Quarter because all the good families were beginning to move out and only Arabs, Jews, and Southerners—people from Campeche, Chiapas, Tabasco, Yucatan—were moving in. She scolded Hector who was already twenty years old, and instead of attending classes at the National University where he was enrolled, spent his days at the Swing Club and in pool halls, cantinas, and whorehouses. His greatest passion was to talk about women, politics, and automobiles. Everyone complains so much about the military, he would say, and just look at what happens to the country when they stick in a civilian president. If they had not cheated my dear General Henriquez Guzman, Mexico would be in as good shape as Argentina is now with General Peron. You'll see, you'll see how things are going to be around here in 1952. I'll lay odds Henriquez Guzman will be president, with the Revolutionary Party or against it.

My father spent all his time at his soap factory, which was rapidly going under due to the competition and marketing of the North American brands. The new detergents were being advertised over the radio: Ace, Fab, Vel, and they proclaimed that soap was a thing of the past. While for most of us (still ignorant of the dangers) all those suds meant cleanliness, comfort, well-being and, for women, a liberation from endless hours at the wash basin, they were, for my family, the crest of a wave that was sweeping away our privileges.

Monseigneur Martinez, the archbishop of Mexico, decreed one day of prayer and penance to halt the advance of communism. I will never forget that morning. During recess, while I was showing Jim one of my Big Little

Books—those illustrated stories with tabs in the upper corners of the pages that look like cartoons when you thumb through them quickly—Rosales, who had never picked on me before, shouted, Hey, look at those two faggots. Let's go beat the shit out of those faggots. And he started to attack me. Your mother's a whore. You son-of-a-bitch. Just you wait and see who's a faggot, you fucking Indian. The teacher pulled us apart. I had a split lip, and his nose was bleeding all over his shirt.

Thanks to that fight, my father taught me not to scorn others. He asked me who I fought with. I said Rosales, that Indian. My father said that in Mexico we are all Indians even if we do not know it or want to be and that if the Indians were not poor, no one would consider it an insult. I called Rosales "trash." My father pointed out to me that nobody is to blame for living in poverty and before judging others I should ask myself if he has had the same opportunities as I.

Compared to Rosales I was a millionaire, but next to Harry Atherton, I was a beggar. The previous year, when I was studying in Mexico High School, Harry Atherton invited me over to his house in Las Lomas: underground pool room, swimming pool, a library with thousands of leather-bound volumes, a butler, wine cellars, gymnasium, steam bath, tennis courts, six bathrooms (why do the homes of wealthy Mexicans always have so many bathrooms?). His room looked out onto a sloped garden with a waterfall and lots of ancient trees. Harry had been sent to Mexico High School instead of the American one so that he could be totally immersed in a Spanish-speaking environment and thus familiarize himself with those people who would be his helpers, his eternal apprentices, his servants.

We ate dinner. His parents did not say a word to me and spoke English throughout the entire meal. Honey, how do you like the little spic? He's a midget, don't you think? Oh Jack, please. Maybe the poor kid is catching on. Don't worry, dear, he won't understand a thing. The next day, Harry said to me: I'm going to give you some advice. Learn how to use your silverware. Last night you ate your filet with your fish fork. And don't make so much noise with your soup, don't talk with your mouth full, chew slowly, and take small bites.

The exact opposite happened with Rosales right after I came to this school, when the problems at my father's factory had already made it impossible for him to pay the tuition at Mexico High School. I went to Rosales's house to copy some civics notes from him. He was an excellent student, the best in composition and spelling, and we all took advantage of him for things of this sort. He lived in a neighborhood constructed out of boards. The broken pipes inundated the patio. Shit floated in the greenish water.

His twenty-seven-year-old mother looked like she was fifty. She was very friendly to me and, although I had not been invited, they shared their dinner with me. Brain tacos. They made me sick. A strange grease similar to car oil oozed out of them. Rosales slept on a straw mat in the living room. His mother's new lover had banished him from the only bedroom.

V. However Deep the Ocean Lies

After the fight with Rosales, Jim was convinced that I was his friend. One Friday, he did something he had never done before: he invited me to his house for an after-school snack. I was sorry I couldn't invite him over to mine. We walked up to the fourth floor and opened the door. I have a key because my mother doesn't like to keep a maid. The apartment smelled of perfume; it was tidy and very clean. Garish furniture from Sears Roebuck. A picture portrait of his mother by Semo Studios, another picture of Jim on his first birthday (the Golden Gate Bridge in the background), many more of the Señor on the Olive Train, in the presidential airplane, in group photos. "The Cub of the Revolution" and his team. The first university graduates to govern the country. Technicians, not politicians. Impeccable moral fiber, the propaganda insisted.

I never thought Jim's mother was going to be so young, so elegant, and above all, so beautiful. I did not know what to say to her. It is impossible to describe how I felt when she gave me her hand. I would have liked to just stand there staring at her. Please, go on into Jim's room. I'll finish preparing your snack. Jim showed me his collection of atomic pens (fountain pens that smelled awful, leaked sticky ink, and were all the rage that year when, for the last time, we used ink wells and blotters); toys the Señor had bought for him in the United States: missile-shooting cannons, jet-propulsion fighter bombers, soldiers armed with flamethrowers, plastic machine guns (plastics were just coming out), a Lionel electric train, a portable radio. I don't bring any of these things to school because nobody in Mexico has toys like this. No, of course not. We, the children of World War Two, had no toys. Everything went into war production. I read in *Reader's Digest* that even Parker and Esterbrook were manufacturing war materials. But I could not have cared less about the toys. Hey, what did you say your mother's name was? Mariana. That's what I call her. I don't call her Mom. What about you? Well, no. I address my mother formally, just like she does my grandmother. Don't make fun of me, Jim. Don't laugh.

Come have a bite to eat, Mariana said. And we sat down. I sat in front of her, looking at her. I did not know which to do: eat nothing or gobble everything down to make her feel good. If I eat, she'll think I'm a starving child; if I don't eat, she'll think I don't like her cooking. Chew slowly. Don't talk with your mouth full. What can we talk about? Fortunately, Mariana breaks the silence. How do you like them? They're called Flying Saucers. I toast them in this machine. I love them, ma'am; I've never eaten anything so delicious. Wonder Bread, ham, Kraft cheese, bacon, butter, ketchup, mayonnaise, mustard. It was all so different from the pozole, birria, tostadas, chicharron en salsa verde my mother made. Do you want another Flying Saucer? I would be more than happy to make one for you. No, thank you anyway, ma'am. They're delicious, but really, please don't bother.

She didn't touch a thing. She talked, she talked to me the whole time. Jim remained silent while he ate one Flying Saucer after another. Mariana asked me: What does your father do? I was ashamed to answer: He owns a factory that makes bath and laundry soap. The new detergents are putting him out of business. Oh, no. I'd never thought about it in that way. Pause. Silence. How many brothers and sisters do you have? Three sisters and a brother. Were you all born here in Mexico City? Only me and the youngest girl, and the rest were born in Guadalajara. We had a big house on San Francisco Street. They tore it down. Do you like school? School's not bad, but our classmates are the pits, don't you think, Jim?

Well, ma'am, if you will please excuse me, I have to go now (how can I explain to her that they'll kill me if I get home after eight?). Thanks a lot, ma'am. Everything was really delicious. I'm going to tell my mother to buy one of those toasters and make me some Flying Saucers. There aren't any in Mexico, Jim interjected, speaking up for the first time. If you want, I'll bring one back for you from the United States when I go.

You are always welcome here. Come back soon. Thank you very much again, ma'am. Thanks Jim. See you on Monday. How I would have loved to remain there forever or, at the very least, take along with me the photograph of Mariana that was in the living room. I walked down Tabasco Street, turned onto Cordoba to get to my house on Zacatecas. The silvery streetlamps only dimly illuminated the streets. A city immersed in semidarkness: the mysterious Roman Quarter of those days. An atom in the immense world, prepared many years before my birth like a stage set for my performance. I heard a bolero playing on a jukebox. Until that time, the only music we had heard was the National Anthem, church hymns, CriCri and his children's songs: "Little Horses," "Parade of Letters," "Little Black Watermelon Boy," "The Cowboy Mouse," "Juan Pestafias," and that circular, dense, absorbing melody by Ravel that Radio XEQ played before beginning its daily broadcast at six-thirty in the morning when my father turned on the radio to wake me up to the clamor of the *Legion of the Dawn Treaders*. When I heard this other bolero that had nothing whatsoever to do with Ravel's, the words caught my attention. "However high the heavens or the skies, / however deep the ocean lies."

I looked down Alvaro Obregon Avenue and said to myself: I'm going to keep my memory of this moment intact because everything that now exists will never be the same again. One day it will all seem to have been part of the most remote prehistoric era. I'm going to preserve it because today I fell in love with Mariana. What will happen? Nothing will happen. Nothing could possibly happen. What will I do? Change schools so as not to see Jim anymore and therefore not see Mariana? Look for a girl my own age? But at my age, nobody can look for a girl. The only thing a person of my age can do is fall in love secretly, silently, like I had done with Mariana. Fall in love knowing that all is lost and there is no hope.

VI. Obsession

You're late. But Mom, I told you I was going to go to Jim's house for a snack. That's right, but nobody gave you permission to stay out until this time of night: it's eight-thirty. I was very worried about you: I thought you had been killed or the Bag Man had kidnapped you. What kind of garbage did you eat? I wonder who *your little friend's* parents are. Is he the same one you go to the movies with?

Yes. His father is very important. He works for the government. For the government? And they live in that filthy building? Why didn't you ever tell me? What did you say his name was? Impossible: I know his wife. She and Aunt Elena are intimate friends. They don't have any children. It is a great tragedy in the midst of all that wealth and power. They're putting one over on you, Carlitos. I don't know why, but they sure are putting one over on you. I'm going to ask your teacher and get to the bottom of this mystery. No, please, I beg of you: don't say anything to Mondragon. What would Jim's mother think if she found out? She was very kind to me. Oh no, this is all I needed! What kind of secrets are you hiding? Okay, tell me the truth: you didn't really go over to this so-called Jim's house, did you?

I finally convinced my mother. In any case, she was left with the suspicion that something strange had occurred. I spent a very sad weekend. I became a child again and went to Ajusco Square to play alone with my little wooden cars. Ajusco Square is where they took me for sunbaths when I was a baby and where I learned to walk. Houses from the era of Porfirio Diaz, some that have already been demolished to make room for horrible buildings. The fountain in the shape of a figure eight; dead insects floating on the water. And Madame Sara P. de Madero lived between my house and the park. It seemed unbelievable to me that I could see, even from afar, a person whose name appeared in the history books, a participant in events that had occurred forty years earlier. That fragile, dignified old woman, still in mourning for her assassinated husband.

As I was playing in Ajusco Square, one part of me reasoned: how can you fall in love with Mariana if you've only seen her once and she's old enough to be your mother? It's stupid and ridiculous because there is not even a remote possibility that she'll feel something for you in return. But the other part of me, the stronger part, was deaf to all reasoning: I kept repeating her name as if the act of enunciating it again and again would bring her closer to me. Monday was even worse. Jim said: Mariana really liked you. She's glad we're friends. I thought: so she knows I exist, she noticed me, she realized—just a bit, at least a bit—the effect she had on me.

For weeks I asked about her, obliquely, using any pretext I could think of so as not to arouse Jim's suspicions. I tried to camouflage my interest while finding out everything I could about Mariana. Jim never told me anything I did not already know. He appeared to be totally ignorant of his own history. I wondered how it could be that everybody else was not. Again and again I begged him to take me to his house to see his toys, his illustrated books, his comics. Jim read comic books in English that Mariana bought for him at Sanborn's. He made fun of our heroes: Pepín, Paquín, Chamaco, Caron, and for the most privileged among us, Billiken, the Argentinian, and Peneca, the Chilean.

Since we always had a lot of homework, Friday was the only day of the week I could go over to Jim's house. At that time of day, Mariana was invariably at the beauty salon, getting ready for her evening out with the Señor. She would always return at eight-thirty or nine o'clock, and I could never wait until then to see her. Our snacks were always ready and waiting for us in the refrigerator: chicken salad, cole slaw, cold cuts, apple pie. Once, when Jim opened a closet, a picture of Mariana at six months old lying naked on a tiger-skin rug fell onto the floor. I felt a great wave of tenderness come over me when I thought about something one never thinks about because it is so obvious: Mariana had also been a little girl, she had been my age, and she would be a woman my mother's age and then an old lady like my grandmother. But at that moment she was the most beautiful woman in the world and I thought about her constantly. Mariana had become my obsession. However high the heavens or the skies, / however deep the ocean lies.

VII. Today Is the Day

And then one day—one of those cloudy days I love and nobody else can stand—I could no longer control myself. We were in National Language Class, as they used to call Spanish. Mondragon was teaching us the past conditional: *Hubiera o hubiese amado, hubieramos o hubiesemos amado, hubierais o hubieseis amado, hubieran o hubiesan amado*. It was eleven o'clock. I asked for permission to go to the bathroom. Then I sneaked out of school. I rang the doorbell to Apartment 4. One, two, three times. Mariana finally came to the door: fresh, beautiful, without any make-up. She was wearing a silk kimono. She was holding a razor just like the one my father used, only in miniature. She had been shaving her legs or her underarms when I rang the bell. She was, of course, surprised to see me. Carlos, what are you doing here? Did something happen to Jim? No, ma'am. Jim is just fine. Nothing happened.

Somehow we were already sitting on the sofa. Mariana crossed her legs. For a split second her kimono opened ever so slightly. Her knees, her thighs, her breasts, her flat belly, her mysterious hidden sex . . . I don't know how to tell you this, ma'am. I'm very embarrassed. What are you going to think of me? Carlos, I really don't understand. This is very strange to see you here like this at this time of day. You should be in class, shouldn't you? Yes, of course, it's just that I couldn't stand it any longer. I can't stand it. I ran away from school without permission. If I get caught, they'll expel me. Nobody knows I am here with you. Please, don't tell anybody I came here. Don't tell Jim. I beg you, least of all Jim. Promise me you won't.

Wait a minute. Calm down and let's see what this is all about. Why are you so worked up? Did something terrible happen at home? Are you having problems at school? Do you want some chocolate milk, Coca-Cola, a sip of mineral water? Trust me. Tell me how I can help you. No, you can't help me, ma'am. Why not, Carlitos? Because I came to tell you—I'll just come out and say it once and for all, please forgive me, ma'am—that I'm in love with you.

I thought she was going to laugh, scream at me, tell me I was crazy. Or maybe, better yet: Get out of here right now. I'm going to tell your parents and your teacher. I dreaded all of these possible reactions: all the ones I could have expected. Nevertheless, Mariana was not outraged, and she did not make fun of me. She sat there looking at me sadly. She took my hand (I'll never forget that she took my hand) and said:

I understand you perfectly. You have no way of knowing how well. Now you have to try to understand me and face the fact that you are a child just like my son and, for you, I am an old lady: I just turned twenty-eight years old. So, not now and not ever will there be anything between us. You understand me, don't you? I don't want you to suffer. Many terrible things await you in the future, you poor boy. Carlos, try to think of this as a joke, like something funny, so when you remember this as an adult, you will smile and not feel any resentment about it. Keep coming here with Jim and treat me just as what I am to you: your best friend's mother. Don't stop coming over; act as if nothing has happened, and in this way the *infatuation*—I'm sorry, love—will die down, and it won't become a problem for you, a tragedy that could cause you lasting damage for your entire life.

I felt like crying. But I controlled myself and said: You're right, ma'am. I understand everything you say. I want to thank you very much for reacting the way you did. Forgive me. In any case, I had to tell you. I thought I would die if I didn't tell you. There is nothing to forgive you for, Carlos. I like it that you are honest and confront your feelings. Please don't tell Jim. I won't say a word. You needn't worry.

I freed my hand from hers. I got up to go. Then Mariana stopped me. Before you go, can I ask you for a favor? Let me give you a kiss. And she gave me a kiss, not exactly on the lips, but on the corner of my mouth. A kiss just like the ones Jim always got before going off to school. I was shaking. I did not kiss her. I said nothing. I went running down the stairs. Instead of going back to class, I walked all the way to Insurgentes Boulevard. I arrived home totally confused. I pretended I was sick and wanted to go to bed.

But the teacher had just called. Surprised at my sudden disappearance, they had looked for me in the bathrooms and throughout the entire school. Jim declared: He probably went to see my mother. At this time of day? Yeah, Carlos is real weird. You never know what's going on in his head. I think he's got a screw loose somewhere. He has a brother who's a half-crazy gangster.

Mondragon and Jim went to the apartment. Mariana confessed that I had been there for a few minutes to pick up my history book I had left there the Friday before. This lie made Jim furious. I don't know how, but he had figured out the whole thing and explained it in full detail to the teacher. Mondragon called the factory and the house to tell my family what I had done, even though Mariana had flatly denied everything. Her denial made me appear even more suspect in the eyes of Jim, Mondragon, and my parents.

VIII. The Prince of This World

I never dreamt you could be such a monster. You couldn't possibly have learned that kind of behavior in this house! Tell me the truth: it was Hector who led you into this foolishness. Anyone who corrupts minors deserves a slow, painful death and all of hell's worst punishments. Come on, speak up, don't just sit there crying like a sissy. Tell me that it was your brother who talked you into doing it.

Listen, Mother, I don't think I did anything so terrible. And you still have the gall to insist you haven't done anything wrong? As soon as your fever drops you are going to confess and take communion so that Our Lord Jesus Christ can forgive you your sins. My father did not even scold me. He simply stated: This boy is abnormal. Something in his head just isn't working right. It must be from that fall on his head in Ajusco Square when he was six months old. I'm going to take him to see a specialist.

We are all hypocrites. We cannot see ourselves or judge ourselves the way we see and judge others. Even I, who never knew anything about what was going on, realized that for years my father had been maintaining another household: a woman—his ex-secretary—and two children. I remember an incident that occurred at the barbershop while I was waiting to get my hair cut. Some copies of *Vea* and *Vodevil* were lying next to the news magazines. I took advantage of the fact that the barber and his customer were engaged in exchanging verbal assaults against the government. I hid *Vea* inside *Hoy* and began leafing through the pages with pictures of Tongolele, Su Muy

Key, Kalantan, all half-naked. Legs, breasts, mouths, waists, buttocks, the mysterious hidden sex.

The barber, who shaved my father almost every day and had been cutting my hair ever since I was a year old, could see my facial expressions through the mirror. Put that down, Carlitos. Those things are for grown-ups. I'm going to tell your father on you. That's when I figured out that children are not supposed to like women. And if you challenge this edict, they create an enormous scandal and tell you that you're crazy. How unfair!

When, I asked myself, was the first time I was conscious of feeling desire? Perhaps it was the previous year when I saw Jennifer Jones's naked shoulder in *Duel in the Sun* at the Chapultapec Theater. Or maybe it was when Antonia lifted up her skirt to mop the yellow-painted floor and I saw her legs. Antonia was very pretty and she was always kind to me. Nevertheless, once I said to her: You're bad because you kill chickens. It would upset me greatly to watch them die. Better to buy them already dead and plucked. But none of that lasted very long. Antonia left the house because Hector refused to leave her alone.

I did not return to school, and they prohibited me from going out anywhere else. They took me to Our Lady of Rosario Church where we attended Mass every Sunday, where I had done my first Holy Communion, and where, thanks to my steady attendance of Mass on the first Fridays of the month, I had accumulated some indulgences. My mother sat down on one of the benches, praying for my soul that was in danger of eternal damnation. I knelt down in front of the confessional. Scared to death, I told Father Ferran everything.

In a soft and slightly panting voice, Father Ferran questioned me on all the details: Was she naked? Was there a man in the house? Do you think she had committed a shameful act before opening the door? And then: Have you ever abused yourself? Have you ever brought on an ejaculation? I don't understand what you are talking about, Father. He then proceeded to give me an explicit description. When he realized that he was talking to a child who was as yet incapable of even producing the raw material necessary for an ejaculation, he regretted having done so and then launched off on a lecture I did not understand at all: as a result of our state of original sin, the devil is the prince of this world, and he is continually setting traps for us, attempting to lure us away from our love of the Lord and tempting us into sin: one more thorn in the crown of our Lord Jesus Christ.

I said: Yes, Father; but somehow I could not conceive of why the devil would personally bother about leading me into temptation. Even less so could I understand why Christ would suffer because I had fallen in love with Mariana. As is expected under the circumstances, I showed myself ready and willing to mend my ways. But I did not regret anything, and I did not feel guilty: to love someone is not a sin. Love is good; only hatred is demonic. That afternoon, Father Ferran's lecture made much less of an impression on me than did his practical guide to masturbation. When I got home, I felt a great longing to abuse myself and bring on an ejaculation. I did not do it. Instead, I recited twenty Our Fathers and fifty Hail Marys. I took communion the next day. In the evening, they took me to a psychiatrist's office with white walls and nickel-plated furniture.

IX. Mandatory English

A young man asked me some questions and wrote down everything I said on lined sheets of yellow paper. I did not know what to say. Since I was totally ignorant of his profession's vocabulary, it was impossible to find a way for us to communicate. He asked me questions about my sisters and my mother that had never even entered my head. Then they made me draw every member of my family and paint trees and houses. Next they gave me the Rorschach test (is there anyone who *doesn't* see monsters in those ink blots?) with numbers and geometric figures and questions I was supposed to answer. The questions were as silly as the answers I gave. "What I like most": to climb trees and scale the walls of old houses; lemon sherbet; rainy days; adventure movies; Salgari novels. No, better yet: to lie awake in bed. But my father always dragged me out of bed at six-thirty in the morning to do exercises, even on Saturdays and Sundays. "What I hate most": cruelty toward people and animals; violence; screaming and shouting; arrogance; the abusiveness of older brothers; arithmetic; the fact that some people have nothing to eat while others have everything; finding garlic cloves in rice or stew; that they trim trees or kill them; watching someone throw bread away.

The woman who gave me the last tests spoke to the man right there in front of me. They acted as if I were a piece of furniture. It is very clearly an Oedipal problem, Doctor. This child is intellectually deficient. He is overprotected and docile. A castrating mother is undoubtedly the primal injury. He went to see that woman, fully aware that he might find her with her lover. I'm sorry, Elisita, but I have reached opposite conclusions: the boy is extremely intelligent and unusually precocious, so much so that by the time he is fifteen, he may become a total idiot. His abnormal behavior stems from a situation of neglect, excessive discipline from both parents, and a strong inferiority complex. Don't forget that he is very short for his age and the youngest male child. Note, if you will, how he identifies with the victim: animals, trees that cannot defend themselves. He is looking for the affection that is lacking within the family unit.

I felt like shouting at them: You idiots, why don't you at least come to an agreement before carrying on with this nonsense in a language you don't even understand yourselves?! Why do you have to label everything? Why don't you just accept the fact that someone can fall in love? Haven't you ever fallen in love? But the man came over to me and said: You can go now, my friend. We'll send the test results to your dad.

My father was sitting solemnly in the waiting room surrounded by worn-out copies of *Life, Look, Holiday* and glowing proudly because he could read them all fluently. He had just passed, at the top of his class, an adult night course in intensive English, and he studied every day with workbooks and records. It was so strange to see a person of his age—an old man of forty-two!—studying. Very early every morning, after his exercises and before breakfast, he reviewed his irregular verbs: *be, was, were, been; have, had, had; get, got, gotten; break, broke, broken; forget, forgot, forgotten;* and he practiced his pronunciation: apple, world, country, people, business. These words came to Jim so naturally and yet were so difficult for my father.

Those were terrible weeks. Only Hector defended me. Wow, you sure got it on! You scored quite some number there. I mean, you start making it now with chicks like her, hot stuff, better than Rita Hayworth, and what won't you do when you grow up? Hey, man? You're all right: trying to catch some action now before you're really up to it, instead of jerking off. I'm sure glad that neither of us turned into faggots even with so many sisters. But watch your step, Carlitos; don't let that bastard set his goons on you and break your ass. But Hector, my God, it's not such a big deal. The only thing I did was tell her I was in love with her. There's nothing wrong with that. I didn't do anything else. Seriously, I don't understand what all the fuss is about.

You were bound to end up at a school for beggars what with your father's greediness, my mother insisted. He throws money away on *other* expenses, but when it comes to his own children, he never has any. Can you believe it: letting the son of a woman *like that* into the school? We must transfer you to a school for our kind of people, from our class. And Hector: But, Mom, what class are you talking about? We are right where we belong: a typical Roman Quarter family on the way down: the essence of the Mexican middle class. Carlos is just fine where he is. That school is precisely for people of our class. Where else are you going to put him?

X. Fire Rain

My mother always insisted that our family—that is to say, her family—was one of the best in Guadalajara. Never any scandals like the one I had created. Honorable, hard-working men. Devout women, self-sacrificing wives, exemplary mothers. Obedient and respectful children. Then came the Indian hordes seeking their revenge against decency and good blood. The revolution—the old chieftains, that confiscated our ranches and our house on San Francisco Street on the pretext that there were too many Cristeros in the family. On top of that, my father—who, despite his degree in engineering, was held in contempt for being the son of a tailor—squandered the inheritance from his father-in-law on one absurd business venture after another, like trying to set up an air route between cities in the interior of the country or exporting tequila to the United States. Then, using money borrowed from my maternal uncles, he bought the soap factory that did well during the war and then went under when the North American companies invaded the domestic market.

And that's why my mother never tired of repeating: We've ended up in this accursed Mexico City. Infamous place, Sodom and Gomorrah awaiting the fire rain, a hell where horrors, the likes of which were never seen in Guadalajara, like the crime I had just committed, were daily occurrences. Sinister Capital City where we had to live among the worst elements. Contagion, bad examples. Birds of a feather flock together. How could it be, she insisted again and again, that a supposedly *decent* school would accept a bastard (what's a bastard?), the illegitimate son of a kept woman? Because there really is no way of knowing who the father is when you consider how many clients that prostitute must have, that corrupter of youth. (What does that mean, an illegitimate son? What's a kept woman? Why do you call her a prostitute?)

My mother had momentarily forgotten all about Hector. Hector boasted about being the *stud* of the university. It was rumored that he was one of the right-wing militants who forced Zubinin, the rector, to resign and erased the sign that read "God does not exist" on the mural Diego Rivera painted in the Prado Hotel. Hector read *Mein Kampf*, books about Field Marshal Rommel, *A Brief History of Mexico* by Vasconcelos, *The Stallion in the Harem, Insatiable Nights, Memoirs of a Nymphomaniac*, pornographic novels published in Havana and sold under the counter on San Juan de Letran and around Tivoli. My father devoured *How to Win Friends and Influence People, Achieving Self-Control, The Power of Positive Thinking, Life Begins at Forty*. My mother listened to all the radio soap operas on station XEW while she did her household chores, and sometimes she read something by Hugo Wast or M. Deily, to relax.

And to see Hector now! What a lean, bald, solemn, elegant fifty-year-old man my brother has become. So serious, grave, devout, respectable, so dignified in his role as a businessman at the service of the multinationals. A Catholic gentleman, the father of eleven children, an important member of the Mexican extreme right (in this respect, at least, he has always been impeccably coherent). But in those remote days: the servants who took flight because "the young boss" would try to rape them (egged on by his gang's motto: "Make it with a maid," he would burst into their room on the roof at midnight, naked, erect, and impassioned by his novels; he would struggle with the girls and ejaculate on their nightgowns before managing to penetrate them, and then the shouts would awaken my parents; they would get up; my sisters and I would watch everything, our mouths hanging open, from the bottom of the winding stairway; they would scold Hector, threaten to throw him out of the house, and at that hour of the night would even fire the servant, an even guiltier party than "the young boss" for going around *leading him on*); venereal diseases contracted from Meave whores or those on Dos de Abril Street; a fight between two rival bands on the banks of the Piety River, one stone's throw that broke his incisors; a locksmith's skull cracked open with a rubber pipe; a visit to the police station because Hector and a bunch of friends from Urueta Park had taken some drugs and ransacked a cafeteria owned by a Chinese couple; my father having to pay the fine and the damages and pull strings in the government so they wouldn't send Hector to Lecumberri. When I heard Hector had taken drugs, I thought he owed some money because in my house debts were always referred to as drugs (as far as that goes, my father was the perfect drug addict). Later, Isabel, my older sister, explained to me what it was all about. It was only natural for Hector to be on my side: I had, at least provisionally, replaced him as the black sheep in the family.

XI. Specters

There was another uproar at the beginning of the year when Esteban became Isabel's boyfriend. In the 1930s, Esteban had been a famous child actor. Logically, when he grew up, he lost his sweet little voice and innocent face. They no longer gave him parts in movies or theater; he made a living reading jokes on Station XEW, drank like a fish, and was determined to marry Isabel and go to Hollywood to try his luck despite the fact that he did not speak a word of English. Whenever he came to see her, he was in a stupor and reeking of booze, without a tie, his suit stained and wrinkled, and wearing dirty shoes.

Nobody could figure it out. But Isabel was his devoted fan. In the absence of Tyrone Power, Errol Flynn, Clark Gable, Robert Mitchum, and Cary Grant, Esteban was Isabel's only chance of kissing a movie star, even if he did only star in the same Mexican movies that had become the butt of family jokes at least as frequently as Miguel Aleman's regime. Did you see Pedro Infante's face? He looks just like a chauffeur. No wonder all the housemaids are in love with him.

One night my father threw Esteban out of the house: he arrived home late from English class and found him in the living room with the lights dimmed and his hand up Isabel's skirt. Hector tossed him out into the street, knocked him down, and then kept kicking him until Esteban managed to get on his feet, all bloody, and run away like a dog. Isabel refused to speak to Hector and began attacking me at the slightest provocation, even though I had tried to stop my brother from kicking poor Esteban on the ground. Isabel and Esteban never saw each other again: a short time later, defeated by failure, poverty, and alcoholism, he hanged himself in an infamous hotel in Tacubaya. Sometimes they show his movies on television and I feel like I am watching a ghost.

The only positive outcome of that period was that I got to have my own room. Up until then, I had slept in twin beds with Estelita, my little sister. Once I was diagnosed as a pervert, however, my mother thought the girl might be in danger. They moved her into the room with the older girls, much to the dismay of Isabel, who was studying in a junior college, and Rosa Maria, who had just gotten her diploma as an English-Spanish bilingual secretary.

Hector wanted to share my room with me. My parents refused. In the aftermath of his most recent adventures with the police and his latest attempts to rape the maid, Hector slept in the basement under lock and key. He had only a few blankets and an old mattress. My father used his old bedroom to store the factory's secret accounts and repeat each lesson from his records a thousand times: *At what time did you go to bed last night, that you are not yet up? I went to bed very late, and I overslept myself. I could not sleep until four o'clock in the morning. My servant did not call me, therefore I did not wake up.* I don't know of any other adult who learned to speak English in less than a year. Clearly, he had no other choice.

Once, without them knowing, I overheard a conversation between my parents. Poor little Carlos. Don't worry, he'll get over it. No, this is going to have an adverse effect on his entire life. What bad luck! How could this have happened to our son? We should think of it as an accident, as if he had been hit by a truck or something, don't you think? Within a few weeks, he won't even remember. If he thinks we have been unfair to him now, he will realize, when he grows up, that it was for his own good. It is all because of the immorality you breathe in this country with this corrupt government: it's the worst we've ever had. Look at the magazines, the radio, the movies: everything is part of a conspiracy to corrupt the innocent.

So, as it turned out, nobody could help me. I was completely alone. Hector saw it all as a mischievous prank, something amusing, like breaking a window with a ball. Neither my father nor my brothers nor Mondragon nor Father Ferran nor the authors of those tests understood anything at all. They were judging me by standards to which my behavior could not conform.

I began the second new school at the end of July. I knew nobody. Once again I was the foreign intruder. There were no Jews or Arabs, no poor kids on scholarships, no battles in the desert, although there was, as usual, mandatory English. The first few weeks were hell. I could not stop thinking about Mariana. My parents thought the punishments, the confession, the psychological tests—the results of which I never saw—had cured me. Nevertheless, on the sly and to the great surprise of the newspaper vendor, I bought *Vea* and *Vodevil* and played with myself without bringing on an ejaculation. Mariana's image reappeared, above and beyond Tongolele, Kalantan, Su Muy Key. No, I had not been cured: love is a disease in a world where the only natural thing is hatred.

I never saw Jim again. I never dared go near his house or back to the old school. When I thought of Mariana, the impulse to go see her was mixed with a sensation of discomfort and ridicule. How stupid of me to have gotten involved in such a mess that could have been avoided by simply repressing my idiotic declaration of love. Too late for regrets: I did what I had to do, and even now, so many years later, I cannot deny that I had fallen in love with Mariana.

XII. The Roman Quarter

There was a big earthquake in October. A comet appeared in November. It was said that these presaged an atomic war, the end of the world or, at the very least, another revolution in Mexico. Then La Sirena Hardware Store burned down, and many people were killed. By the time Christmas vacation came around, everything had totally changed for us. My father had sold his soap factory and had just been appointed manager of the North American company that had bought him out. Hector was studying at the University of Chicago, and my older sisters were in Texas.

One day at noon I was returning home after playing tennis at the Junior Club. I was seated sideways on a bus on the Santa Marta line reading a Perry Mason novel when, on the corner of Insurgentes and Alvaro Obregon, Rosales boarded the bus and asked the driver for permission to sell the Adams Chewing Gum he was carrying in a small box. He saw me. Ashamed, he jumped off the bus as fast as he could and hid behind a tree near Alfonso y Marcos, where my mother used to get her permanents and manicures before she had her own car and could go to a salon in Polanco.

Rosales: the poorest boy in my old school, whose mother was an orderly in a hospital. Everything happened in a matter of seconds. I jumped off the Santa Marta while it was in motion; Rosales tried to escape; I caught up with him. Ridiculous scene: Rosales, please don't be ashamed. It's great that you're working (look at me, who'd never worked a day in his life). You shouldn't be ashamed of helping your mother (look at me, playing the role of *Doctor Lovesick from Her Soul Clinic*). Hey, come on, I'll buy you an ice cream at La Bella Italia. You can't imagine how happy I am to see you (look at me being magnanimous with money to spare, in spite of devaluation and inflation). Rosales: sullen, pale, retreating. Finally he stopped and looked me in the eyes.

No, Carlitos, I would rather you bought me a sandwich, if you don't mind. I haven't eaten breakfast. I'm really starving. Listen, aren't you still mad at me because of our fights? What are you talking about Rosales? Those fights don't matter now (look at me, the generous one, capable of forgiving because I had become invulnerable). Okay, Carlitos, let's sit down and talk.

We crossed Obregon, then Insurgentes. So, tell me: did you get through the school year? How did Jim do on his exams? What did they all say when I never returned to school? Rosales kept quiet. We sat down in a sandwich shop. He ordered one sausage and two steak sandwiches and a soda. And you, Carlitos, aren't you going to eat? I can't: they're expecting me at home.

Today my mother made roast beef, my favorite. If I eat anything now, I won't be able to eat later. Just bring me a Coke and make it very cold.

Rosales put the box of Adams on the table. He looked out onto Insurgentes: the Packards, Buicks, Hudsons, the yellow streetcars, silver-colored lampposts, multicolored buses, the pedestrians who were still wearing hats: a scene and a moment that will never be repeated. The building in front: General Electric, Helvex Heaters, Mabe Stoves. A long silence; mutual discomfort. Rosales very restless, avoiding my eyes. He wiped his damp hands on his worn-out tweed pants.

They brought the food. Rosales took a bite out of the sausage sandwich. Before chewing it, he took a sip of water to wet it down. It was nauseating. Drawn-out hunger and anxiety: he devoured it. He asked me with his mouth full: And you? Did you get through the year even with the change of school? Are you going somewhere for vacation? On the jukebox, "La Mucura" ended and "Ghost Riders in the Sky" began. We are going to meet my brothers and sisters in New York for Christmas. We already have reservations at the Plaza Hotel. Do you know what the Plaza is? But listen, why don't you answer my questions?

Rosales swallowed saliva, sandwich, and soda. I thought he was going to choke. Well, Carlitos, it is just that, look, I don't know how to tell you this. Everybody in our class knew everything. What's everything? That thing about his mother. Jim told every single one of us. *He hates you.* We all thought that what you did was pretty funny. You're really nuts. And to top it off, someone saw you confessing in church after your declaration of love. And somehow word got out that they had taken you to the nut house.

I didn't respond. Rosales kept eating in silence. Suddenly he lifted his eyes and looked at me: I didn't want to tell you, Carlitos, but that isn't the worst part. No, someone else should tell you. Let me finish my sandwiches. They're delicious. I haven't eaten for a whole day. My mother lost her job at the hospital because she was trying to organize a union. And the guy who lives with her now says that since I'm not his son, he has no obligation to support me. Rosales, really, I'm sorry to hear that, but it's none of my business and I have no reason to get involved. Eat whatever you want and however much you want—I'm paying—but tell me the worst part.

Well, okay, Carlitos, it's just that it makes me real sad, you have no idea. Out with it, Rosales, once and for all, don't play around with me. It's just that, look Carlitos, I don't know how to tell you: Jim's mother is dead. Dead? What do you mean, dead? Yes, yes, Jim isn't at school anymore. In October he went to live in San Francisco. His real father came and got him. It was horrible. You have no idea. It seems like she had some kind of argument or something with that Señor who Jim said was his father but wasn't. He and his mother—her name was Mariana, right?—were in a cabaret or a restaurant or a very elegant party in Las Lomas. They were arguing about something she had said about the thieves in the government, about how they squandered the money they stole from the poor. The Señor didn't like that, and he raised his voice in front of all his powerful friends: ministers, foreign millionaires, his top associates in all his business schemes, whatever. And he slapped her right there in front of everybody, and he screamed at her that she had no right to talk about honor because she was a whore. Mariana got up and went home in a taxi and took a bottle of Nembutal and slit her wrists with a razor blade and shot herself, and she did all of it at once, I'm not sure how it was exactly. Anyway, Jim woke up and found her dead, lying in a pool of blood. He almost died too from pain and fear. And since the doorman of the building wasn't there, Jim went to Mondragon: he had nowhere else to turn. You should have seen the crowds of curious onlookers and the Green Cross and the agent from the public prosecutor's office and the police. I didn't dare look at her dead, but when they brought her out on the cot the sheets were covered with blood. For all of us, it was the worst thing that had ever happened to us in our lives. She left Jim a letter in English, a long letter asking him to forgive her and explaining to him everything I just told you. I think she also left some other notes—maybe there was even one for you, but there'd be no way of finding out—but they disappeared because the Señor covered everything up immediately, and they forbade us to talk about it among ourselves and especially at home. But you know how gossip flies and how difficult it is to keep a secret. Poor Jim, poor old buddy, how much we teased him at school! I really feel bad about it.

Rosales, this isn't possible. You're pulling my leg. You invented everything you just told me. You saw it in some fucking Mexican movie, the kind you like. You heard it on some sleazy soap opera on station XEW. Those things can't happen. Don't joke with me like that, please.

It's true, Carlitos. I swear to God it's true. May my mother drop dead if I told a lie. Ask anyone you want to at school. Talk to Mondragon. Everyone knows, even though it didn't come out in the papers. I'm surprised you didn't find out about it until now. Remember, I didn't want to be the one to tell you: that's why I hid, not because of the chewing gum. Carlitos, don't look at me like that: are you crying? I know, it's really terrible and horrible what happened. I was also very upset by it, you have no idea. But you're not going to tell me that seriously, at your age, you were in love with Jim's mom.

Instead of answering, I got up, paid with a ten-peso bill, and walked out without even waiting for the change or saying good-bye. I saw death everywhere: in the little pieces of animal about to become sandwiches and tacos, along with the onions, tomatoes, lettuce, cheese, cream, beans, guacamole, jalapeno peppers. Live animals like the trees they had just finished pruning on Insurgentes. I saw death in the soft drinks: Mission Orange, Spur, Ferroquina; in the cigarettes: Belmont, Gratos, Elegantes, Casinos.

I ran down Tabasco Street telling myself, trying to tell myself: It's one of Rosales's bluffs, an idiotic joke, he has always been a jerk. He wanted to get his revenge because I saw him starving to death with his little box of chewing gum and me with my tennis racket, my white suit, my Perry Mason in English, my reservations at the Plaza. I don't care if Jim opens the door. I don't care if I make a fool of myself. Even though everyone is going to laugh at me, I want to see Mariana. I want to prove that Mariana isn't dead.

I arrived at the building, dried my tears with a Kleenex, walked up the stairs, rang the doorbell to Apartment 4. A girl about fifteen years old answered the door. Mariana? No, no one by the name of Mariana lives here. This is the home of the Morales family. We moved here two months ago. I don't know who might have lived here before. Maybe you should ask the doorman.

While the girl was talking, I looked past her into a different living room: dirty, poor, disorderly. No pictures of Mariana at Semo's or of Jim at the Golden Gate Bridge or of the Señor serving his country with the president's team. Instead of all that, the Last Supper in metallic relief and a calendar with pictures from *The Legend of the Volcanoes*.

The doorman in the building was also new. The one from before wasn't there anymore: Don Sindulfo, Zapata's old ex-colonel who had become Jim's friend and sometimes told us stories about the Revolution and cleaned the apartment because Mariana didn't like having maids. No, son, I don't know any Don Sindulfo or this Jim you're talking about. There's no Mariana here. Forget it kid, don't insist. I offered him twenty pesos. Not even if you give me a thousand, kid. I can't accept it because I don't know nothing about nothing.

Nevertheless, he did take the money and let me carry on my search. At that moment I remembered that the building belonged to the Señor, and he had hired Don Sindulfo because his father—who Jim called "my grandpa"—had been a friend of the old man when they had both fought in the Revolution. I rang all the doorbells. I was so ridiculous with my little white tennis suit and my racket and my Perry Mason, asking questions, my face on the verge of tears peering in through the door. The smell of rice soup, the smell of chiles rellenos. In all the apartments they listened to me almost fearfully. My white suit was so incongruent! This was the house of death, not a tennis court.

No. I've been in this building since 1939 and as far as I know, no one by the name of Mariana has ever lived here. Jim? Don't know him either. In Apartment 8 there is a kid about your age named Everardo. In Apartment 4? No, an old couple without children lived there. But I came over here to Jim and Mariana's house a million times. You're imagining things, kid. It must have been on another street, in another building. Okay, good-bye. Don't waste any more of my time. Don't get involved in what's none of your business and create more problems. Enough kid, please. I have to get lunch ready; my husband gets home at two-thirty. But, ma'am. Go away or I'll call the police, and they'll take you straight to the juvenile authorities.

I returned home and I can't remember what I did afterward. I must have cried for days. Then we went to New York, I stayed at a school in Virginia. I remember, I don't remember even what year it was. Just these bursts, these flashes of light that bring everything back and the exact words. Just that little song that I will never hear again: "However high the heavens or the skies, / however deep the ocean lies."

How ancient! How remote! What an impossible story! But Mariana existed; Jim existed; everything I went over in my head existed even after such a long time of refusing to confront it. I will never know if the suicide really happened. I never again saw Rosales or anybody else from that period. They demolished the school; they demolished Mariana's building; they demolished my house; they demolished the Roman Quarter. That city came to an end. That country was finished. There is no memory of the Mexico of those years. And nobody cares: who could feel nostalgic for that horror? Everything came to an end just like the records on the jukebox. I will never know if Mariana is still alive. If she is, she would be sixty years old.[1]

Pedro Infante, *Nosotros los pobres* (1948); Luis Buñuel, *Los olvidados* (1950). Watch either film.

The immediate years after World War II overlap with the Golden Age of the mass media, especially the movies. To celebrate the movie industry during this time, we identified two significant films that can be used as an introduction for each of the themes in the chapter. Watch the movies on DVD or one of the video-streaming system such Netflix, Amazon Prime, iTunes, or YouTube. Both are available with either dubbing or subtitles or both. An overall topic might consider how the films represent either the Golden Age or the postwar society or both.

10.2. POLITICS: TWO IMAGES

"I was in the Grey Automobile Gang! I am in the Cadillac Gang!"
Jueves de Excelsior (March 15, 1951). Used by permission.

Abel Quezada, "I Had a Dream"
The Best of Impossible Worlds **(Englewood Cliffs, NJ: Prentice-Hall, 1963).**

THE MOST POWERFUL COUNTRY IN THE WORLD

1

LAST NIGHT I DREAMT THAT **MÉXICO** WAS THE **POWERFUL** COUNTRY AND THE **U.S.** THE **WEAK** ONE...

AMERICA FOR MEXICANS!

2

THAT AUTOMOBILES SOLD THE WORLD OVER HAD NAMES LIKE "GONZÁLEZ", "LÓPEZ" AND "RODRIGUEZ"...

GONZALEZ SUPER CUSTOM
THERE'S A GONZALEZ IN YOUR FUTURE

3

I DREAMT WE ORGANIZED COMMITTEES FOR FAIR PLAY AND ELBOW ROOM FOR NORTH AMERICANS BECAUSE SOME MEXICAN RESTAURANTS REFUSED TO SERVE THEM...

SORRY, NO SERVICE.

TASTY TACOS.

4

...THAT WE WENT IN FOR THE GOOD NEIGHBOR POLICY AND HIRED NORTH AMERICAN FIELD HANDS TO HARVEST OUR CORN AND BEAN CROPS.

5

...THAT WE HANDED OUT **PESOS** BY THE BUCKET TO HELP THE **U.S.** AND OTHER UNDERDEVELOPED PEOPLE, CHARGING ONLY A MODEST INTEREST...

6

...AND I WOULD LOVE TO GO ON DREAMING, BUT I WOKE UP.

10.3. MILITARY AND POLICE: JOE RICHMAN AND ANAYANSI DIAZ-CORTES, "MEXICO'S 1968 MASSACRE: WHAT REALLY HAPPENED?"

Listen to the National Public Radio report and watch a short video on the Tlatelolco massacre.[2]

Examine the digital archive of declassified National Security Agency documents on the subject.[3]

10.4. FAMILY: EARTHQUAKE—FILM AND CORRIDO

The 1985 Mexico City earthquake struck in the early morning, 7:17 a.m. on September 19, with a monumental magnitude of 8.0 and Mercanti intensity of X. Watch the earthquake video and listen to the associated corrido.[4]

10.5. POPULAR GROUPS: ALONSO ARREOLA, "10 MONSTERS OF POP CULTURE"

Everything was bigger in the seventies. Cars were almost as big as trucks, bell-bottoms reached historic dimensions, and peso bills sported a string of zeroes. The personalities of the decade seemed larger than life, too.

How can we forget Gena Montes swinging her hips hypnotically, multiplied by six, a dozen, or even two dozen clones on the small screen, dancing as if it were the last day of her life in the finale of *La Carabina de Ambrosio*? A grain of sand on the beach of the seventies, Montes, like all the pop artists of her day, was the product of a specific context. In a society in conflict, many of these "seventies monsters" cast a ray of hope in the shadow of the student protests of '68, the tyranny of a presidential government and a thirst for football arenas. It was in the seventies that President Echeverría Alvarez decked the country's economists out in guayaberas and when his successor, José López Portillo, true to his turtleneck style, ruled with a nepotism that went down in history. This was the time when guerilla movements, ideologies, and personalities from cultural, artistic, and entertainment circles emerged, all determined to mold a new nation. It was a time when—and please forgive us for the inevitable omissions—these giants that marked a decade were born.

Jacobo Zabludovsky

With the birth of Televisa in 1973, Emilio Azcárraga Milmo, alias the Tiger, took the reins of the broadcast company he inherited from his father, along with the most influential programs and figures of Mexican television.

One of his right-hand men was journalist Jacobo Zabludovsky (Mexico City, 1928), a conservative man who, as host of the legendary news program *24 horas,* came to be the standard-bearer of public opinion in a decade when journalism was still subordinated to the country's political apparatus. Brother of the architect and artist Abraham Zabludovsky, Jacobo studied law at the UNAM, graduating in 1967. He began his career as editor at Cadena Radio Continental before moving on to XEX-AM and from there to Televisa, where he remained until 2000. He is currently a program host for the Radiocentro group. Some of the highlights of his career include covering Fidel Castro's entry to Havana and the 1985 Earthquake in Mexico City.

Raúl Velasco

A native of Guanajuato, Raúl Velasco was born in 1933 and began working as an accountant and bank clerk. At 27 he moved to Mexico City, where he began to climb the ladder of the entertainment business. At the express request of the "Tiger" Azcárraga, he was hired as host of *Siempre en Domingo,* a show that was to bring him international fame. It was from this platform that he launched the careers of a mixed bunch of artists and contributed to the creation of festivals like the OTI, Valores Juveniles, Juguemos a Cantar, and Acapulco. As an entertainment guru, Raúl Velasco had no equal and remained a popular television celebrity for more than three decades. He died at his home in Acapulco in 2006.

Roberto Gómez Bolaños, "Chespirito"

A fan of the classic comedians of silent movies, Gómez Bolaños first saw the light of day in Mexico City in 1929. He left his mark on the collective unconscious of Mexico with two creations born of poverty and tragedy, *El Chavo del 8* and *El Chapulín Colorado*. The misadventures of the characters, full of aspirations doomed to failure, were popular throughout the entire continent in an age when television was prone to the repetition of formulas. Architect, amateur boxer, singer-songwriter, and closet caricaturist and playwright was the second of three children of an secretary and an artist. The brains behind the dialogue of Viruta and Capulina, and Pedro Vargas, this miniature prolific Shakespeare (hence the nickname Chespirito) leapt to fame in 1969 at Telesistema Mexicano to become a prominent figure of the seventies and opened international markets for Mexican television.

Octavio Paz

Winner of the Nobel Prize for literature, Paz built up a conservative elite that was to be vital to the Mexican arts, first as editor of *Plural* and later of *Vuela*. Born in Mexico City in 1914, Paz was one of our finest poets and essayists and perhaps the Mexican author with the greatest international exposure. However, his ideological shifts caused a rift between him and contemporaries like Carlos Monsiváis. While José Agustín was fueling the literary "onda" movement and Carlos Fuentes was publishing *Terra Nostra*, Paz was criticizing communism, conquering public opinion abroad, and closing ranks with Televisa to become the intellectual with the highest media profile of his time.

José José

In the seventies, Mexico City's Zona Rosa was a parade of bell-bottoms, ruffled shirts, turtlenecks, and platform shoes. It was also the operations center of one of the greatest singer-songwriters in history. Every week thousands would cram into the 00 disco at the Camino Real Hotel or the Patio at Atenas 9 to applaud José, otherwise known as the Prince of Song. The son of the tenor José Sosa Esquivel and the pianist Margarita Ortíz, José Rómulo Sosa Ortíz (Mexico City, 1948) got off to a shaky start in choirs and student festivals. After making his debut in 1965 with the Orfeón label, he met the producer Rubén Fuentes and embarked on two decades of success that would escalate into an alcoholic roller-coaster ride. Looking back, we can safely say that no one has yet matched this authentic crooner's rendition of the urban ballad.

Rubén "El Púas" Olivares

The seventies were the glory years for boxers. Although soccer was in good health, it was pugilists like "Pipino" Cuevas and "El Púas" Olivares who hogged the limelight before they were overshadowed by up-and-coming soccer players like Hugo Sánchez (who was already a champion scorer for the university team) and Fernando Valenzuela, bought by the Dodgers of Los Angeles in 1979. Constantly parodied on television, Rubén "El Púas" Olivares (Mexico City, 1947) epitomized the troublemaking hero who was too fond of booze and ill-equipped to handle fame and fortune. The four-time world champion's fall from grace coincided with historic events like the discovery of the Aztec moon goddess Coyolxauhqui during excavations of the Templo Mayor and the first visit of Pope John Paul II at the end of the decade.

Eduardo del Río "Rius"

Eduardo del Río (1934), alias Rius, an exceptional self-taught caricaturist from Michoacán, escaped a life as a priest at the hands of the Salesian Catholic sect but ended up doing society a service by publishing books like

Los agachados and *Los Supermachos*. These works launched a movement that Magú, El Fisgón, and Ahumada would soon join. In his time, Rius produced a disciplined body of work that pays tribute to Mexico's graphic past, while criticizing the politics of the government in direct effort of a counterbalance. The author of *Cuba para principiantes* and *Marx para principiantes*, Rius and his imperialist ideology underscored dozens of titles that brought him recognition on all five continents, so much that the movie director Alfonso Arau made a film based on his characters in 1973. Rius began his career 53 years ago at the magazine *Ja-Ja* and there isn't a cartoonist in Mexico who can deny his influence.

Alex Lora

At the first Avándaro Festival in September, 1971, bands like Three Souls in the Mind (today known as Los Tri), Los Dug-Dugs, and White Ink played to 200,000 youths, including the "Avandaro Stripper" at the first mass concert in Mexico. The counterculture movement was crushed by government repression, giving rise to underground rock venues. Those were the days of the guitar of Javier Bátiz, the piano of Eugenio Toussaint and the voices of other nonconformists, like Alejandro Lora. Born in Puebla in 1952, Lora became a pioneering force in Mexican rock by recording in Spanish when custom dictated that rock ballads could be recorded in English. First a bass player and then a guitarist, this singer songwriter is the lead vocalist of El Tri and remains a living icon of Mexican rock as he proved at the Vive Latino Festival 2007 when he played to an audience of more than 80,000.

Sasha Montenegro

Born in the former Yugoslavia 57 years ago, Sasha was Mexico's most beloved sex kitten of the seventies. As she showed off her body on the big screen and women cried over their household disasters on the small screen, Rosario Ibarra de Piedra spoke out against the government. But Sasha wasn't alone. Numerous vedettes, including Zulma Faiad, Lyn May, Wanda Seux, aroused passions on the stages of the Regis, the Fru, the Blanquita, and the Capri. Riches and wealth were in store for Sasha unlike many of her contemporaries, when she became the lover and later wife of former President José López Portilla. Subsequently, she disappeared from the public eye.

Rigo Tovar

The seventies saw the first Cervantine Festival and a memorable poetry gathering in Morelia, Michoacán, yet far from the high-flown yearnings for modernity, other monsters reared their heads. One of these was Roberto

Tovar García (1946), better known as Rigo Tovar, who began his musical career in Houston and went on to found the group Costa Azul in his native Matamoros, a group that was to invent a new musical genre by fusing cumbia, ballads, and rock. Today a symbol of the kitsch culture (together with Chico Che), Rigo made movies and appeared on television sporting a huge pair of dark sunglasses and employing a funny hop. These peculiar traits were enough to persuade society to adopt him and dance *El Sirenito*. He died of illness in 2005, denied of the sweet taste of fame and fortune.[5]

ADDITIONAL READING

Garcia y Griego, Manuel. "Responses to Migration: The Bracero Program." In *Binational Study on Migration Between Mexico and the United States* 3: 215–21. Online at https://lbj.utexas.edu/uscir/binpapers/v3c-1garcia.pdf.

Leer en español

Loaeza, Soledad. "Modernización autoritaria a la sombra de la superpotencia, 1944–1968." In *Nueva historia general de México*, 653–98. Mexico City: El Colegio de México, 2010.

NOTES

1. José Emilio Pacheco, *Battles in the Desert and Other Stories*, translated by Katherine Silver (New York: New Directions Publishing, 1987). Reprinted by permission of New Directions Publishing.
2. Online at http://www.npr.org/templates/story/story.php?storyId=97546687.
3. The National Security Agency archives are maintained at George Washington University and they are available online at http://nsarchive.gwu.edu/search.html.
4. Mexico City's earthquake is discussed on the website of the US Department of the Interior, US Geological Survey, http://earthquake.usgs.gov/earthquakes/world/events/1985_09_19.php, which provides links to various sources. News stories on film can be seen online on Bing.com, YouTube, and other video upload sites. The earthquake was memorialized in various corridos, one of which is discussed in document 71 of *Mexican History: A Primary Source Reader*, ed. Nora E. Jaffary, Edward Osowski, and Susie S. Porter (Boulder, CO: Westview Press, 2009). Also see Bing videos.
5. Alonso Arreola, "Ten Monsters of Pop Culture," *Vuelo, Especial de Colección "Mex '70s: La década que vivimos en onda"* [in-flight magazine of Mexicana Airlines] (July 2007): 118–26.

CHAPTER 11

The Lost Decades, 1982-2000

The Miracle collapsed in some 8 billion dollars in national debts, plummeting peso values (recorded in several devaluations), inflation, unemployment, sky-rocketing crime, and increased migration to the United States. The economic collapse brought international assistance at the price of austerity demands from international agencies and foreign governments as the condition for bailout loans. Some political leaders made the first order of business the reform of the official party that controlled government and political system. Their efforts created the democratization campaign from 1980 to the present (11.1). They could not achieve their reforms overnight, but eventually they had an impact on both politics and government and the election of an opposition party candidate as president in 2000. For members of the general public, personal, family, and community security held paramount importance, including the decline of corruption in official agencies (11.2). In another effort to address the crisis, President Carlos Salinas undertook a number of political, economic, and social changes. He reflected on these events in his book *The Policy and Politics of Modernization* and discussed them in the Shell Distinguished Lecture 2002 (11.3). The North America Free Trade Agreement (NAFTA) and its myths (11.4) created an environment that changed Mexico immediately with the revolt of the Zapatista National Liberation Army (11.5).

11.1. POLITICS: THE DEMOCRATIZATION OF MEXICO

Watch the interviews conducted by William H. Beezley and Roderic A. Camp with Cuauhtémoc Cárdenas (leading spirit of the democratization) and Miguel Bisañez (leading pollster and former Mexican ambassador to the United States).[1]

11.2. SECURITY: "MEXICO POLICE AND LAW ENFORCEMENT ORGANIZATIONS"

Mexico's rural indigenous peoples periodically have risen in protest against poverty and encroachment by large farmers, ranchers, and commercial interests on contested land. The most recent and serious such uprising occurred on January 1, 1994, when the Zapatista National Liberation Army (Ejército Zapatista de Liberación Nacional—EZLN) rebelled, capturing four municipalities in Chiapas state. Some of the group, believed to number about 1,600, were armed with semiautomatic and assault rifles, whereas others were armed only with sticks and wooden bayonets. Although the group's attacks seemed well planned, army units, supported by air force strikes, were able to regain control after the initial surprise. At least 12,000 troops were transported to the scene. Officials announced that 120 deaths had resulted, although church officials said 400 lives had been lost. Five rebels apparently were executed while bound, and other deaths may have been the result of extrajudicial executions. Many disappearances of peasants were reported, and there was indiscriminate strafing of hamlets. The government declared a unilateral cease-fire after twelve days and announced several goodwill gestures as a prelude to reconciliation talks with the rebels, who were represented by their masked leader, Subcommander Marcos.

According to government sources, the EZLN, commonly known as the Zapatistas, is not a purely indigenous movement, but is instead an alliance of middle-class intellectuals and radicalized indigenous groups dating from the early 1980s. The EZLN began as an offshoot of the National Liberation Forces (Fuerzas de Liberación Nacional—FLN), a Maoist guerrilla group that had been largely dormant since the 1970s. At the start of the Zapatista rebellion, command of the Zapatista army was jointly held by FLN veterans from Mexico City and a "clandestine committee" of Chiapas Indians representing the various ethnic groups residing in the area.

In February 1995, on the eve of a new offensive against rebel strongholds, the government identified Subcommander Marcos as Rafael Sebastián Guillén, a white, middle-class graduate in graphics design from the National Autonomous University of Mexico (Universidad Nacional Autónoma de México—UNAM). In the initial January 1994 Zapatista raids, the charismatic guerrilla leader had become an international media star, quickly assuming the status of a folk hero among many Mexicans. Capitalizing on his newfound fame and his proximity to the rebel army, Marcos is believed to have wrested control of the EZLN from its Mexico City leadership.

Despite a formidable government offensive involving approximately 20,000 army troops venturing into Zapatista-held territory, Subcommander Marcos and his rebel force eluded capture. By late February 1995, a second cease-fire had been declared. Soon thereafter, the government and the rebels embarked on a second major round of peace talks. In early 1996, the Zapatistas declared their willingness in principle to lay down their arms and become a legal political party pending major reforms of the political system. Despite their ability to grab headlines and attract international support, the Zapatistas remain a marginal political force and are not considered a serious military threat outside of Chiapas.

Police and Law Enforcement Organizations

A number of federal, state, and local police and law enforcement organizations exist to provide for internal security. Their responsibilities and jurisdictions frequently overlap, a factor acknowledged in 1984 when the government created a national consulting board designed to "coordinate and advise police forces" throughout the country. The senior law enforcement organization in Mexico is the Federal Judicial Police, which is controlled by the attorney general. The plainclothes force acts as an investigative agency with arrest power for the Office of the Attorney General. The foremost activity of the Federal Judicial Police is carrying out investigations and making apprehensions related to drug trafficking. Espionage, arms trafficking, and bank robberies also fall under its purview. The Federal Judicial Police serves as the government's liaison with the International Criminal Police Organization (Interpol). Its role can be compared to a combination of the United States Federal Bureau of Investigation (FBI) and the United States Drug Enforcement Administration (DEA).

The jurisdiction of the Federal Judicial Police encompasses the entire nation. For control purposes, its jurisdiction is divided into thirteen zones with fifty-two smaller detachment headquarters. Under the coordination of the local federal prosecutor, each zone is headed by a second commandant of the Federal Judicial Police, who in turn directs the group chiefs in the outlying detachments. Individuals arrested by the Federal Judicial Police are placed at the disposition of the local federal prosecutor, who appoints subordinate attorneys to assess each case.

Although it remains one of the smaller law enforcement agencies, the Federal Judicial Police tripled in size between 1982 and 1984, from 500 personnel to an estimated 1,500. In 1988 an assistant attorney general's office for investigating and combating drug trafficking was formed with an additional 1,500 Federal Judicial Police agents. In 1990 the office was expanded and given interagency coordinating functions in the battle against narcotics.

The principal Mexico City police force, the Protection and Transit Directorate, also known as the Traffic Police, consists of some 29,000 officers organized into thirty-three precincts. It is the largest law enforcement organization in Mexico. More than 100 serious crimes are reported each day in Mexico City, and on average in the Federal District in the first quarter of 1997 one police officer was killed and one injured weekly. A sense of insecurity prevails among many citizens because of the lack of confidence in the police and the fear of police misbehavior and crime.

The Federal District police are poorly paid; in 1992 they earned between US$285 and US$400 a month. Double shifts are common, although no extra pay for overtime is provided. Incomes can be supplemented in various ways, including from petty bribes (*mordidas*) from motorists seeking to park in restricted zones. Police are said to be obliged to pay for more desirable assignments where the possibilities of extorting payments from drivers in lieu of fines is greater. However, junior officers are forced to pass along a daily quota of bribes to more senior officers. In one case, a tow truck driver admitted that he had paid more than US$1,000 for his lucrative job and said that he had to contribute US$32 daily to his superior. In 1992 after a number of officers expressed their objections to the system, the mayor of Mexico City set up offices to receive and investigate citizen complaints.

A number of smaller law enforcement bodies exist at the state and local level. Each of the country's thirty-one states and the Federal District has its own judicial police—the State Judicial Police and the Federal District Judicial Police. State police are under the direction of the state's governor; the Federal District Judicial Police fall under the control of the Federal District attorney general. The distinction between crimes investigated by State and Federal Judicial Police is not always clear. Most offenses come under the state authorities. Drug dealing, crimes against the government, and offenses involving several jurisdictions are the responsibility of the federal police.

Cities and municipalities have their own preventive and municipal police forces, which are responsible for handling minor civil disturbances and traffic infractions. The Federal Highway Police patrols federally designated highways and investigate traffic accidents. Highway police are assisted by military personnel on national holidays.

Both state and municipal forces operate from precinct stations, called *delegaciones*. Each *delegación* has an average of 200 police officers attached to it. The ranking officer is known as a *comandante*, equivalent to a first captain in the military. Most of the remaining personnel hold the ranks of first sergeant, second sergeant, and corporal.

Immigration officers, directed by the Mexican Immigration Service under the Secretariat of Government (Secretaría de Gobernación), have the right to detain suspected undocumented aliens and, under certain conditions, to deport them without formal deportation proceedings. Customs officers, controlled by the Secretariat of Finance and Public Credit (Secretaría de Hacienda y Crédito Público), are deployed at borders and at international airports to interdict contraband entering Mexico. The Bank of Mexico also operates its own security division, which is charged with enforcing banking and monetary laws, including cases of counterfeiting, fraud, and money laundering.

A number of unofficial paramilitary groups incorporating various police officials have existed in the past to deal with rural and urban guerrillas and illegal groups. The most notorious paramilitary group was the White Brigade (Brigada Blanca) whose existence was officially denied, although it was known to be active from 1977 until 1980, when the government dismantled it. The White Brigade consisted of a group of officers from the army and the police forces that used illegal tactics to destroy guerrilla movements. Published reports held that the White Brigade was responsible for the "disappearance" of several hundred leftists, most of whom the government claimed were killed in fights between rival leftist groups. Politically motivated "disappearances" tapered off sharply during the 1980s, but were once again being reported in the mid-1990s in connection with the unrest in Chiapas.

The government has repeatedly denounced abuses and corruption by the Federal Judicial Police and other police forces. Numerous reforms have been announced, personnel shifted, and codes of procedures adopted. Allegations of police brutality have declined, but torture, wrongful arrests, and involvement in drug trafficking have not been eliminated because abuses are so deeply rooted in the police agencies, and violators for the most part have been able to act with impunity.

In 1991 Attorney General Enrique Álvarez del Castillo, who was reported to have impeded several human rights investigations against the police, was abruptly removed from office and replaced by Ignacio Morales Lechuga. Morales quickly announced a crackdown on corruption, including a reorganization of the Federal Judicial Police, the creation of special anticorruption and internal affairs units, as well as a unit to protect citizens against crimes committed by the police. In addition, all federal police units were placed under the control of a civilian deputy attorney general. New high-level officials supervised police activities in sensitive border areas. These reform measures were announced soon after a jailed drug lord took over a prison in Matamoros, claiming that agents of the Federal Judicial Police aligned with another drug lord were threatening his life.

Despite Morales's reputation as an upright official prepared to dismiss police agents and government prosecutors suspected of ties with drug traffickers, he was replaced in early 1993. Later reports accused some of Morales's subordinates of drug-related corruption. The new attorney general, Jorge Carpizo MacGregor, was a respected human rights activist. Carpizo acknowledged in a detailed report the close relations between criminals and law enforcement agencies and produced his own program to eliminate deficiencies and corruption among the police. His reforms brought some progress; some members of the security forces were charged and sentenced, and human rights violations declined, but the so-called "culture of impunity" still prevailed. Carpizo resigned as attorney general in early 1994 and was replaced by Diego Valádez.

The 1994 assassinations of PRI presidential candidate Luis Donaldo Colosio Murrieta and PRI Secretary General José Francisco Ruiz Massieu shook the highest levels of federal law enforcement. After failing to make significant progress in investigating the Colosio case, Attorney General Valádez was replaced in May 1994 by Humberto Benítez Trevino. Initially declaring that the Colosio assassination was the work of a lone gunman, the Attorney General's office later revised its theory based on videotape evidence that suggested a conspiracy of up to six individuals working in concert to allow the alleged gunman to approach the candidate during a crowded campaign rally. The post of attorney general underwent yet another change in early 1996 when incoming President Zedillo replaced Benítez with an opposition congressman, Fernando Antonio Lozano Gracia. Lozano's tenure was significant because it was the first time a non-PRI official held the post.

Late in 1994, the assassination of José Francisco Ruiz Massieu prompted a special investigation headed by Deputy Attorney General Mario Ruiz Massieu, brother of the slain politician. After calling dozens of PRI officials to testify, Ruiz resigned abruptly in November, accusing high-level PRI functionaries of complicity in the killing and of impeding further progress in the investigation. In early 1996, the investigation still had produced no results.[2]

11.3. CONSTITUTION: CARLOS SALINAS, "SHELL DISTINGUISHED LECTURE SERIES—MEXICO: THE POLICY AND POLITICS OF MODERNIZATION"

President Carlos Salinas, during his six-year term in office from 1988 to 1994, worked to remake the constitutional framework that governed everyday life, especially by removing or revising those rules that he and his advisors believed no longer served the nation. Amendments reshaped land provisions, citizenship definition, and redefined the rights of the Church, including the restoration of political rights to its hierarchy. An obvious model for some of his early actions came from Lech Wałesa's solidarity movment in Poland.[3]

11.4. FAMILY: NAFTA: ITS BACKGROUND, COMMISSIONS, AND MYTHS

While NAFTA could be considered as a political or economic agreement, the creation of free trade across North America has had and will continuing having im-

plications for families, including migration from Mexico to both the United States and Canada, by men seeking work and sending home remittances that finance family life. This pattern has also resulted in women taking on increased and new roles in Mexican life. Examining the following document challenges readers to go beyond economic and political aspects to find the everyday lived, family experiences of NAFTA.

"NAFTANOW.ORG: NORTH AMERICAN FREE TRADE AGREEMENT" (LAST MODIFIED 2013)[4]

A number of NAFTA institutions work to ensure smooth implementation and day-to-day oversight of the Agreement's provisions.

Free Trade Commission

Made up of ministerial representatives from the NAFTA partners.

Supervises the implementation and further elaboration of the Agreement and helps resolve disputes arising from its interpretation.

Oversees the work of the NAFTA committees, working groups, and other subsidiary bodies.

NAFTA Coordinators

Senior trade department officials designated by each country.
Responsible for the day-to-day management of NAFTA implementation.

NAFTA Working Groups and Committees

Over 30 working groups and committees have been established to facilitate trade and investment and to ensure the effective implementation and administration of NAFTA.

Key areas of work include trade in goods, rules of origin, customs, agricultural trade and subsidies, standards, government procurement, investment and services, cross-border movement of business people, and alternative dispute resolution.

NAFTA Secretariat

Made up of a "national section" from each member country.

Responsible for administering the dispute settlement provisions of the Agreement and for administering dispute resolution processes under Chapter 14, Chapter 19 and Chapter 20. Also has certain responsibilities related to the Chapter 11 dispute settlement provisions concerning investment.

Maintains a court-like registry relating to panel, committee, and tribunal proceedings. Maintains a tri-national website containing up-to-date information on past and current disputes.

Commission for Labor Cooperation

Created to promote cooperation on labor matters among NAFTA members and the effective enforcement of domestic labor law.

Consists of a Council of Ministers (comprising the labor ministers from each country) and a Secretariat, which provides administrative, technical, and operational support to the Council and implements an annual work program. Departments responsible for labor in each of the three countries serve as domestic implementation points.

For more information, please visit www.naalc.org.

Commission for Environmental Cooperation

Established to further cooperation among NAFTA partners in implementing the environmental side accord to NAFTA and to address environmental issues of continental concern, with particular attention to the environmental challenges and opportunities presented by continent-wide free trade.

Consists of a Council (comprising the environment ministers from each country), a Joint Public Advisory Committee (a 15-member, independent volunteer body that provides advice and public input to Council on any matter within the scope of the environmental accord), and a Secretariat (which provides administrative, technical, and operational support).

For more information on topics that have been reviewed by the Council, please visit www.cec.org/council.

NAFTA Background

In 1994, the North American Free Trade Agreement (NAFTA), a state-of-the-art market-opening agreement, came into force. Since then, NAFTA has systematically eliminated most tariff and non-tariff barriers to trade and investment between Canada, the United States, and Mexico. By establishing a strong and reliable framework for investment, NAFTA has also helped create the environment of confidence and stability required for long-term investment. NAFTA was preceded by the Canada-U.S. Free Trade Agreement.

For details about NAFTA's impact on North Americans, please see Results: North Americans Are Better Off After 15 Years of NAFTA.

NAFTA: Chronology of Events

June 10, 1990: Canada, the U.S., and Mexico agree to pursue a free trade agreement.

February 5, 1991: NAFTA negotiations begin.

December 17, 1992: NAFTA is signed by leaders from Canada, the U.S., and Mexico.

August 1993: Additional side agreements on labor and the environment are negotiated.

January 1, 1994: NAFTA enters into force.

The Canada-U.S. Free Trade Agreement

Negotiations toward a free trade agreement between the United States and Canada began in 1985. Sixteen months later, the two nations came together and agreed to the Canada-U.S. Free Trade Agreement (FTA). It was a historic agreement that placed Canada and the United States at the forefront of trade liberalization.

Key elements of the Agreement included the elimination of tariffs and the reduction of many non-tariff barriers to trade. The FTA was also among the first trade agreements to address trade in services. It also included a dispute settlement mechanism for the fair and expeditious resolution of trade disagreements, and established a ground-breaking system for the binational review of trade remedy determinations, thereby providing an alternative to domestic judicial review.

In practical terms, Canada and the United States agreed to remove bilateral border measures on traded goods, which included the removal of tariffs on goods such as meat products, fruits and vegetables, beverages, processed foods, live animals, wine, clothing and textiles, fuels, electrical goods and machinery.

Canada-U.S. FTA: Chronology of Events

September 26, 1985: Canada proposes a free trade agreement with the United States.

October 4, 1987: Substantive negotiations conclude and agreement is reached on the Canada-U.S. Free Trade Agreement.

January 2, 1988: The Agreement is signed by leaders from Canada and the United States.

January 1, 1989: The Canada-U.S. Free Trade Agreement enters into force.

Myths and Realities

A review of the myths and realities surrounding NAFTA reveals the extent to which its critics have been proven wrong.

Myth 1: NAFTA has not achieved its core goals of expanding trade and investment between Canada, the United States, and Mexico.
Reality: Since NAFTA came into effect, trade among the NAFTA countries has more than tripled, reaching US$949.1 billion. In 2008, Canada and the United States' inward foreign direct investment from NAFTA partner countries reached US$469.8 billion. Meanwhile, Mexico has become one of the largest recipients of foreign direct investment among emerging markets, and received more than US$156 billion from its NAFTA partners between 1993 and 2008.

Myth 2: NAFTA has resulted in job losses.
Reality: Since NAFTA came into effect, the overall job growth has been strong in all three partner countries. Across North America, total employment has grown by almost 40 million jobs since 1993.

Myth 3: NAFTA hurts workers by eroding labor standards and lowering wages.
Reality: The NAFTA partners negotiated and implemented a parallel agreement on labor cooperation, the North American Agreement on Labor Cooperation (NAALC). The NAALC adds a social dimension to NAFTA. Through the NAALC, the regional trading partners seek to improve working conditions and living standards, and to protect, enhance, and enforce basic workers' rights.

Over the years, the NAALC has helped to improve working conditions and living standards in Canada, the U.S., and Mexico. It has also raised the public profile of major labor rights issues, including pregnancy-based discrimination, secret ballot voting, protection contracts, and protection of migrant workers.

The NAALC promotes the effective enforcement of domestic labor laws in all three countries and highlights cooperation on labor matters in three key areas: industrial relations, occupational health and safety, and employment standards.

In addition, NAFTA has promoted higher wages. In Mexico, for example, export firms employ one in five workers; these workers are paid 40% more on average than those in non-export jobs. Firms with foreign direct investment employ nearly 20% of the labor force and pay 26% more than the domestic average manufacturing wage. For more information on the Commission for Labor Cooperation, please visit the website.

Myth 4: NAFTA undermines national sovereignty and independence.

Reality: NAFTA is a trilateral agreement designed to facilitate trade and investment between Canada, the United States, and Mexico. It respects the unique cultural and legal framework of each of the three countries and allows them to maintain their sovereignty and independence.

Myth 5: NAFTA does nothing to help the environment.

Reality: The NAFTA partners negotiated a parallel agreement on environmental cooperation, the North American Agreement on Environmental Cooperation (NAAEC). The NAAEC commits the NAFTA partners to work cooperatively to better understand and improve the protection of their environment. The agreement also requires that each NAFTA partner effectively enforce its environmental laws.

The Commission for Environmental Cooperation, established under the NAAEC, has produced concrete improvements in the management of North American environmental issues. With a budget of US$9 million annually, some initiatives of the Commission include the development of North American management practices for toxic chemicals; establishment of the first Mexican national air emissions inventory; launch of the North American Bird Conservation Initiative, which provides a resource for bird conservation programs in the three countries; promotion of best practices to address the linkages between the environment, the economy, and trade.

Additionally, the United States and Mexico created two binational institutions. The Border Environment Cooperation Commission provides technical support for the development of environmental infrastructure projects in the U.S.-Mexico border region (www.cocef.org). The North American Development Bank finances these projects (www.nadbank.org). To date, they have provided nearly US$1 billion for 135 environmental infrastructure projects with a total estimated cost of US$2.89 billion and allocated US$33.5 million in assistance and US$21.6 million in grants for over 450 other border environmental projects. The Mexican government has also made substantial new investments in environmental protection, increasing the federal budget for the environmental sector by 81% between 2003 and 2008. For more information on what has been accomplished by the parties under the NAAEC, please visit the Commission for Environmental Cooperation website at www.cec.org/.

Myth 6: NAFTA hurts the agricultural sector.

Reality: NAFTA has led to increasingly integrated agricultural and agri-food trade within the North American market. Since 1993, agricultural and agri-food trade and investment flows between the NAFTA partners has grown, with overall agricultural trade reaching about US$50 billion.

The NAFTA partners are one another's largest agricultural export markets: Canada and Mexico are the two largest agricultural suppliers to the United States, and the United States is the leading agricultural provider to both the Canadian and Mexican markets. U.S.-Mexico agricultural trade reached US$26.9 billion in 2008.

As NAFTA has contributed to further integration of the trading partners' agricultural sectors, Mexican industries have required more U.S. agricultural inputs. For example, U.S. feedstuffs have increased Mexican meat production and consumption; likewise the importance of Mexican produce to U.S. fruit and vegetable consumption is growing. Grains, oilseeds, meat and related products make up three-fourths of U.S. agricultural exports to Mexico, while beer, vegetables and fruit account for three-fourths of U.S agricultural imports from Mexico.

Myth 7: NAFTA negatively impacts the North American manufacturing base.

Reality: Since NAFTA came into effect, North American manufacturers have enjoyed better access to materials, technologies, capital, and talent available across the continent. Thousands of manufacturers have capitalized on this to improve efficiency and better refine technology, making them more competitive at home and around the world.

U.S. manufacturing output rose by 62% between 1993 and 2008, compared with 42% between 1980 and 1993. In 2008, U.S. manufacturing exports reached an all-time high of US$1.0 trillion.

Canadian manufacturing output (real GDP) increased by 62% between 1993 and 2008 compared with 23% between 1981 and 1993. Over the same period (1993–2008), Canadian manufacturing exports grew at a much faster pace (up 103.6%).

NAFTA has empowered Mexico's industrial base by facilitating modernization. As a strategic manufacturing center in North America, Mexico enhances the region's competitive status in the global marketplace. Since NAFTA's implementation, Mexico's international presence has been invigorated by the growth of manufacturing output, which has since tripled. In addition, Mexico's manufactured exports have multiplied five times over the past 15 years.

11.5. POPULAR GROUPS: THE ZAPATISTA ARMY OF NATIONAL LIBERATION

"Zapatista Rebels and Inter Milan"

In 2005, Subcomandante Marcos wrote to Milan International Futbol Club president Massimo Moratti with an invitation for Inter to play a friendly match, as a gesture of appreciation and solidarity, against the EZLN Football Club.[5] Marcos proposed the Argentine star Diego Maradona as referee.

Zapatista Army of National Liberation
Mexico
May 25, 2005
To: Massimo Moratti, President of the Milan International F.C. Milan, Italy
From: Subcomandante Insurgente Marcos EZLN Chiapas, Mexico
Don Massimo,

We have received the letter in which you inform us that your football team, the International F.C., has accepted the fraternal challenge we made to you. We appreciate the kindness and honesty of your response. We have learned through the media of statements by the Inter's management, coaching staff and players. They are all simply more examples of the nobility of your hearts. Know that we are delighted to have met you along our now long path and that it is an honor for us to be a part of the bridge which unites two dignified lands: Italy and Mexico.

I am letting you know that, in addition to being spokesperson for the EZLN, I have been unanimously designated Head Coach and put in charge of Intergalactic Relations for the zapatista football team (well, in truth no one else wanted to accept the job). In this role I should, perhaps, make use of this letter to move forward in fixing details about the match.

Perhaps, for example, I might suggest that, instead of the football game being limited to one match, there could be 2. One in Mexico and another in Italy. Or one going and one on return. And the trophy known the world over as "The Pozol of Mud" would be fought for.

And perhaps I might propose to you that the game in Mexico would be played, with you as visitors, in the Mexican 68 Olympic Stadium, in CU, in DF, and the stadium receipts would be for the indigenous displaced by paramilitaries in Los Altos of Chiapas. Although then, obviously, I would have to send a letter to the UNAM university community (students, teachers, researchers, manual and administrative workers) asking them to lend us the stadium, not without previously solemnly promising them that we wouldn't ask them to remain silent . . . and then imposing Don Porfirio's word on them. And perhaps we might agree, given that you would already be in Mexico, that we would hold another game in Guadalajara, Jalisco, and that the proceeds would go to provide legal help for the young altermundistas unjustly imprisoned in the jails of that Mexican province and to all the political prisoners throughout the country. Transportation would not be a problem, because I have read that someone here in Mexico, generous as before, has offered his help.

And perhaps, if you are in agreement, for the games in Mexico the EZLN would turn to Diego Armando Maradona and ask him to be referee; to Javier El Vasco Aguirre and to Jorge Valdano and ask them to act as assistant referees (or linesmen); and to Sócrates, midfielder who was from Brazil, to be 4th referee. And perhaps we might invite those two intergalactics who travel with Uruguayan passports: Eduardo Galeano and Mario Benedetti to do the play by play of the game for the Zapatista System of Intergalactic Television ("the only television which is read"). In Italy, Gianni Mina and Pedro Luis Sullo could be the commentators.

And, perhaps, in order to differentiate ourselves from the objectification of women which is promoted at football games and in commercials, the EZLN would ask the national lesbian-gay community, especially transvestites and transsexuals, to organize themselves and to amuse the respectable with ingenious pirouettes during the games in Mexico. That way, in addition to prompting TV censorship, scandalizing the ultra-right and disconcerting the Inter ranks, they would raise the morale and spirits of our team. There are not just 2 sexes, and there is not just one world, and it is always advisable for those who are persecuted for their differences to share happiness and support without ceasing to be different.

Rushing headlong now, we might play another game in Los Angeles, in California, the US, where their governor (who substitutes steroids for his lack of neurons) is carrying out a criminal policy against Latin migrants. All the receipts from that match would be earmarked for legal advice for the undocumented in the USA and to jail the thugs from the "Minuteman Project." In addition, the zapatista "dream team" would carry a large banner saying "Freedom for Mumia Abu Jamal and Leonard Peltier."

It is quite likely that Bush would not allow our spring-summer model ski masks to create a sensation in Hollywood, so the meeting could be moved to the dignified Cuban soil, in front of the military base which the US government maintains, illegally and illegitimately, in Guantánamo. In this case each delegation (from the Inter and from the Ezeta) would commit themselves to taking at least one kilo of food and medicines for each of their members, as a symbol of protest against the blockade the Cuban people are suffering.

And perhaps I might propose to you that the return games would be in Italy, with you as the home team (and us as well, since it is known that Italian sentiment is primarily pro-zapatista). One could be in Milan, in your stadium, and the other wherever you decide (it could be in Rome, because "all games lead to Rome" . . . or is it "all roads lead to Rome?" . . . ah well, it's the same). Some of the receipts would be to help migrants of different nationalities who are being criminalized by the governments of the European Union and the rest for whatever you decide. But we would certainly need at least one day in order to go to Genoa to paint caracolitos on the statue of Christopher Columbus (note: the likely fine for damages to monuments would be covered by Inter) and in order to take a flower of remembrance to the place where the young altermundist Carlo Giuliani fell (note: we would take care of the flower).

And, if we are already in the Europe, we could play a game in Euzkal Herria in the Basque Country. If "An Opportunity for the Word" couldn't happen, then we'd try for "An Opportunity for the Kick." We would demonstrate in front of the head office of the racists from the BBVA-Bancomer who are trying to criminalize the humanitarian aid received by the indigenous communities (perhaps in order to divert attention from the criminal proceedings against them for "tax evasion, secret accounts, illegal pension funds, secret contributions to political campaigns, bribes in order to buy banks in Latin America and wrongful appropriation of goods"—Carlos Fernández-Vega. "Mexico, S.A." in La Jornada 2S/V/05). Hmm . . . It looks like there's going to be 7 games now (which isn't bad, because that way we can compete for the audience for the European Cup, the Liberators and the qualifiers for the World Cup). The one which wins 4 of the 7 games will win "The Pozol of Mud" (note: if the zapatista team loses more than 3 games, the tournament will be canceled).

Too many? Fine, Don Massimo, you're right, perhaps it's better to leave it at 2 games (one in Mexico and the other in Italy), because we don't want to tarnish the Inter's record too badly with the certain defeats we're proposing.

Perhaps, in order to balance your evident disadvantage a bit, I might pass on to you some secret information. For example, the zapatista team is mixed (that is, there are men and women); we play with so-called "miner's" boots (they have steel toes, which is why they puncture balls); according to our uses and customs, the game is only over when none of the players of either team is left standing (that is, they are high resistance); the EZLN can reinforce itself at its discretion (that is, the Mexicans "Bofo" Bautista and Maribel "Marigol" Domínguez can appear in the lineup . . . if they accept). And we have designed a chameleon-like uniform (if we're losing, black and blue stripes appear on our shirts, confusing our rivals, the referee . . . and the public). And also we've been practicing, with relative success, two new plays: the "marquiña avanti fortiori" (note: translated into gastronomical terms it would be something like a pizza and guacamole sandwich) and the "marquiña caracoliña con variante inversa" (note: the equivalent of spaghetti with stewed beans, but spoiled).

With all this (and a few other surprises), we might, perhaps, revolutionize world football, and then, perhaps, football would no longer be just a business, and once again it would be an entertaining game. A game made, as you put it so well, of true feelings.

Perhaps . . . Nonetheless, this is just to reiterate to you and to your family, to all the men and women of the Inter and the nerazzurro fans, our appreciation and admiration for you (although I'm warning you that, in front of the goalposts, there will be neither mercy nor compassion). As to all the rest, well . . . perhaps . . . but . . .

Vale. Salud and may the green-white-red that clothes our dignities soon find themselves on both lands.

From the mountains of the Mexican Southeast.
Subcomandante Insurgente Marcos (D. T. Z.)
(designing plays on a chalkboard and fighting with Durito because he's insisting that, instead of the traditional 4-2-4, we should present 1-1-1-1-1-1-1-1-1-1, which, he says, is confusing).
Mexico, May of 2005.
P.S. for the Mexican Federation of Football, the Real Madrid, the Bayern Munich, the Osasuna, the Ajax, Liverpool and the Ferretería González team—I'm sorry, but I have an exclusive contract with the Ezetaelene.
P.S. in the tone and volume of a sports announcer—The Sup, using the tactics of the Uruguayan Obdulio Varela in the final against Brazil (World Cup, Maracaná Stadium, Rio de Janeiro, 7/16/1950), ball in hand, having traveled as if in slow motion (since May of 2001), from the zapatista goalpost. After complaining to the referee about the illegitimacy of the goal, he puts the ball in the center of the field. He turns around to look at his compañeros and they exchange glances and silences. With the scorecard, the bets and the entire system against them, NO ONE has any hope for the zapatistas. It starts to rain. A watch reads almost 6. Everything appears ready for the game to resume . . .

F. C. Internazionale Milano
Dear Subcomandante Insurgente Marcos,

I am exceedingly pleased to have the privilege of writing in response to your extremely pleasant and kind challenge. I am addressing you, and through you to all the EZLN, in order to thank you for the opportunity you have given all of us to experience this special relationship. Allow me also to express my thoughts in response to your very, very kind letter. We will play. We will play our game, and I thank you for that. It will be a great match. Perhaps in a field, like we did as children, perhaps surrounded by giant trees. Or in a stadium, in the capital or on a rectangle drawn out in chalk on the earth, with the dust rising up until it makes us cough. Exhausted, but happy.

Since we are in agreement, we will bring the balls and you the bitter pozol. If you accept, we will begin discussing the organization with the respective representatives and managers. We hope we can play soon. I think we could send a good group of players to Mexico, we'll see about the timing. Let us know what location would be best. Whether in DF or San Cristóbal, or in a community or a Caracol. Football can be an instrument for achieving important objectives, but it is something that turns us all into children and all equals. Dreamers all. We imagine great things, and we take pleasure in the small ones: a dribble, a scissors kick, a header, all make us happy. And we discover later that these small things are made of true feelings.

Dear Subcomandante, I am happy and proud to have known you and to have developed this relationship with the indigenous peoples of Mexico, in the name of the men and women of the FC Internazionale. The Inter peoples, like this football society, will try to always be close to you, exactly as you, with your example, are close to us. The game will truly be a simple and important moment. Every revolution begins from its own penalty area and ends in the opponent's goalpost. With so very much admiration and affection, I am sending you and all the zapatista indigenous men and women, my most personal best wishes, as well as those of my wife, my children and the nerazzurro peoples.
Un abrazo,
Massimo Moratti
[translated by irlandesa][6]

Unfortunately, the match was never actually played—but EZLN's futbol team did find chances to compete on the pitch against international teams. The Easton Cowboys, an anarchist team (whose sign-up sheet said players should bring boots, shin pads, and sideburns) representing the Plough, a neighborhood pub in inner-city Bristol, England, in 1999 became the first European football team to travel to Chiapas, but that is another story.[7]

ADDITIONAL READING

Simpson, Will, & Malcolm McMahon. *Freedom through Football: The Story of the Easton Cowboys and Cowgirls*. Bristol: Tangent Books, Ltd., 2012.

Leer en español

Beltrán, Enviada, and Claudia Herrera. "En septiembre, la reforma a la educación secundaría: Fox." *La Jornada Virtual*, May 19, 2005. www.jornada.unam.mx.

NOTES

1. These are available through the *Oxford Research Encyclopedia for Latin America*, http://latinamericanhistory.oxfordre.com/page/videos/ [For those without institutional access to this Oxford online source, a discussion of the democratization process is available in Roderic A. Camp, *Mexican Politics* (New York: Oxford University Press, 2013; 6th edition).]

2. Online at http://www.photius.com/countries/mexico/national_security/mexico_national_security_police_and_law_enfor~516.html. Per the website, data is

"re-published from The Library of Congress Country Studies and the CIA World Factbook" and is valid as of June 1996.

3. This lecture is available online from Rice University's Baker Institute, https://www.youtube.com/watch?v=dy5deIZUvLc.

4. The North American Free Trade Agreement is available at https://www.nafta-sec-alena.org/Home/Legal-Texts/North-American-Free-Trade-Agreement. Text in this section is available online at or clearly linked from http://www.naftanow.org/about/default_en.asp.

5. "Zapatista rebels woo Inter Milan," BBC News, May 11, 2005, http://news.bbc.co.uk/2/hi/4537859.stm. Also William H. Beezley and Roderic A. Camp, interview with Jaime Serra Puche, available through the *Oxford Research Encyclopedia for Latin America*, http://latinamericanhistory.oxfordre.com/page/videos.

6. The story is shown as it appeared on FootballBar, November 14, 2012, https://footballbar.wordpress.com/2012/11/14/zapatista-rebels-and-inter-milan/.

7. See William H. Beezley, "The Ski Mask," in *Objects and Episodes in Latin American Lively Arts* (Latham, MA: Wiley-Blackwell, forthcoming).

CHAPTER 12

Contemporary Issues, 2000–

Since the mid-1990s, dramatic forces have shaped Mexico's path in each of the five networks. Documents consider the recent impact of immigration, the drug war, democratization, popular culture, and globalization. Many features of contemporary life in Mexico can be examined as problems rather than as characteristic descriptions of the society—as some critics do. Corruption (12.1); drugs (12.2); unfair international treatment, obesity and psychological depression (12.3); and childhood pregnancy (12.4) are examples. Here we demonstrate some of the ways Mexicans respond to these problems through effigies and images, using humor to combat their difficulties (12.5).

12.1. POLITICS: MAURICIO MERINO, "THE FIGHT AGAINST CORRUPTION"

(A review of ongoing reforms to promote transparency and curtail corruption.)

I

Though neither of the two recent episodes that sparked Mexico's largest public awareness movement since the beginning of this century were anything out of the ordinary, they marked a tipping point in Mexican politics. First off, the forced disappearance of 43 students in Iguala, Guerrero, on September 26, 2014, caused a wave of protests against human rights violations and impunity.[a] Soon after, leading journalist Carmen Aristegui published a report on First Lady Angélica Rivera's dubious acquisition of the "Casa blanca," a high-end residence in Mexico City. Aristegui pointed out that Grupo Higa, which built the residence for Rivera "according to her specifications," had been awarded several public-works concessions during Enrique Peña Nieto's governorship of the State of Mexico, as well as during his presidency, provoking widespread public discontent toward corruption in Mexico.[b] In less than 45 days, the social discontent that had accumulated over the course of almost 15 years came to the forefront, with collective outrage focusing on two main issues: impunity and corruption.

I use the term "movement" with a certain reserve—public resistance toward the scandals has not responded to a defined political organization, has no visible leadership, has not been reflected in party competition, has not sought representation, and has not orchestrated a common agenda. Nevertheless, the movement has clearly manifested in social and other non-traditional media outlets. People have taken to the streets, with a wide range of civil and academic organizations successfully putting forward their demands. Still, this form of resistance has none of the characteristics of a typical movement. Nevertheless, since the closing months of 2014, this movement has not only defied the Mexican political class' discourse and practices but has also signaled out impunity and corruption as the two nemeses of Mexican democracy. Thus, I would lean toward calling this an awareness movement, whose main contribution thus far has been to open

---

[a] On September 26th, 2014, students from the Normal Rural School "Raúl Isidro Burgos," in the town of Ayotzinapa, Guerrero, were attacked by municipal police forces from the municipalities of Iguala and Cocula, Guerrero. Mayor of Iguala José Luis Abarca ordered the police to detain the students and stop them from entering the municipality. During the attacks, six people died—three of whom were students—and 25 people were injured. The 43 disappeared students were detained by the police, who "turned them in" to a criminal organization known as "Guerreros Unidos." On October 6th, 11 days later, the federal government started investigations via the Attorney General's Office. The investigation concluded that the students had been murdered and cremated in a dump in the municipality of Cocula. The disappeared students' families, together with a number of activists, have disputed the investigation's findings. These parties have been protesting since the events took place.

[b] The report, which was supported by Connectas and the International Center for Journalists, is titled "La casa blanca de Enrique Peña Nieto (investigación especial)" ("Enrique Peña Nieto's White House [special investigation]"), and was originally published in the news outlet aristeguinoticias.com (http://aristeguinoticias.com/0911/mexico/la-casa-blanca-de-enrique-pena-nieto/). In December 2014, after the Ayotzinapa and "Casa blanca" episodes, presidential approval reached its lowest point in two years, according to a poll by El Universal/Buendía & Laredo. Approval rates fell to 41 percent (Peña Nieto started his presidential term at 43 percent) and disapproval rates were at 50 percent. Just one year earlier, his approval rates were at 50 percent. According to Ulises Beltrán's telephone surveys, presidential approval dropped to 25 percent. Beltrán, Ulises, "El desacuerdo con los presidentes (1994–2015)," *Nexos*, March 2015. The newspaper *Reforma* registered polls for the last four months of 2014, with presidential approval at 39 percent and disapproval at 58 percent. According to another *Reforma* poll, conducted March 17th, 2015, 78 percent of university students (from public and private universities alike) disapprove of the president and his government.

a window of opportunity for proposing and promoting reforms to fight impunity and corruption.[c]

The processes by which public administrations make choices are usually jumbled, obscure, and confusing. It is a well-known fact that arbitrary and imprecisely regulated practices are diametrically opposed to honesty. It is also known that the multiplication and fragmentation of administrative regulations increase the chances of arbitrary practices taking place.[d] Nevertheless, the institutions in charge of fighting corruption in Mexico are fragmented and have their own sets of regulations for public officials to follow. From this perspective, the smartest public officials are not those who focus their programs on public issues that need solutions, nor those who submit their decisions, resources and results to public scrutiny. Rather, the public officials on top are those who know how to adhere to the right bureaucratic procedures. Meanwhile, officials who make mistakes in procedures and cause irregularities in the system are punished.

Today, we have valuable information on which procedures generate the most irregularities. The five highest rates can be found in the following areas of management: 1) in the distribution of allocated posts and the reaping of their benefits, as well as in certain schemes to obtain millions of pesos in severance payments for unjustified lay-offs; 2) in the granting of public-works contracts for government purchases, which, at least on the surface, appear to follow impeccable bidding procedures; 3) in the authorities' granting of concessions, licenses, or permits of all kinds—for everything between housing-development to informal business projects; 4) in the transfer of public funds via subsidies or aid programs, whose growth directly benefits public officials, both politically and financially; and 5) in face-to-face interactions with public officials providing services—especially, in interactions with officials who claim to serve in the name of justice and security. Despite the fact that more and more information on the corruption permeating these areas is coming to the fore, efforts against corruption remain fragmented and procedural. Instead of addressing the causes of corruption, public officials causing irregularities in the system are prosecuted on a case-by-case basis.[e]

---

[c] The "window of opportunity" concept pertains to the moments and conditions that instigate change in public agendas, especially when caused by circumstantial or inconstant environmental factors, even though these factors may be part of a larger and older problem. See John Kingdon's book, *Agendas, Alternatives and Public Policies*, Harper Collins, New York, 1995. To Kingdon, a "window" opens when three "streams" flow together—the problem, the policies, and politics. The window of opportunity opens after an issue has been established as a public problem and once there are options and incentives for politicians to implement change.

[d] See Cass Sunstein's book *Simpler: The Future of Government*, Simon & Schuster, New York, 2013.

[e] Cfr. "Evaluación de la política de combate a la corrupción," Superior Auditing Office. This document pertains to the Superior Auditing Office's 57th, 58th, and 59th amendments, as well as to the Report on Superior Auditing Results for Public Accounts.

Evidently, the Ayotzinapa and "Casa blanca" scandals were not exceptional in Mexico's long history of corruption and impunity. However, these events pushed society to the limit for their severity, coupled with the global interest they sparked. The Ayotzinapa scandal's international scope stems from the cruelty and cynicism with which the 43 students in Guerrero were massacred, as well as from the fact that the responsible criminals were acting under the orders of the mayor of Iguala (and his wife) with the collusion of local police—and the initial indifference of federal authorities. With Ayotzinapa in the backdrop, the disclosure of First Lady Angélica Rivera's tactics to increase her private wealth, coupled with the president and his wife's ambiguous and insufficient public response, which widely circulated in the media, only exacerbated public discontent—finally opening a window of opportunity to make in-depth modifications to Mexico's institutional design and fight corruption at its roots.

III

Over the course of the 21st century, several notable advances in terms of access to public information—namely, transparency—have already taken place. Both the Felipe Calderón and Enrique Peña Nieto administrations ascribed to the Open Government Partnership, with the creation and strengthening of pertinent legal regulations and transparency institutions on the rise since 2002. Thanks to these institutions and regulations, public information has undoubtedly multiplied, become increasingly accessible, and been continually put to better use. However, files and management records for decision-making processes in the public sphere are yet to be made available. Public finance accounts—including the promising concept of national accounting harmonization—are still insufficient and obscure. Meanwhile, budgetary allocations still rely on the arbitrary and ambiguously regulated trends mentioned above, and errors in financial-oversight processes are yet to be corrected. Transparency has helped find and report abuse, sparking scandals in turn. However, transparency can also function as an alibi for corruption: with more information published, better online portals, and increased propaganda, public officials can maintain the processes that propagate the abuse of power for personal gain.

This patchy diagnostic sparked the creation of an Accountability Network (Red por la Rendición de Cuentas) in May 2011. At the time, the network was under the oversight of the Center for Economic Research and Teaching (CIDE), a university research institution for the social sciences, which is part of the National Council of Science and Technology (Conacyt). The Accountability Network was created by a group of researchers that had undertaken the task of studying and documenting how Mexico's lack of a comprehensive, coherent, and articulated policy on accountability was directly behind corruption and impunity. After publishing several papers,[f] the group decided to formalize their dialogue, which had already made an impact on public, civil, and academic organizations.

The Accountability Network's main goal is to use academic studies, public debate, and social-impact assessments to promote the design and implementation of an accountability policy. Their initiative has been unprecedented. Not only did it stem from a public academic institution that was funded and governed by the Mexican State, but it also included members of other public institutions, such as the Federal Institute for Information Access and Data Protection (IFAI), which was created under the first set of pro-transparency reforms; the Superior Auditing Office (ASF), which is the Chamber of Deputies' auditing office for public finances; the General Archive of the Nation (AGN), which is formally housed under the Ministry of the Interior; the former Federal Electoral Institute (IFE), which was a national autonomous body in charge of conducting federal election processes; and the Mexican Conference for Access to Public Information (COMAIP), an umbrella organization for the bodies guaranteeing transparency in each of Mexico's states. In other words, the Accountability Network amalgamated several public institutions that would be relevant to the design of said policy—all of which agreed to join the academic team that gave birth to the project.[g]

Since the Accountability Network's founding, the above public institutions have engaged with civil-society organizations, which had already been using applied knowledge and public assessment for transparency and accountability measures in Mexico for a long time. These civil-society organizations had already formed a true community around the issue, exerting their influence upon the media and decision-makers alike. However, aside from a few occasional projects, these civil-society organizations never established a permanent channel for collaborating among themselves—and even less so, for collaborating with public institutions. In this sense, the Accountability Network constituted a step forward, with a wide network of scholars from various public and private universities and research centers becoming active participants as well. For the first time, Mexico's large and influential community of civil-society organizations could join scholars and public officials (who usually functioned independently) to engage in debates and work to address the issues at hand.

---

[f] The studies published through the Accountability Network's initiative or mediation may be viewed here: www.rendiciondecuentas.org.mx. Among others, the most relevant study to the organization's structuring was *La Estructura de la Rendición de Cuentas en* México, edited by Mauricio Merino, Sergio López Ayllón, and Guillermo Cejudo. CIDE, 2010.

[g] The full list of the 75 social, public, and academic organizations that have formally convened with the Accountability Network can be found in the website cited above.

Since its founding, the Accountability Network has committed to three main principles. First of all, the network is not made up of natural persons, but of legal persons and collectives that have voluntarily ascribed to the CIDE's project. Thus, the network has kept the names, careers, and freedoms of the people in the organization separate from the network's initiatives. The Accountability Network does not take ownership of the research, findings, or projects that its members conduct individually, but does foster their works' public distribution via the network's website, which has become a comprehensive database as well as a channel for everyday communication among its followers and member organizations. Secondly, the network does not emit its own communiqués: rather, member organizations share their opinions separately. Only when documents are consensually drafted during open deliberations are these presented under the Accountability Network's name. The same rule applies to its editorial guidelines: the books in the series "Cuadernos de la Red" (The Network's Notebooks), as well as the articles published throughout the network's trajectory, have invariably respected the original author's rights over their works. Lastly, the network has never changed or increased the scope of its original aim: to show why Mexico needs to prioritize the design of a public policy to guarantee accountability. Thus, even though all its members have their own agendas, collective efforts seek to promote the drafting of said public policy. The way this unprecedented collective of institutions and organizations has upheld its principles without compromising any of its members, together with the fact that the network's work has focused on defining and creating a method for the proper drafting of said public policy, have turned the Accountability Network into an invaluable project. Furthermore, the network's professional, efficient, and committed executive management and Advisory Board, which was designed to represent its members' plural interests, have been critical to the development of the network's projects.

Among other fundamental changes, President Peña Nieto's initiative was broadened to include certain transparency obligations for political parties, unions, public trusts or funds of any kind, as well as the judicial branch. At the same time, the reform ensured the autonomy of the organ in charge of guaranteeing information access (the IFAI) and secured the scope of said organ's resolutions, which are valid throughout Mexico.[h] Surely, these changes would have never taken place without the aforementioned technical and political dialogue between senators and civil society organizations—especially since the Chamber of Deputies and some of the PRI's parliamentary representatives actively tried to check the revamped right to transparency's scope throughout the legislative process. Nevertheless, senators remained

---

[h] The full text of the constitutional reform on transparency, which was published in February of 2014, can be found on the Accountability Network's website, cited above. A narration of the events that led up to the initiative's conclusion may also be found on said website.

firm and—after several months of tug of war between both chambers, the federal government, and civil society organizations—managed to overcome their opponents' attempts at resistance. Without a doubt, the constitutional reform for transparency passed on February 2014, is, to date, the most advanced in the world in terms of the extent to which it guarantees citizens' fundamental right to access information.

This reform also gave the Senate the faculty to revise IFAI memberships and, if necessary, appoint new commissioners tasked with guaranteeing the right to information access under the newly created National Transparency System. Thus, after publically discussing the IFAI commissioners' performance and openly considering academic and civil-society perspectives, the Senate chose to completely overhaul the IFAI—which was composed of seven commissioners. After summoning the candidates who met the established requirements and had strong enough careers to fill these posts, the Senate established a procedure to meticulously study each of the candidates' careers, credentials, and qualities. In an unprecedented move, a "complementary committee" of ten scholars, activists, and professionals—who had all collaborated with the Accountability Network in the past (but were not required to have done so for the purposes of this committee)—was invited to participate in the evaluations as well.[i] Despite its controversies, the process to renew the revamped IFAI's members marked a precedent that cannot be ignored: candidates for Senate-designated public posts were compared and evaluated according to public criteria, with the support of a team of specialists who worked independently of the legislative branch.

Without a doubt, the most relevant product of this open dialogue was the joint creation of the General Transparency Law, which, in turn, stemmed from the constitutional transparency reform. In another unprecedented move, the same group of senators behind the aforementioned changes decided to create a "writing group" for the bylaws—bringing together representatives from the Collective for Transparency (Colectivo por la Transparencia), Mexico Get Informed (México Infórmate), and the Accountability Network.[j] These organizations' representatives worked alongside the senators' technical and legal consultants to draft a legislative proposal that both adhered to the February 2014 constitutional reform and safeguarded Mexico's previous advances in terms of information access. Thus, after

---

[i] Those who wish to read about the details of the procedure and its results may consult the Accountability Network's website as well.
[j] While the first two organizations are also part of the Accountability Network, it was more convenient for them to participate in the writing group on their own behalf. Meanwhile, the Accountability Network chose a CIDE investigator to act as the network's representative. Ana Cristina Ruelas, from Colectivo por la Transparencia; Gabriela Morales, from México Infórmate; and Natalia Calero, from CIDE, served as writers and as messengers between the Senate and the Accountability Network's organizations. It is worth noting that their performance was commended by both legislative chambers, as well as by their respective communities.

approximately 250 hours of drafting and deliberating, in early November 2014, Senators Arely Gómez, Alejandro Encinas, Laura Rojas, and Pablo Escude publically announced the end of said stage and the beginning of a new process to consult senators and other officials who would be subject to the new legislation.

Still, it is hard to know whether public pressure would have sufficed to stop the government's attempts at halting the legislation's progress if it had not been for the political window of opportunity that came with the two deplorable events mentioned above. While there is no doubt that public discontent helped make progress in terms of transparency, there is no way of determining to what extent this discontent bolstered the civil organizations and senators leading Mexico's transparency efforts.

In any case, on March 2nd, the senators opened a new round-table session to discuss possible changes to the initial bill. Just a few days earlier—on February 23rd—the Office of the President, directed by Aurelio Nuño, had invited the Accountability Network's civil-society organizations, which had participated in the transparency-reform debates, to join him at the presidential residence, Los Pinos, to discuss Legal Counsel Humberto Castillejo's objections to the bill. While this meeting was not easy, it was highly productive: Counsel Castillejo took the civil organizations' arguments into account, and the civil organizations considered the executive branch's reasons for making changes to the original project. By the end of the meeting, the Office of the President agreed to send the Accountability Network a written note with the legislation's modifications—at that point, there were still no official accounts of the modifications, which the senators had only encountered through rumor.

The Senate received the note a few hours before the public hearing was held on February 28th. The note was published online that same day. Thus, the hearing's deliberations were based on well-founded legal arguments, rather than on assumptions and abstract allegations.[k] Many of the objections that had been leaked over the weeks preceding these debates were removed (some of them, perhaps, were never more than rumors), and the Senate agreed with the remaining, well-founded objections. Even with the modifications, the version of the bill the Senate ultimately approved satisfactorily reflected the aspirations that the Accountability Network's civil and academic organizations had for the bill. After being sent to the Chamber of Deputies for ratification, the General Transparency Law was approved on April 16, 2015. I have no doubt that as time goes by, this will be a date worth remembering.

---

[k] Details on this publication may be found on the Accountability Network's website.

VI

If successful, the anti-corruption reform's premises will prove highly ambitious. Before concluding this text, I will present a summary of the reform's central premises and components, citing the document that gained the most support from the Accountability Network.[1] The reform's first premise states that corruption should be addressed at its roots rather than solely focusing on its effects—it would be impossible to truly curtail corruption with a punitive and individualistic approach that only punishes corrupt acts after they have already been committed and proven. Fighting corruption with an individualistic crime-and-punishment perspective not only ignores the causes of corruption (regulations, responsibilities, procedures, and decision-making environments) but also produces "social vaccines" that end up normalizing corrupt practices.

Rather than changing the environments that present opportunities for corruption, viewing the issue through the lens of corrupt persons that need to be sanctioned would only bring about a never-ending chain of punished individuals, with no practical consequences for the causes behind corruption. This, in turn, would multiply detection rates for corrupt acts, with media coverage increasing in response. In the end, increased exposure could prompt society to start viewing corruption as a customary part of everyday political and social relations. Thus, institutional reactions against corruption should not be limited to the detection and prosecution of corrupt acts. Instead, institutions should permanently and deliberately detect and modify the regulations and processes that generate corruption.

The second premise is that an institutional intelligence design should be implemented to effectively address the causes of corruption. Varying interpretations of legal frameworks and operational criteria inevitably affect day-to-day public administration, creating loopholes for corruption and arbitrary decision making. Thus, there is an urgent need to design the right instruments to detect these loopholes—namely, the imprecise or sub-par legal regulations, the confusing procedures, the inadequate distribution of faculties and attributions among public officials and offices, the fragmentation or weakening of decision-making responsibilities, the lack of connectivity among processes and results, the absence of public surveillance and internal control, etc.—, which create environments (and even incentives) for public officials to use their assigned authority and monetary resources for personal gain.

Indeed, fighting corruption requires institutional intelligence to detect and curtail any opportunities to gain control over public resources and de-

---

[1] While said document was written by me, Eduardo Bohórquez, José Roldán Xopa, José Octavio López Presa, Max Kaiser, and Marco Fernández also participated in its elaboration. I would like to take this opportunity to thank them for their hard work and valuable contributions once again.

cisions with the purpose of deflecting them for personal gain. Rather than basing these efforts on generalizations or abstractions, this institutional intelligence should look to accumulated experience and institutional histories on the application of regulations, procedural quality, spaces for interaction between society and the authorities, and decision-making processes that have generated corruption in the past.

Institutional intelligence should be founded upon a registry of cases in which corruption has been detected effectively, recurrently, and even systematically. It should be based on these cases' accumulated evidence, drawing conclusions from a system of precedents. At the same time, the institutions in charge of combating corruption should have enough authority to change the conditions that heighten the risk of gaining control over public resources and decisions and using them for corrupt acts. Nevertheless, the authorities responsible for fighting corruption should under no circumstances take over the responsibilities of the public offices where corruption is taking place, nor should these offices ignore the authorities' institutional intelligence recommendations.

The third premise is that there should be a system of checks and balances for the institutions combating corruption. The only way to create a long-term solution for corruption is to have not just one but many institutions with the authority to jointly address corruption. It is important to note that limiting these efforts to a single national entity could increase the risks of mismanagement and politicization, whereas having multiple institutions would help create a mutual vigilance system. Having institutions that specialize in corruption—that is, internal and external oversight, and the development of institutional intelligence and processes of prevention, investigation, and sanction—does not imply that efforts will be fragmented. Rather, institutions should coordinate and adapt in synergy. These institutions should expressly create a mechanism for collaboration and information exchange.

Building a system of checks and balances based on having myriad institutions collaborating among themselves could strengthen their ability to identify, prevent, investigate, and make changes in situations that cause corruption. Individual power and resource mismanagement could be more assertively punished according to the offenses' severity: going from minor administrative offenses to serious cases of corruption to outright crimes. Evidently, this should be coordinated with a comprehensive, articulate, and coherent system.

The National Anticorruption System will be composed of four main institutions—two of them already exist but should be reformed and strengthened, and another two are new. Firstly, the Ministry of Public Service (SFP) will be in charge of internal control and of administrative innovation in the Federal Public Administration. The SFP will have the authority to coordinate a national internal control system, which will involve the State's autonomous organs as well as state and municipal governments. To fulfill this task, the SFP will need to be strengthened and reformed.

At the most basic level, strengthening the Ministry of Public Service (SFP) will imply establishing a professional career system for the federal government's internal auditors. To maintain impartiality and professionalism, the SFP should appoint internal auditors for their professional skills and not for their closeness to department heads. In our view, building a professional system of internal auditors is critical to the National Anticorruption System's success.

Besides sanctioning minor administrative offenses and ensuring the legality of internal public-administration processes, the SFP should seek to promote institutional innovation. Essentially, the SFP should use its institutional intelligence to fight the causes of corruption.

Lastly, the SFP will have the authority to coordinate the national internal-control system, which would bring best practices beyond the federal public administration by including the State's autonomous organs as well as municipal and state governments. For all these reasons, the head of the SFP will still be appointed by Mexico's president, but will need Senate ratification as well.

The Superior Auditing Office (ASF), which was reformed and strengthened just like the Ministry of Public Service, will still be the nation's top external controller for the fight against corruption. Thus, the ASF should have full constitutional autonomy, even though the Chamber of Deputies will still have exclusive control over public-finance evaluations.

In order for external control to effectively complement internal control in terms of checks and balances, the Superior Auditing Office (ASF) will need to overcome the restrictions that keep it from taking action during current tax years or from revisiting previous events that have sparked subsequent corrupt acts. We propose that the ASF should have the authority to take real-time action for specific incidences of corruption. Furthermore, the ASF would draft records that could eventually lead to the sanctioning of corrupt public officials. Likewise, auditing calendars would have to be modified so that the external control's findings may efficiently influence each tax year's public-spending programming. The ASF would also have the faculty to check state-level public spending deriving from the National Fiscal Coordination System, with no exceptions.

As stated in the proposal, internal and external control efforts should be both preventative and innovative. Thus, the ASF should have the authority to coordinate the National Auditing System so that state-level superior auditing organs, which are in charge of external control for each locality's resources and attributions, comply with shared technical regulations and criteria. Both the SFP and the ASF will have the authority to: i) sanction minor administrative offenses, ii) initiate sanction procedures for serious corruption offenses before the Federal Court of Auditors, and, if necessary, iii) provide assistance to the Special Prosecutor's Office for Corruption for cases of corruption crimes.

However, for corruption crimes, the Special Prosecutor's Office for Corruption will be in charge of investigating, creating files, and representing parties before Mexico's judicial branch. Thus the judicial framework for criminal law will need to be revised so that the Special Prosecutor's Office for Corruption can investigate and prosecute corruption crimes independently of the branch, institution, level of government, or autonomous organ in which corruption is committed. The Special Prosecutor's Office for Corruption may sanction all individuals involved in corruption-related crimes, regardless of whether said individuals are public officials or civilians. The Special Prosecutor's Office for Corruption is to take action based on the corruption reports issued by the internal and external control organs or by civilians. However, it may also act on its own accord.

Lastly, a Special Chamber within a revamped Court of Administrative Justice would also be a central component to the proposed system. The Chamber, to be composed of a central group as well as several regional chambers, will bring together all the records of serious cases of corruption registered in all internal control and auditing organs in Mexico. Judges will conduct the due processes corresponding to these records and will have the power to issue disqualification sanctions and fines for all individuals and public officials who participate in proven acts of serious corruption.

It is worth highlighting that the Court will only try serious acts of corruption, whereas the internal and external control organs will still be in charge of prosecuting minor administrative offenses, and the Special Prosecutor's Office for Corruption would manage all corruption crimes. Thus, Mexico's administrative and criminal proceedings system needs to be reformed so that corruption-related offenses and crimes may be addressed in all their forms.

Basically, the National Anticorruption System will be composed of the four institutions described above, independently of any other anticorruption measures the Mexican State decides to take—including cultural or public-ethics efforts. In addition to these four institutions, the Judicial Council of the judicial branch, the IFAI, and representatives from a council of citizens will be responsible for supervising the system's operation and issuing recommendations to ensure its efficacy. The system's design will require a constitutional reform as well as new laws on responsibilities and corruption that take advantage of international best practices. In addition, bylaws for the proposed institution's proper functioning will need to be drafted as well. Likewise, the National Anticorruption System will include a coordination and information-exchange mechanism for all its institutions.

The mechanism will issue recommendations based on the institutional intelligence process—these recommendations will apply to all three federal branches and to all state-level authorities.

In summary, the National Anticorruption System will i) create a history of the country's institutional experiences with corruption; ii) establish an active channel of interaction between the three federal branches, autonomous organs, and local governments; iii) prevent the fragmentation of current institutions and create separate, specialized, and mutually-reinforcing courts to sanction administrative offenses, serious acts of corruption, and federal crimes in accordance with the agreements Mexico has drafted with the Organization of American States, the United Nations, and the Organization for Economic Co-operation and Development (OECD); iv) promote the creation of a system that would address corruption beyond the federal level by focusing on state and municipal governments as well; v) use a system of checks and balances to comprehensively fight corruption; vi) investigate and prosecute those responsible for committing corrupt acts—both in the government and among private citizens—and go further by addressing the causes of corruption; and vii) establish measures to create institutional intelligence, prevent corruption, support innovation, and promote a national culture that stands against corruption.

VII

The ongoing transparency and corruption reforms have been the subject of much public debate. These reforms have built upon academic and social organizations' years of research and dialogue to draft comprehensive, articulate, and coherent public policy on accountability as a way to fight the corruption that has plagued Mexico's public institutions. Corruption hinders institutions from performing as expected, deteriorates trust and social relationships, violates rights, wastes resources, limits economic growth, and stops income distribution. Corruption is the number one cause of inequality, impunity, and exclusion from Mexico's political regime.

The constitutional reform that will create the National Anticorruption System will by no means be the sole component of the fight against corruption—which will require further changes in bylaws and public-administration practices. However, the reform will pave the way for the fight against corruption. This reform is not unaffected by the progress that has already been made in terms of transparency, nor will it be unaffected by the pending legislation on personal files and information protection. Without the corruption reform, however, there would still be something missing. If the strengthening of the right to information access had been approved without the creation of institutions specifically designed to combat corruption, Mexico would still be missing an integral part of its new foundation.

Both reforms have paved the way to change Mexico's system for corruption-related administrative and criminal proceedings—the Achilles heel of Mexico's political regime. Changing this will counter the institutional fragmentation that has hindered institutional work from prospering ever since Mexico's democratic transition. The reform will bind these institutions, along with all of Mexico's state governments, to the same accountability policy. It will promote a system of checks and balances so that no states or entities are excluded from the fight against corruption. Instead, they will all be responsible for transparency and social vigilance—mutually supervising each other and creating an influx of institutional intelligence in order to correct the processes, regulations, and environments that cause corruption today. The reform will counter the deep-rooted misconception that combating corruption is limited to punishing corrupt individuals without addressing the causes of corruption. Lastly, it will highlight the need to fully overhaul the government's operations and public administrations—which has been a pending issue ever since Mexico's democratic transition.

None of these changes will take place in the short term, which makes the need to start now that much more urgent. The events that opened a window of opportunity for the enactment of the transparency and corruption reforms bring the promise of a completely different political scene. For the first time in the history of Mexico's public administration, all public officials would have to document what they are doing and how they are doing it, recording their proceedings in accessible public files. Also for the first time, citizens could become directly involved in supervising public management. Traditional bureaucracy's corrupt practices will have to give way—not just because the right to information access implies that corruption will be publicly exposed, but also because for the first time, comprehensive regulations will define corrupt practices within Mexico's administrative and criminal proceedings. Once these practices are detected and documented, professional external and internal auditors can address the issues, which would then be sanctioned in a new Special Chamber within the Court of Administrative Justice. Not only that, but the Special Prosecutor's Office for Corruption would be able to prosecute corruption, with its central group systematically and publically addressing corruption issues. If the reform is successful on its own terms, Mexico will have to reassess its public spending, supervision, and sanctioning practices. Never before has there been a reform this ambitious to tackle, however slowly, the trends in Mexico's illegitimate spending of public resources. As I write these notes, I sincerely trust that, despite it all, this story will have a happy ending.[1]

12.2. MILITARY AND POLICE: MEXICO'S DRUG TRAFFICKING ORGANIZATIONS: SOURCE AND SCOPE OF THE RISING VIOLENCE[2]

Illegal drugs and related criminal activities represent the most severe challenge for the police and military in contemporary Mexico. The profits from the illegal drug industry have financed the organization of many other criminal enterprises. In this excellent government document prepared for members of the United States Congress and its committees, the analyst provides a useful summary and conclusion (although anyone interested in the question should read the entire document).

Summary

In Mexico, the violence generated by drug trafficking organizations (DTOs) in recent years has been, according to some, unprecedented. In 2006, Mexico's newly elected President Felipe Calderón launched an aggressive campaign—an initiative that has defined his administration—against the DTOs that has been met with a violent response from the DTOs. Government enforcement efforts have had successes in removing some of the key leaders in all of the seven major DTOs. However, these efforts have led to violent succession struggles within the DTOs themselves. In July 2010, the Mexican government announced that more than 28,000 people had been killed in drug trafficking-related violence since December 2006 when President Calderón came to office. Although violence has been an inherent feature of the trade in illicit drugs, the character of the drug trafficking-related violence in Mexico seems to have changed recently, now exhibiting increasing brutality. In the first ten months of 2010, an alarming number of Mexican public servants have been killed allegedly by the DTOs, including 12 Mexican mayors and in July, a gubernatorial candidate. The massacres of young people and migrants, the killing and disappearance of Mexican journalists, the use of torture, and the phenomena of car bombs have received wide media coverage and have led some analysts to question if the violence has been transformed into something new, beyond the typical violence that has characterized the trade. For instance, some observers have raised the concern that the Mexican DTOs may be acting more like domestic terrorists. Others maintain that the DTOs are transnational organized crime organizations at times using terrorist tactics. Still others believe the DTOs may be similar to insurgents attempting to infiltrate the Mexican state by penetrating the government and police. The growing security crisis in Mexico including the March 13, 2010, killing of three individuals connected to the U.S. consulate in Ciudad Juárez, Mexico, (two of the victims were U.S. citizens) has drawn the attention of the U.S. Congress and has raised concerns about the stability of a strategic partner and neighbor. Congress is also concerned about the possibility of "spillover" violence along the U.S.

border and further inland. The 111th Congress held more than 20 hearings dealing with the violence in Mexico, U.S. foreign assistance, and border security issues. The 112th Congress is likely to be interested in progress made by the Calderón government in quelling the violence and asserting its authority in DTO strongholds, and in the implications for the United States. Members are also likely to continue to conduct close oversight of U.S.-Mexico security cooperation and other related bilateral issues. This report provides background on drug trafficking in Mexico, identifies the major drug trafficking organizations operating today, and analyzes the context, scope, and scale of the violence. It examines current trends of the violence, analyzes prospects for curbing violence in the future, and compares it with violence in Colombia. For background on U.S. policy responses to the spiraling violence in Mexico and information on bilateral cooperation between the United States and Mexico see: CRS Report R41349, U.S.-Mexican Security Cooperation: the Mérida Initiative and Beyond, by Clare Ribando Seelke and Kristin M. Finklea. For a discussion of the problem of violence "spilling over" into the United States, see CRS Report R41075, Southwest Border Violence: Issues in Identifying and Measuring Spillover Violence, coordinated by Kristin M. Finklea. For general background on Mexico, see CRS Report RL32724, Mexico-U.S. Relations: Issues for Congress, by Clare Ribando Seelke. Mexico's Drug Trafficking Organizations: Source and Scope of the Rising Violence. . . .

12.3. FAMILY: DANIELA MOLINA, "MEXICANS: MORE POUNDS AND LESS HAPPY"

The mood of the population has been diminished by the conditions of insecurity, violence, poverty, and social discontent that the country has lived

Mexicans suffer personal depression because of insecurity.

through for several years, that has caused nearly 10 percent of inhabitants in Mexico to be diagnosed with depression and with an inclination for up to 25 million people to develop some affective disorder throughout their lifetime.

While economic forecasts are not favorable and the political climate continues to upset a good number of Mexicans, now in the field of health is seen an encouraging picture.

With 32 percent of the Mexican population suffering obesity (almost 40 million) and 10 million with depression, experts agree that both conditions are multifactorial and they can be linked, one can lead to the other, exacerbate their symptoms, and also cause the development of other diseases such as diabetes, high blood pressure, or even lead to suicide.

"We are inter-related, we cannot think that human beings are only body or mind—only," says in an interview with SinEmbargo, Gabriela Camera Cáceres, President of the Group of civic organizations Voz Pro Salud Mental (Voice for Mental Health) and a specialist in the subject.

She, who also served as National Counsel for Health, says: "It has been a difficult year for all Mexicans, independent of the statistics that indicate that 10 percent of the population has or has suffered depression at some moment in their lives, but in general there has been much social unrest that has been reflected in the streets, in the news, in everything that has been experienced, we have dealt for so many years with problems of insecurity, in some cities there has been much more than in others, like spending years in war, and when something like this happens, there is discontent and a sense of insecurity that greatly increases psychiatric and emotional problems, the people are more depressed and, of course, there is more anxiety because of the uncertainty that is felt in society. When people live in an environment in which they feel secure, and feel protected and at the same time have reached a maturity to demand and contribute, these are countries where things work better, but when there is social unrest and insecurity, obviously the mental experience is affected."

For her part, Blanca Pardo, graduate in nutrition from the Nutrition and Metabolism Services unit of Mexico's Juárez Hospital mentioned in an interview, "As has been seen sometimes diet has a relationship with some level of depression in adults as well as children. There are many factors. Sometimes individuals eat out of anxiety and that exacerbates obesity." And, she continues, "On the other hand, the patient who is obese is an easy target for bullying because society rejects him, always saying that he looks bad or cataloguing him as a fatty and that also affects people."

The president of the association specializing in giving workshops, courses, and care for depressed persons, says in this regard, "We cannot deny that many people have depression and anxiety, some eat more or sometimes eat less, these are people who get thinner, but the majority begin to have compulsive eating behavior to reduce anxiety and this affects physique and health.

It also relates to the lack of concern about self-care that can leave you without energy to exercise or to have a healthy diet that results in personal carelessness in several respects. She says, "Of course, people with depression have more disease comorbidities, such as obesity, diabetes, to heart disease or HIV because they ignore care."

At the beginning of year the Mexican Association on Management of Human Resources (Amedirh) revealed that Mexican companies function with depressed, overweight and tired employees. The document "Best practices of health in Human Resources [RH] 2013" reads that 50 percent of the workers in the country are obese, 33 percent have high cholesterol, 30 percent are depressed, 20 percent have high blood pressure and 12 percent diabetes, which influences the productivity and quality of work that they carry out.

According to the data of the United Nations Food and Agriculture Organization (the FAO), during a six-year period an obese person experiences an increase of 50 percent in lost productivity and requires 88 percent more doctor visits than a healthy person.

While depression is responsible for 54 percent of absenteeism among workers of the Federal District according to a survey conducted in 2012 by the civil society Voz Pro Salud (Voice for Health), it also mentions that absences for this cause can reach 25 days a year, most of them (64.8 percent) as a result of the working conditions.

The Saddest

The Ministry of Health places between 12 and 20 percent of the incidence of depression among adults from 18 to 65 years old, with women being the most affected, almost doubling the percentage of men with this condition, with 14.4 and 9.9 percent, respectively.

Camera Cáceres points out that this increased incidence in females could be due to that throughout life women have more hormonal changes than men and it has been observed that the symptoms vary depending on the sex in particular; for men there is seen increased anger and moodiness from having been educated largely to repress showing their feelings; the depression is expressed through anger, and they also resort to alcohol and illegal drugs.

Depression is a common mental disorder characterized by the presence of sadness, loss of interest or pleasure, feelings of guilt or lack of self-esteem, disorders of sleep or appetite, feeling tired, lack of concentration and it affects about 350 million people around the world, according to the World Health Organization (WHO). Depending on the timing and intensity of the condition this may become chronic, cause suffering, and obstruct work, school, and family activities.

"The number one symptom to identify depression is a lack of energy, not having wishes, nor desire nor energy to do things that previously produced pleasure," said Gabriela Cámara.

"We have also observed that the depression can be reflected in specific symptoms of pain in the body, that makes everything complicated, because on the one hand the physical pain can make you depressed, and depression can cause a muscular contraction, for example, or puts one in such a nervous condition that it causes stomach or back aches. Something that is very important is that we should see the entire person, no longer separating the mind from the body. It is necessary to drop the stigma that depression is not a disease, because it is a real illness of the brain caused by a neurochemical imbalance."

The De la Riva Group, a research company that since 2012 has produced rankings to measure the mood of Mexicans, recorded the month of October of this year [2014], one of the lowest indices, in which only 29 percent of the adults surveyed reported having a positive mood, the majority of the rest expressed a feeling of anger, an emotion that doubled compared to the previous month. The age range in which the most people said to be "very angry," was the so-called generation X, now between 30 and 45 years; the most critical regions in this respect are the Center and the North.

It is [a] social attitude that has lasted for several years in the country, especially in the Center and the North.

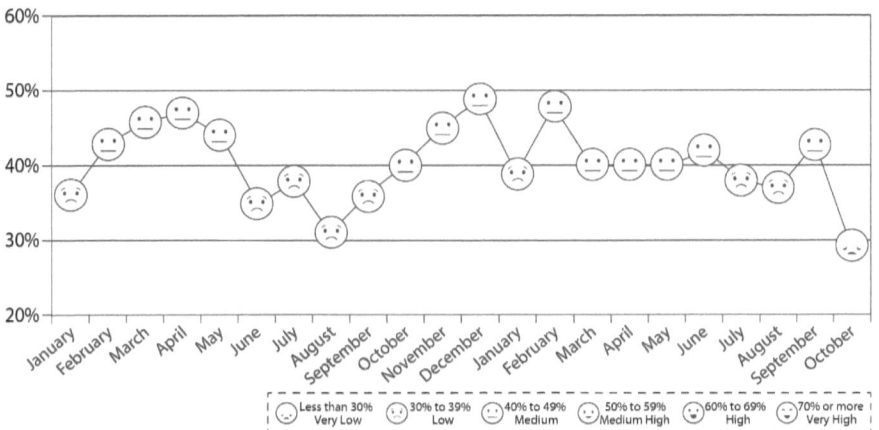

Percentage of adults in Mexico who report having a positive mood (October 2014).
SinEmbargo (December 27, 2014).

Elizabeth Campero, director of opinion studies for *De la Riva Group*, told SinEmbargo that one year to another there are variants above all the social situation that exist in the country at the moment of the survey, for example, in December 2012, 56 percent of those polled reported a very positive mood, in part because "there existed the circumstance of expectations for the new Government."

Last year it was higher than the rest of the months, but dropped compared to 2012, because 49 percent of workers surveyed were adults who said they felt in a good mood, a state of mind formed by several factors: social and family relationships, the question of the family economy and also social expectations.

"In the last month we had a level of very strong anger, she said, although persons between 18 and 29 years old continue being less angry, if they are compared over the last month, certainly there is a dreadful fall in the mood, nevertheless, they always have greater expectations that things will be better," she says.

And, she continued, "it moves from one state of mind to another, sometimes we are sad, sometimes we are afraid, what we saw right now, this past month, that is from September to October, anger increased greatly, practically doubling the number of angry people.

Reports of the De la Riva Group have observed that the low months are usually August and September, "between the return to school and the purchase of supplies, and the end of vacation, and getting organized again as it comes to an end," says Campero.

Recommendations and Care

- Exercise daily (30–40 minutes) keeping the endorphins at standard
- Maintain a balanced diet, lower carbohydrates
- Reduce the consumption of caffeine, especially after 1 p.m.
- Create a healthy environment in a room to have a peaceful moment and sleep well
- Avoid what can make us feel bad or distressed at night, not reading things that cause anxiety
- Practice yoga and meditation
- Eat a piece of bittersweet chocolate
- If you turn to a psychologist, you must be careful that it is someone who has preparation and experience in psychiatry
- Seek out civil groups that have psycho-educational courses for relatives and patients, support groups, and talks

More Obese

Obesity has multiple causes; it is said that we live today in a world conducive to obesity where everything around us leads us to gain weight, from eating habits, to lifestyle, and lack of physical activity," says Blanca Brown, an expert on diabetes and obesity.

In 2013, Mexico unseated the United States as the most obese country in the world, according to the study "The State of Food and Agriculture 2013" of the United Nations Food and Agriculture Organization (FAO), which indicated that our country has an estimated 32.8 percent of adults obese, above the United States with a reported 31.8 percent. In addition, it mentions that seven of 10 adults are overweight and obesity among children has tripled in the last decade, with about 30 percent of adolescents being fat. At that time, the *Global Post* website published an article called "How Mexico got so fat," which reveals that 70 percent of adult residents of Mexico are overweight, and that four of five children who currently suffer from obesity will remain with that condition the rest of their lives.

The expert consulted regarding the increase in obesity of Mexicans from the lack of physical activity and the lifestyle, that influences social situations, says: "In the case of children, each survey they do less exercise since they have less opportunity to do so, their lifestyle has changed because they spend more hours in front of the TV than playing in the street, owning to several factors such as insecurity, before they could go out freely and play, now that is not recommended.

With the adults it is the same, each survey they report doing less exercise, work more, spend more time sitting and obviously have less time to exercise, little time for cooking, and therefore consume easy processed foods that are characterized by being very high in calories, saturated fat and simple carbohydrates, salt and sodium."

Physical inactivity is a severe problem among the inhabitants of Mexico, according to a statement issued by the National Institute of Statistics and Geography (INEGI) in June of this year, 57.6 percent of those over 18 years living in the urban areas of the country do not practice any sport or any type of exercise. Of this total inactive population women form the majority with 60.2 percent, according to the results of poll of the Sports and Physical Exercise Unit (Mopradef), carried out in 32 cities of the country in the first days of May 2014. The study noted that the academic level is related to physical activity, because of people who exercise, 57.3 percent have a higher education, while 73 percent who identified themselves as inactive have no basic education.

In his report, the nutritionist Alejandra Oropeza, Coordinator of Obesity and Metabolic Syndrome Clinic of Mexico's "Eduardo Liceaga" General Hospital also blames bad eating habits. "The problem is the amount and schedule of food eaten, all foods contain calories and everything is fattening in different proportions, the problem is the amount consumed. Mexicans tend to eat many foods with high energy content and simple carbohydrates, such as tortilla, bread, rice, pasta and they eat too much of this," the expert told SinEmbargo.

"Then more than such food alone [. . .] the problem is the portions that we consume, and the question of eating fast food, which is now done, as people have gone more for manufactured food, that comes already packaged, that is easily accessible, low cost and can be eaten at any time," continues the Nutrition graduate.

What Awaits Us?

The increase in both conditions is a health problem requiring immediate action to stop its growth, prevent deaths, diseases and also costs to the government. Alfonso Miranda, specialist in health economics from the Center for Research and Teaching Economics (CIDE), says that Mexico faces "a public health emergency that every day has human and economic costs of catastrophic proportions." Alejandro Calvillo, from El Poder del Consumidor [*Consumer Power*], for his part, says that "obesity is significant problem for the national economy because it could lead to a collapse in the public health system." He projects that if rates of obesity and the overweight in Mexico could be reduced only about 1 percent by 2030, it could save a total of $43 million dollars and $85 million dollars by 2050. If the situation were better, say a decrease 5 percent of obesity, it would save $117 and $192 million dollars in the same years, he explained.

"Numbers for obesity, both child as well as adult levels, have been increasing. In general, I think that we need more nutrition education, making people aware of the importance of health care based on food, we need campaigns to tell people the importance of having a healthy weight, eating balanced meals," stated nutritionist Blanca Brown.

The incidence of overweight and obesity is increasing, and it is a disturbing health problem because it means higher costs to treat obesity and its complications, such as diabetes, hypertension, metabolic syndrome, alterations of the spine, kidney failure. All of these diseases are also increasing and require more spending to care for all those patients," she concluded.

Ángel Gurría, Secretary General of the Organisation for Economic Cooperation and Development (OECD), the organization that reported that 32 percent of Mexican adults suffered from obesity, and that in the past five years the rate had risen between 2 and 3 percent, also published in May this year that "Mexico's strategy to deal with obesity is promising."

"We cannot finance the economic and social consequences of having more than half the population overweight or obese. Mexico has shown

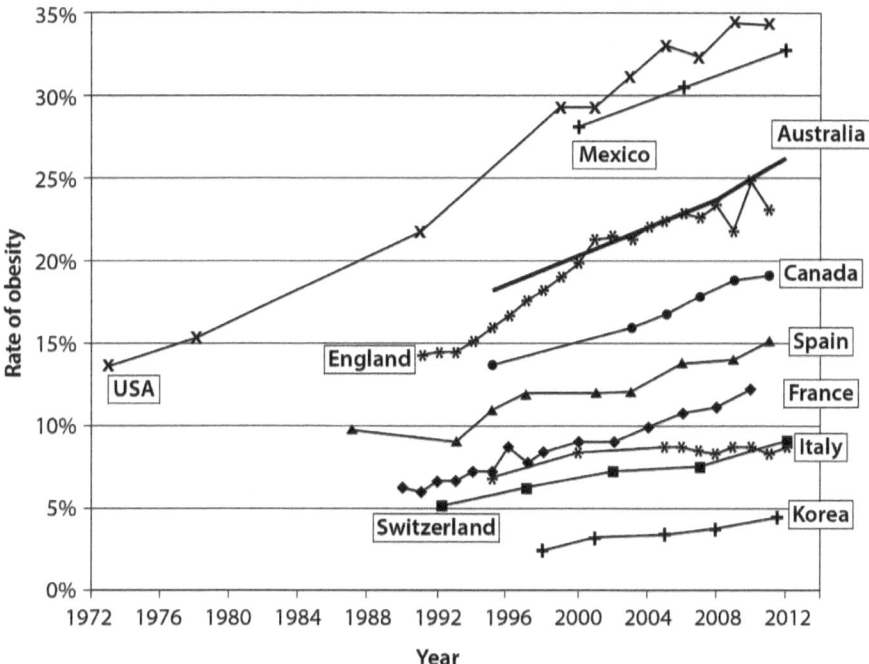

Chart showing the increase in the rates of obesity in Mexico.
Organisation for Economic Co-operation and Development (OECD).

that it is possible to take decisive action to deal with this epidemic; setting a good example for countries facing a similar challenge," Gurría then said.

There are mentioned a series of measures that have been taken to improve the health of Mexicans in this regard, such as actions to raise public awareness, improve medical care, regulating the labeling and advertising of foods to children as well as taxing food and drinks potentially harmful to health.

The expert on depression, for his part, called for finding a personal balance to avoid the socio-economic context and diminish politics in the mood, "depression is a biological, chemical, psychological, social disease and of course the social environment affects it a lot, in times of economic crisis suicides are increased, which we saw in Europe recently, and also in Mexico when we had serious economic crisis." He concludes, "We must achieve self-care to avoid feeling worse and so external things do not hit us so hard, to try to realize what is what we do not like and to be aware that there is no obligation to be happy."[3]

12.4. CHURCH: "IN OAXACA, INDIGENOUS FEMALES HAVE THEIR FIRST PREGNANCY STARTING AT 11 YEARS"

Oaxaca, well known for the strength of its commitment to Roman Catholicism, especially in small communities, also has problems of pregnancy among unmarried young women, despite religious prohibitions against premarital sex. This newspaper report describes the problem of these pregnancies.

Silvia Chavela Riva

The Network for Sexual and Reproductive Rights (Ddeser) disclosed that in some indigenous regions of Oaxaca, women have their first pregnancy between eleven and nineteen years of age.

Mayra Morales, of Ddeser, stressed that regrettably the rights to health are the most violated in the state by misinformation, myths, prejudices, and taboos. She stated that there are numerous needs to address, among them, to provide all health institutions medications, organization, and contraceptive methods. She commented that Oaxaca is first in the nation in the negative statistics of maternal mortality, abortion, and adolescent pregnancy.

Therefore, she called on Oaxaca's elected federal legislators "to make a real commitment to ensure access to health across the population, especially the vulnerable indigenous people, women and children." She pointed out that the legislature has an obligation in the field of sexual and reproductive rights.

12.5. POPULAR GROUPS: HUMOR—ROBBEN, PIÑATAS, AND PEÑATAS

The Mexican soccer team lost to the Dutch in overtime of one of the 2016 World Cup quarterfinals. The referee awarded a penalty kick when Dutch player Arjen Robben went down in the penalty box (Mexican fans believed he faked being fouled).

Mexicans made piñatas of Robben and told the following joke: "We won against the Dutch, but the referee Robben-ed us." In a subsequent election, voters marked their ballots, "It Was Not a Penalty."[4]

Gerardo Zúñiga Pacheco, "'La Peñata': Fabricantes lanzan modelo inspirado en EPN "'para que la gente se desahogue,'" dicen (2014)

Piñatas are made of clay pots or cardboard and decorated with multicolored paper. Usually, they are filled with fruits and candies. They have the shape of stars, ships, fruit or fictional personalities. They are hung up in

Piñata of Dutch soccer star.
Excelsior, July 7, 2014. Used with permission.

order to break them with a stick or a bat. Piñatas form part of the tradition celebrating the Christmas season, New Year's festivities, or birthday parties.

Piñata manufacturers created a new design inspired by the image of the president of Mexico, Enrique Peña Nieto, to celebrate New Year parties: the "Peñata."

"You have to update it. For such a problem as there is, well, we make 'Peñas Nieto' [*play on words Grandson Penalties*]," said the manager of Susy Piñatas, Martha Aguilera, quoted in today's edition of *Reforma*.

Popular opinion of Peña Nieto.
SinEmbargo, December 28, 2014.

The piñata, in human form, is covered with paper simulating a black suit, white shirt, and a presidential sash decorated in green, white, and red, that crosses the chest, while the person's head shines with a pronounced crest.

"There is a great deal of hostility (because of the violence in Mexico), so we have to find something so that people can vent their frustration," added the manager of a piñata business in the Monterrey, Nuevo León, in the north of the country. The "peñata," a word that joins the last name Peña with piñata, sells for 150 pesos (around 10 dollars).

The manufacturer released the Peñata inspired by Enrique Peña Nieto and a woman piñata representing his wife, the actress Angelica Rivera (the pendant on her necklace is the Televisa logo). The manager of the company suggested Mexicans could vent their frustrations on the effigies.[5]

For these and other political piñatas, see the informercial "Breaking the Peñata," on the Web.[6]

Effigies of the President and First Lady.
SinEmbargo (December 28, 2014).

Ayunzinpan: The murder[er]s are in Los Pinos. Students at the Universidad Autónoma Metropolitana expressed their outrage and broke a piñata of Peña in protest of the Ayotzinapa case.
Photo by Hugo Cruz, *Revista Proceso* (December 28, 2014).

The national organization demanding information on the missing 43 students burned images of the president at the Zócalo, as Villa and Zapata watched.
Photo by Hugo Cruz, *Revista Proceso* (December 28, 2014).

ADDITIONAL READING

Ley, Sandra. "Violence and Citizen Participation in Mexico: From the Polls to the Streets," January 9, 2015. Provided online by the Mexico Institute at the Wilson Center, https://www.wilsoncenter.org/publication/violence-and-citizen-participation-mexico-the-polls-to-the-streets.

Leer en español

Calaverita for the forty-three students, by Grupo Saltimbanqui[7]

Ya murió el mal Gobierno que se quería burlar del pueblo
quiso entregar nuestra tierra y el pueblo le hizo la guerra
¡El petróleo pa los gringos, carreteras para España!
Así gritaba el Gobierno, y mató estudiantes con saña . . .
Pero ahora está enterrado como se debe: bocabajo
por si se quiere salir, pos que le cueste su trabajo.
¡Pero sale a la luz el verso y . . . hoy no es Día de los Muertos!
¡No importa, porque en México, todos los días son de muertos

NOTES

1. Provided online by the Mexico Institute at the Wilson Center, https://www.wilsoncenter.org/sites/default/files/mexico_the_fight_against_corruption.pdf. Reprinted by permission of the Wilson Center.

2. Congressional Research Service 7-5700 www.crs.gov R41576, June S. Beittel, Analyst in Latin American Affairs, January 7, 2011.

3. *SinEmbargo*, December 27, 2014, http://www.sinembargo.mx/27-12-2014/1197566. Reprinted by permission of SinEmbargo.

4. *Excelsior*, July 7, 2014, http://www.excelsior.com.mx/nacional/2014/07/07/969345.

5. *SinEmbargo*, December 28, 2014, http://www.sinembargo.mx/28-12-2014/1202232.

6. "Romper la PEÑATA" is available on YouTube, https://www.youtube.com/watch?v=lWXs8b8xJBY.

7. Grupo Saltimbanqui is a Mexican puppet group; see http://www.saltimbanquimexico.com/.

Appendix

Readings for Armchair Historians

These essays for "armchair historians" offer different methodologies for making a historical analysis of the documents. The authors of the essays come from history, anthropology, and journalism, and their provocative approaches encourage readers to do history. The essays can be accessed through the connecting links.

1. Becker, Carl L. "Everyman His Own Historian." Annual address of the president of the American Historical Association, delivered at Minneapolis, December 29, 1931. *American Historical Review* 37, no. 2, 221–36. http://www.historians.org/about-aha-and-membership/aha-history-and-archives/presidential-addresses/carl-l-becker.

2. Geertz, Clifford. "Thick Description: Toward an Interpretive Theory of Culture." *The Interpretation of Cultures: Selected Essays*. New York: Basic Books, 1973), 3–30. http://www.sociosite.net/topics/texts/Geertz_Thick_Description.php.

3. Ginzburg, Carlo. "Morelli, Freud, and Sherlock Holmes: Clues and Scientific Method." *History Workshop* no. 9 (Spring 1980): 5–36. http://www.jstor.org/stable/4288283. Readers can also consult this essay in the journal or in Ginzburg's collection, *Clues, Myths, and the Historical Method* (Baltimore: Johns Hopkins University Press, 2013).

4. Roberts, Sam. "Object Lessons in History." *New York Times*, September 27, 2014. http://www.nytimes.com/2014/09/28/sunday-review/object-lessons-in-history.html.

Index

Abad y Queipo, Manuel, 7–10
accountability network, 254–64
Alemán, Miguel, President, 137, 202–3, 205, 225
Altimirano, Ignacio Manuel, 94
ALZATI news, 87
American Revolution, 27
Angeles, Felipe, 114
Apaches, 27, 50
Arab-Israeli Wars, 203–4
Armas, Justo (Maximilian?), 74, 75–83
Arista, General Mariano, 61–2
Armendariz, Pedro, 140
Arozamena, Juan, 138
Arozamena sisters, 138
Atl, Dr., 138, 150–1, 152
atomic age, 203
Atristain, Miguel, 44
automobiles, 202, 225
Avila Camacho, Manuel, President, 173, 174–5, 176, 179–80
Ayotzinapa 43, 252, 254, 277, 278
Azcárraga, Raúl, 137

ballet folklórico, 138, 139, 167
bandits, 95
Barrón y Forbes Company, 37–8
Basañaz, Miguel, 233
baseball, 41, 202
"Battles in the Desert," 202–25

beatitudes of the family, 197
Becker, Carl, 2, 279
Best Maugard, Fito, 138
Beteta, Ignacio, 163–8
Blanquet, Aureliano, 115
border, U.S.-Mexican, 46–8
bracero program, 232
Brown, John, 70–3
"Buen Amigo" program, 159, 164

Calderón, Felipe, President, 254, 265–6
Calleja, Félix, 30–32
Calles, Plutarco, President, 143–4, 149
"Cangrejos, Los," ("The Crabs"), 84, 87
Cárdenas, Cuauhémoc, 159, 162–3, 233
Cárdenas, Lázaro, President, 137, 146, 205; expropriates foreign oil, 160–2; presidency, 159–171
Carlota, Empress: "Adiós, Mamá Carlota," 83–8
Carreño, Manuel Antonio, 100–105
"Casa blanca" scandal, 252, 254
Caso, Alfonso, 138
Catalina de Guisa (opera), 69, 70
Catholicism, Roman, 24, 25, 37; Constitution of 1824, 35–6
Celnart, Madame, etiquette manual, 99–100, 102

282   *Index*

Central American Games (1938), 164–5
Champion Folk Art Collection, xiv, 141, 147
"Charleston," 141–2
charra, la, 139
charro, el, as national type, 124–5, 137, 138
"Chespirito" (Roberto Gómez Bolaños), 229
"Chiapaneca, La," 138
child's history, 60–4
china poblana, 137
chica moderna (flapper), 141, 146–7
church, 1, 2, 173; confession, 215–6; and family, 197; provision of 1917 Constitution, 117–9
Cinco de Mayo (May 5) battle, 69; board game, 69–70; video reenactment, 70
Ciudad Juárez, battle of (1911), 109–11
clothing, 17–8, 140; laws (hats and trousers), 89–91
Colosio Murrieta, Luis Donaldo, 238
Commanches, 27, 50
Constitution, of 1824, 35–6; of 1857, 63, 64–5; of 1917, 117–24, 142; Salinas Amendments, 238; Transparency Amendment, 255–8
contemporary issues, 251–78
Coronela, La (ballet), 159, 170
Cornish miners, 107
corruption, 205–6, 236, 251–64
corridos, "Agrarista, Corrido del," 137, 159, 168–70; "Cucaracha, La" (Villa), 127–8; Earthquake (1985), 228, 232n4; Porfirian, 91, 92, 94–7; of Tragic Ten Days, 116–7;
Couto, Bernardo, 44
Covarrubias, Miguel, 138
Cristeros and Cristero Rebellion, 165, 205, 217
culture, pop, of 1970s, 228–32
curios, 137

Del Rio, Dolores, 140
Del Río, Eduardo (Rius), 230–1

depression and health, 267–73
Díaz, Félix, 113–5
Díos Cañedo, Juan de, 61–2
disease, 27, 145, 146, 202
domestic life, 124–6, 142, 207
d'Orsay, Count, 102, 108n11
drugs, illegal, and violence, 265–6
Durango, the ship, 159, 163–8

earthquake (1985), 228, 229
Easton Cowboys and Cowgirls, 249
education and nationalism, 138
Eighth Regiment Band, 88
El Salvador, 74–83
electricity, appliances, 124–6, 207
etiquette manuals, 99–105
evacuation of U.S. troops from Mexico, 45–6, 53
excommunication, 8–10, 43

family, 1, 2
Federal District Judicial Police, 236
Federal Electoral Institute (IFE), 255
Federal Judicial Police, 235
Félix, María, 140
Ferdinand, King, VII, 25
Fernandez, Indio, 140
floating signifier, 167–8
flying saucers, 209–10
foreigners in Mexico, 107; property ownership, 121; visit the revolution, 138
French Intervention (1862–1867), 69–88
French Invasion of Mexico, 28, 29, 40–1
French Invasion of Spain, 8, 28–9
French Revolution, 8, 28
Frías, Heriberto, 60, 94

Gamio, Manuel, 138, 155
Garibaldi, José, 110
Geertz, Clifford, 2, 279
General Transparency Law (2015), 257–8
Ginzburg, Carlo, 2, 279

Gonzaga Cuevas, Luis, 44
Gonzalez Camarena, Jorge, 138
Great Britain, 27, 29
Green Woodpecker, The, 87
Grito de Dolores, 5–6
Guadalupe Hidalgo, Treaty of (1848), 43–59
Gulf of California, 48

Haiti, 8–9
Havana, 27
Haya de la Torre, Víctor Raúl, 165
health, public, 142–6, 266–74
Health Service in the States, Federal, 145
Hermosa, Jesús, 85
Hernandez, Amalia, 139–40
Herrera, General José Joaquín de, 61, 62,
Hidalgo, Padre Miguel, 5, 29, 139; excommunicated, 8–10; wanted dead or alive, 11–12
honor codes, unwritten, 36–8
Huerta, Victoriano, 114–6
Hugo, Victor, 70–3
human rights issues, 237–8
humor, 226–7, 274–7
hygiene, 142; First National Congress of Rural Hygiene (1935), 146

Ildegonda (opera), 70
Immigration Service, Mexican, 236
Indigenous Mexico, 156, 274
independence, 5–21, 23; heroes of, 6, 8–10; 11–12; rebellion for, 29–34. *See also* Plan of Three Guarantees
internment of Japanese and Japanese-Latin Americans, 182–95
interpreting the documents, 2–3
Iturbide, Agustín, 24–27, 34

Jalisco, 37
Japanese, in World War II, 177. *See also* internment of Japanese and Japanese-Latin Americans
"Jarabe Tapatío," 107, 137, 167
José José, 230

Juárez, Benito, 64, 65–6, 74; and French Intervention, 69; letter from Victor Hugo, 70–3

land and farming, 16; provision of 1917, 119–24
Liberal era, 43–68
Liszt, Franz, 73
López Portillo, José, President, 231
Lora, Alex, 231
Lost Decades, The (1980–2010), 233–50
Louisiana, 28, 43, 59
Lozada, Manuel, 36–8

Madero, Gustavo, 114–5
Madero, Francisco, 109–11, 198; and Tragic Ten Days, 111–17
Madero, Sara, 116
mariachi, 137, 138–9
marriage: civil marriage oath, 66–7; Perfect Wife, 12–9
Maximilian, 69; escape (?), 73–83; execution, 73; Hugo's plea for, 70–3; Manet's painting of, 80
Merida, Carlos, 138
mestizaje, 166
Mexican Folkways, 154–5
Michoacán, 83–8
Miracle, The (1945–1985), 201–32
military, 1, 2; duties, 25; and health campaign, 142–6; and independence, 26–35; music, 92–3; Porfirian, 91–8
militia, 28–35
Mistral, Gabriela, 138
Mondragón, Manuel, 114
Montenegro, Sasha, 231
movies, 140, 225; U.S., 206–7, 215, 219
music, 137, 138–9, 197–8, 202; "La Bamba," 137; in Chile, 16–7; recordings, 105–7; Tehuana song, 138. *Also see* corridos

Nava, Carmen, xiv
Napoleon, 6, 129
Napoleon III, 84, 87

national identity, 135–41
National Liberation Forces (Fuerzas de Liberación Nacional—FLN), 234
Nazis, 175–6, 178–9
networks, social, 1, 2; and independence, 5–21
North American Free Trade Agreement (NAFTA), 238–44
Nosotros los pobres (1948), 225

Oaxaca, 65–6, 274
obesity, 267–73
Obregón, Alvaro, President, 142
Obregón, Carlos, 151–2, 154
Ocampo, Melchor, Epistle, 66–7
oil expropriation, 160–3
Olivares, Rubén (El Púas), 230
Olvidados, Los (1950), 225
Open Government Partnership, 254
Orozco, José Clemente, 138, 153, 154
Orozco, Pascual, 110–11

Pancho Pistolas, 198
Panchos, Los, 198
Paniagua, Cenobio, 69
paramilitary groups, 237
Pastry (or Pie) War, 40–1
Payno, Manuel, 94
Paz, Octavio, 139, 229–30
Peña Nieto, Enrique, President, 252, 254, 256, 274–7
"Perfidia," 198–9
piñatas, 274–7
Poe, Edgar Allan, 167–8
Pino Suárez, José María, 115–6
Plan of Iguala. *See* Plan of Three Guarantees
Plan of Three Guarantees, 23–27
Plan of San Luis Potosí, 109
poetry, military, 92, 93, 94, 97–8
police, 1, 2, 234–8
politics, 1, 2
Pope John Paul II, 230
Pope Pius IX, 43, 64–5
popular groups, 1, 2
Porfirian era (1876–1911), 88–108
Posada, José Guadalupe, 60

Prieto, Guillermo, 84, 94
prisoners, U.S.-Mexican War, 46
Protection and Transit Directorate (Traffic Police), 235–6
public health, current situation, 266–73; Department of, 142, 151; pregnancy, 274
puzzles (riddles), 38–9

radio, 202, 210, 229
Revueltos, Silvestre, 159
revolution: in 1910–1920, 109–33; in 1920–1934, 135–56; in 1934–1940, 159–171; and culture, 136–7; definition of the people, 136
revolutionary deaths, 109
Reyes, Bernardo, 113–4
Riva Palacio, Vicente, 84–8
Rivera, Angélica, First Lady, 252, 254, 276
Rivera, Diego, 138, 147–9, 152, 154
Roberts, Sam, 2, 279
Rockefeller, Nelson, 173
Rockefeller Foundation, 144
Rudolf, Crown Prince, 74, 76–8
Ruíz, Eduardo, 85, 86
Ruiz Massieu, José Francisco, 238

Sáenz, Moisés, 149–50, 153
Salinas, Carlos, President, 233, 238
Sanitary Code (1926), 144
Santa Anna, Antonio López de, 34, 62–3; leg, 41–2; memory cards, 39–42
sewing machines, 163
"Solamente una vez," 198
Solórzano de Cárdenas, Amalia, 162–3
Spaniards (Guachupines), 6, 34
spanglish, 203
sport, 164–6, 244–9, 274–5
Squadron 201, 174, 180–1
State Judicial Police, 236
Subcommander Marcos (Rafael Sebastián Guillén), 234–5

taxes, 6, 37
Tehuana, costume, 138

television, 229, 276
tequila, 140
Tepic, 36-8
"Three Caballeros, The," 198
Tlatelolco Massacre, 228
Toor, Frances, 153, 154-5
tourism, 137-8
Tovar, Rigo, 231-2
transparency in government, 254-64
Trist, Nicolas, 44
trade and commerce (1848), 53-7
Tragic Ten Days, 111-17

U.S., and illegal drugs, 266
U.S.-Mexican War, 43-61
U.S. payment to Mexico by 1848 Treaty, 51-2, 61

Velasco, Raúl, 229
Vasconcelos, José, 138, 166
Veracruz, 27, 29, 34

Villa, Pancho, 110, 135, 140, 198; corrido "La Cucaracha," 127-28; sketch of, 129-133
Villar, Lauro, 113-4
Virgin of Guadalupe, Crowning (1895), 98-9; and independence, 6, 7, 8, 19-21; and York Rite Masons, 35
Virgin of Remedios, 19-21; and Scottish Rite Masons, 35

World War II in Mexico, 173-200; nurses (picture), 197; soldiers (picture), 197

Zabludovsky, Jacobo, 228-9
Zapata, Emiliano, 124, 135
Zapatista National Liberation Army (Ejército Zapatista de Liberación Nacional—EZLN), 234; and Milan International Futbol Club, 244-9

About the Editors

William H. Beezley has achieved an international reputation for his investigations of Mexico's history and culture through publication of the classic *Judas at the Jockey Club* and the fundamental anthologies *A Handbook of Mexican History and Culture* and *The Oxford History of Mexico*. He has authored or edited over twenty-five additional books, including *Latin American Popular Culture*, edited with Linda Curcio-Nagy, and *The Human Tradition in Latin America*, edited with Judith Ewell. His books have been translated into Spanish and Chinese. He has appeared in over a dozen PBS episodes of *The Desert Speaks* and *In the Americas*, and, as of 2016, he and Roderic Ai Camp are interviewing former Mexican presidents and politicians for a video production on the democratization of Mexico. He has taught at North Carolina State University and has held endowed chairs at Texas Christian University and Tulane and visiting positions at the universities of Texas, Calgary, British Columbia, and the Colegio de Mexico. He now teaches at the University of Arizona, directs the Oaxaca (Mexico) Summer Institute, sits on numerous editorial boards, and serves on the wine cultural commission at Toulouse University. He is the editor-in-chief of *The Oxford Research Encyclopedia for Latin America*.

Monica Rankin is an associate professor of history at the University of Texas–Dallas and the director of the Center for U.S.–Latin America Initiatives. She specializes in the history of Mexico, Latin America, and U.S.–Latin American relations. She is the author of *¡México, la patria! Propaganda and Production during World War II*, along with various articles and chapters dealing with Mexican foreign policy, gender, and popular culture during World War II. She is the coauthor of a general textbook on Latin American history for Oxford University Press and is writing a history of the (US) Office of the Coordinator of Inter-American Affairs during the 1940s. Her research has been supported by grants from the Fulbright Program, the Roosevelt Institute, the Truman Institute, and the UT–Dallas Center for U.S.–Latin America Initiatives. In the area of pedagogy, she was the winner of the 2015 Regents' Outstanding Teaching Award for the University of Texas system. She is known for her use of Twitter, animation, and other forms of emerging media in the classroom. Notably, La Casona del Llano Restaurant in Oaxaca, Mexico, has named "la sopa Mónica" in her honor.

www.ingramcontent.com/pod-product-compliance
Lightning Source LLC
Chambersburg PA
CBHW030108010526
44116CB00005B/143